Article by Article

Also by Johannes Morsink

The Universal Declaration of Human Rights: Origins, Drafting and Intent (1999)

Inherent Human Rights: Philosophical Roots of the Universal Declaration (2009)

The Universal Declaration of Human Rights and the Challenge of Religion (2017)

The Universal Declaration of Human Rights and the Holocaust: An Endangered Connection (2019)

Article by Article

The Universal Declaration of Human Rights
for a New Generation

Johannes Morsink

PENN

University of Pennsylvania Press

Philadelphia

Published by
University of Pennsylvania Press
Philadelphia, Pennsylvania 19104-4112

www.upenn.edu/pennpress

Printed in the United States of America on acid-free paper

10 9 8 7 6 5 4 3 2 1

Library of Congress Cataloging-in-Publication Data
Names: Morsink, Johannes, author.
Title: Article by article : the Universal Declaration of Human Rights for a
    new generation / Johannes Morsink.
Other titles: Pennsylvania studies in human rights.
Description: 1st edition. | Philadelphia : University of Pennsylvania Press, [2022] |
    Series: Pennsylvania studies in human rights | Includes index.
Identifiers: LCCN 2021019352 | ISBN 9780812253504 (hardcover)
Subjects: LCSH: United Nations. General Assembly. Universal Declaration of
    Human Rights. | Human rights.
Classification: LCC K3238.31948 .M663 2021 | DDC 341.4/8—dc23
LC record available at https://lccn.loc.gov/2021019352

ISBN 978-0-8122-5350-4

History, despite its wrenching pain, cannot be unlived,
but if faced with courage need not be lived again.

—*Maya Angelou*

Pennsylvania Studies in Human Rights
Bert B. Lockwood, Series Editor
A complete list of books in the series is available from the publisher.

Contents

Preface

You may or may not be familiar with what the Universal Declaration of Human Rights (UD) looks like or how it is organized. It is quite a simple document, starting out with seven "recitals" in which the drafters give us their reasons for proclaiming this text on December 10, 1948. Then we read in the "operative paragraph" that education is the purpose of this proclamation, which is also the main reason I wrote this brief article-by-article commentary. After that come the thirty articles of this famous text, some of which my reader may be familiar with, many probably not. So the UD has three parts to it: a preamble, a statement of purpose, and thirty articles.

Throughout, the reader will discover that the declaration's drafters were in a militant mood that went beyond simply educating the public on what human rights it has. They also wanted to enlist people to help them beat back future attacks of Hitlerian authoritarianism and illiberal populism, which theme I will refer to as a "battle" or a "fighting back" with human rights as our weapons of choice. After they had won World War II militarily, many UD drafters saw themselves as part of a continuing ideological warfare between democratic states and authoritarian regimes. That is how most North Atlantic and Latin American nations and their friends saw the fight. Communists were also happy to see fascism defeated, but they were not afraid of their own kind of authoritarianism, which they referred to as "democratic socialism," but which was not at all what we today mean by that phrase. The Nordic model of political and economic organization is nothing like the one-party totalitarianism that communist UD drafters were pushing. However, their drafting colleagues resisted these communist attempts to inject a strong role for the authoritarian or absolutist state into the text of the declaration. Those other drafters wanted the UD to stand in judgment over national legal systems, something the communists resisted. The reader will detect this tension everywhere, in the preamble as well as in many of the thirty articles.

I have written this book not just to tell you that the UD drafters were worried about a recurrence of Hitler's fascism and communist authoritarianism of the 1930s, 1940s, and 1950s. I wrote it also to enlist you in the combat against a recurrence of these movements today in the different countries we call home. I have in mind the intellectual climate of our own day as painted by authors like Timothy Snyder in his *On Tyranny: Twenty Lessons from the Twentieth Century* and Anne Applebaum in her *Twilight of Democracy: The Seductive Lure of Authoritarianism.* These authors have summarized decades of their research in slim volumes that help us understand the dangerous times in which we live.

Applebaum tells us how she experienced shifts toward authoritarianism in leading public figures on the ground in Poland, Egypt, Hungary, Turkey, the United Kingdom, France, Spain, Hong Kong, and, yes, the United States. Snyder's last lesson from his twentieth-century research tells us, "Be as courageous as you can." That fits the Maya Angelou epigraph I picked for this book: "History, despite its wrenching pain, cannot be unlived, but if faced with courage need not be lived again." We do not want and cannot go back to the horrible dictatorial times of the 1930s, 1940s, and even 1950s. But if these authors are correct, that is the danger that Western democracy faces. Even the foundational values of our own country, the United States, are at stake in this fight. Readers who are aware of what happened in the Trump presidency will know about the hollowing out of every department of our government, with public norms and legal precedents being set aside on a daily basis. There is no telling how long it will take to heal this oldest of all democracies.

This book therefore asks you to put on the armor supplied by the Universal Declaration of Human Rights, to pick a human rights violation that enrages you, and go and do battle against that violation. I stretch the reasons behind the adoption of each article in this iconic text into a lesson for our own time and place. The UD drafters worried about the same dangers the aforementioned authors describe. They sharpened their resolves and used their pens to show us where the moral high ground is in our fight for the human-rights-based world order they bequeathed to us but that is now so obviously threatened.

Against this background of doing battle with authoritarianism and populism, each UD article also presented the narrower goal of protecting its own particular human right, however that right had been shaped in each nation's domestic context. All these national human rights interests had to be universalized against the larger background of fighting off a recurrence of Nazism, fascism, sexism, colonialism, workers' neglect, illiteracy and ignorance, and all types of discrimination. Also, workers knew that World War II was fought on *their* backs and they wanted their welfare taken care of in this declaration. Thus you will see a large union influence on the drafting of the economic and social human rights in the second half of the declaration. That second half reads like a veritable blueprint for the socialist half of today's "democratic socialism," the democratic half of this equation having been set down in the first half of the UD text.

Toward the end of the drafting process—when the communists forced the Western powers to launch the 1948 Berlin Airlift—most UD drafters also realized they needed to fight off the threat of communist authoritarianism. My reader will see that this Cold War tension did not stop the proceedings, nor did it prevent the communist delegations from continuing to give input into the kind of declaration they wanted. Their very objections, you will see, led to a much better list of human rights than we would have had without their opposition to aspects of the new world order being created. All of the UD drafters, on either side of the Iron Curtain, wanted to set the world on fire for human rights. What we therefore get when the archives of these debates are laid bare is a veritable triumph of nations in the battle for human rights. No one quit, and they were not made to stick it out by any external force.

Right after the Third Committee had adopted the third paragraph of UD Article 21 with a resounding vote of thirty-nine votes to three, with three abstentions, Alexei Pavlov of the Soviet Union was exuberant. His delegation, he said, "had voted in favor of the compromise that had been adopted, and which had been arrived at as a result of sincere collaboration between many delegations. It was one of the all too rare cases when the Committee had adopted progressive ideas. The conciliatory spirit manifested on that occasion was very encouraging, and gave grounds for unbounded hope in the future of the United Nations. That new spirit of co-operation had just led to concrete and positive results" (A/C.3/SR.134/473). As I said, the adoption of the Universal Declaration in 1948 was a triumph of nations willing to align their own positions with the good of the world. Would that was so today.

Seventy-five years later, we do not have the same enthusiasm, not in general and not for the United Nations. But the evils we face today can all be found in these 1948 UD debates. We too must fight back with human rights, the same ones that were proclaimed in 1948.

Now that the fog of the 2020 health pandemic is lifting and we see the rubble around us, the Universal Declaration presents itself as the perfect tool for the reconstruction of our world. If Americans are going to have a third founding, let us do it with human rights. We should use the human rights articles of the declaration as our weapons of choice to fight against authoritarian leaders who seek to abuse the pandemic to aggrandize their power and subvert the democratic order of their nation-states. This iconic text was forged in the afterglow of the greatest battle against authoritarianism and absolutism in the 1940s when the world faced a series of crises not unlike our own. The declaration gives us a common moral ground that links the silos of information we choose for ourselves.

That glow is evident in what Jorge Carrera Andrade from Ecuador told his Third UN Assembly colleagues in 1948. As far as he was concerned, that reconstruction glow spread over the whole of the declaration and not just a few isolated parts. I quote him at length:

From the ruins of the destruction wrought by the Second World War, man had once again fanned the immortal flame of civilization, freedom, and law. The multiplicity of origins of human rights could be detected in reading the articles of the declaration. It was true that some of the [UD] articles had already become part of the Constitutions of many Member States whose democratic systems made their exercise possible, but it gave added strength to the declaration, as it was proof that that international document was based on political realities and not on utopianism.

Many of the rights established in the declaration had been the heritage of mankind for several years, but others had only recently come into existence, such as the right of man to work and his right to benefit from his leisure, the right to a decent standard of living, and the right to social security. All those rights constituted the real triumph of the twentieth century, and were the foundation for the modern democratic system which believed that social peace depended on the well-being of the individual. In the social systems being developed, there existed a close inter-dependence between man, the State and world order; thus if man were given peace and economic security the whole world would also enjoy that peace and security.

Nazism and fascism having been destroyed, so had the brutal totalitarian States. The United Nations should strive for a new democratic internationalism which would have as its objective not war or conflicts, but the establishment of a lasting peace. It was the duty of democratic systems to create a just social order so as to make a century of progress possible.

The declaration of human rights contained a number of new rights which were the logical result of the victory of democracy and of the birth of that internationalist spirit to which he had just referred. Certain clauses dealt with social order while others dealt with the universal protection of human rights. All men had the right to live in a world ruled by justice and where laws were respected and freedoms recognized. The inclusion of those provisions was one of the great triumphs of the United Nations. (A/PV.183/918)

The amazing thing is that in spite of the tensions I mentioned, the Universal Declaration came into being as the result of genuine cooperation among nations that had very different legal and political systems, as well as different religious and cultural traditions. The previously cited Soviet praise for what it took to get UD 21(3) adopted is proof of that cooperative spirit. Time and again the reader will see nations listening to each other and compromising to get a certain article written and move on to the next one.

Though the world has changed a great deal in the intervening decades and the old liberal and international order constructed after the war is crumbling, the UD is still the best tool with which to construct a new one. Those who wrote it were intimately and even physically familiar with authoritarian tactics and threats. One of them had a Gestapo arrest warrant posted on his Paris apartment door. On an almost daily basis our bookstores, social media, and podcasts warn us against fascism's past and present and tell us how it works. They now also regularly warn us against attacks on our democracy by white supremacist groups. But none of them give us uniform advice on how to fight these dangers across the board. In this brief commentary on the UD, I supply some thirty different fighting platforms (if not local strategies) from which to combat different violations. They give readers a moral lift with which to view the chaos around them and then to join us in the reconstruction of our world.

Readers will have to find their own local applications for each fight in whatever branch of the human rights movement they have an interest. There is such a branch for pretty much each UD article in most countries, provinces, and towns the world over. My own comments are therefore mostly historical. I do, however, make regular references to our own time of need. My epigraphs and interspersed comments give this article-by-article commentary its twenty-first-century slant. Given the extraordinary time in which we live, with its threats of recurrent fascism, I do not see how else I could have portrayed the spirit of this iconic liberal text.

One last point. The reader should not forget to read what I say about the drafters' "statement of purpose" at the end of the preamble, which is officially referred to as the "operative paragraph" of the text. It shows you how I wrote each of these thirty drafting stories and includes a flow-chart of the eight debate stages that the UD text went through to its final adoption. You will see that the declaration resulted from an amazing international cooperative effort that exceeded all expectations. The cumulative knowledge of how this historic text was constructed should give us confidence in our own time to fight against the same 1940s evils presenting themselves in different garb to us today.

A Note on Sources

Most of the citations in this book direct you to the United Nations Archives. You will find pretty much all the UN references used here on this one UN website: http://research.un.org/en/undhr. When you go there, remember that the bulk of the work was done in the years 1947 and 1948, so the timeline is important. Also, remember that in the flowchart you find in my comments on the operative paragraph, I explain how the UD text went through different drafting stages, such as the commission and its different sessions, its drafting subsidiary, the Third Committee, and lastly the General Assembly.

You will find those organs listed on the previously mentioned website. If careful use of that website fails, you can try any of these sites: http://www.un.org/en/ga/documents (which searches for specific documents), http://research.un.org/en (which searches the whole UN library).

Preamble

The word "preamble" has two Old Latin parts to it, *prae*, meaning "before," and the verb *ambulare*, meaning "to go." Together they make the Latin verb *praeambulare*, meaning "going before." That gives us the standard use of a preamble as an introduction to something that follows. In this case what follows (after the operative paragraph) are the thirty articles of the Universal Declaration of Human Rights. As are most introductions, this one was written after most of the rest of the declaration was close to being finished. The seven paragraphs of this preamble are called "recitals." They tell us why the Third General Assembly of the United Nations decided to declare this list of universal human rights on December 10, 1948, in Paris, France. Here I cite and comment on the seven reasons the drafters gave for making this declaration.

These recitals give the reader more of the historical background I mentioned in the Preface. They mostly speak for themselves. Still, if we are going to use this iconic text as a weapon against different kinds of antidemocratic authoritarianism, then I should spell out how I interpret the first three of these recitals, for they give us the moral underpinnings for that fight.

In my comment on the first recital, I explain why the drafters thought that human rights are part of people's moral DNA and why they wanted to keep the declaration a secular text accessible to religious and nonreligious people alike. In my comments on the second recital, I explain that we get our knowledge of human rights through our conscience and also that the UD drafters were aware of US president Franklin Roosevelt's Four Freedoms speech. In those on the third recital, I explain that while historically the rights of rebellion and petition form a pair, the drafters honored the latter and dropped the former from their slate of rights. The last four recitals are important for they link the declaration to the United Nations Charter and give the document its international legal grounding.

1) *Whereas recognition of the inherent dignity and of the equal and inalienable rights of all members of the human family is the foundation of freedom, justice and peace in the world,*

This recital was the brainchild of the Committee on the Preamble that was appointed rather late in the drafting process. It consisted of the representatives of the United States, China, France, and Lebanon, all of which were (in various degrees) supporters of the idea that human rights are inherent in all members of the human family and not just the result of extraneous factors like government actions or judicial procedures, whether domestic or international. This view holds that people have moral rights that constrain the behavior of others regardless of whether those moral rights are matched (as they should be) in the realm of legality. The Third Committee, which had representatives on it from all fifty-six UN Member States, adopted this recital unanimously. Two things immediately come to mind upon reading the foregoing text.

First, the terminology of "inherent dignity and of the equal and inalienable rights of all members of the human family" leads many to think of the eighteenth-century Enlightenment. The 1776 Virginia declaration of rights says that "all men . . . have certain inherent rights," and the US Declaration of Independence asserts that all men are "endowed by their creator with certain unalienable rights." US founding documents are replete with these kinds of references, which not infrequently have served as a model the world over.

This idea of inherence was not just the pet project of some drafters around the North Atlantic. For instance, Peng-Chun Chang from China defended Article 18 (on freedom of thought and religion) as "one of the most important principles in the Declaration" because "from the eighteenth century, when the idea of human rights was born in Western Europe, freedom of thought had figured among the essential human freedoms and had covered the idea of religious freedom" (A/C.3/SR.127/397). In the discussion of UD 15 (on nationality), Eduardo Anze Matienzo from Bolivia insisted that "nationality was an unalienable human right," adding that in law it "might be regarded as transitory; but as a right it was inherent" (A/C.3/SR.123/351). At one point the Egyptian delegation submitted an amendment that described all the UD rights as "inherent attributes" of the human person (A/C.3/264). Uruguay told the General Assembly that "the inherent rights and freedoms of the human being" were enshrined in the UD (A/PV.181/887).

At one point communist Yugoslavia lobbied for the practice of "establishing, as rights inherent in the human person, the principle of freedom of trade union association and any other safeguards such as minimum wages, equal pay for equal work for men and women, abolition of racial discrimination in economic and social activities, full employment, effective struggle against unemployment especially in a period of crisis and compulsory social insurance, as may provide the basis for a minimum of well-being within the reach of all the workers in the world" (A/C.3/187, as found in W. A. Schabas, "The Universal Declaration of Human Rights," in *The Travaux Preparatoires*, vol.1 [Cambridge: Cambridge University Press, 2013], 967–68). Today, in the midst of a worldwide pandemic that hits lower-income workers most and with marches against systemic racism all over the United States and its former colonialist allies, this Yugoslav list of "rights inherent in the human person" does not sound nearly as far flung as it struck the members of the Economic and Social Council, which passed on it in the late 1940s but could not prevent it from influencing the work-related rights we have in the declaration. Some seventy-five years after the UD adoption, the belief that a wide range of human rights are part of people's moral DNA has come to be shared around the globe.

The second thought I need to share on this first recital is that it lets inherence and inalienability fend for themselves without grounding these ideas in any way in religion. This lack of reference to the sacred was not the result of a lack of trying. In the Third Committee the Dutch delegation proposed to insert the part I have italicized into the text: "Whereas recognition of the inherent dignity and of the equal and inalienable rights of all members of the human family, *based on man's divine origin and immortal destiny*, is the foundation of freedom, justice and peace in the world" (A/C.3/219).

The Dutch argued that their "amendment affirmed the relation between the Creator and man, stated the latter's origin and referred to his destiny" (A/C.3/SR.164/755). L. J. C. Beaufort made the observation that "for those who were agnostics or atheists, the Netherlands amendment was merely devoid of any meaning, but it could not harm them or offend their conscience. . . . On the other hand, if the amendment were adopted, it would give satisfaction to the majority of the world's population, which, generally speaking, still believed in the existence of a Supreme Being" (ibid.). Beaufort said his proposal was also "required for practical reasons, because the rights of man had to be protected in countries where the omnipotence of the State had precedence over the rights of individuals" (ibid.).

The communist delegates rightly felt themselves addressed and responded in force. In an overstatement, Alexandre Bogomolov of the USSR reminded Beaufort that "the dispute on the divine origin of man had been fought out in Paris as long ago as 1789 when the Declaration of the Rights of Man and of Citizen had included no reference to the divine origin" (A/C.3/SR.165/758–59). He overlooked the fact that the French Assembly noted in its preamble that it proclaimed this otherwise secular bill "in the presence of the Supreme Being." Fryderyka Kalinowska of Poland pointed out that the Dutch amendment "failed to take into account the fact that the Declaration was a United Nations' document which could not properly deal with metaphysical questions" (ibid., 762). Opponents of the Dutch view got help from some theistically inclined friends of the Dutch. Adrian Carton de Wiart from Belgium admitted that he was "personally inclined to favour [the Dutch proposal] because it provided the idea of equality of man with perhaps the only possible ultimate argument and would thus strengthen the Declaration" (ibid., 760). But he did not think that the committee should try to resolve this kind of question by a vote. Hernan Santa Cruz of Chile explained that his country, "where the bulk of the nation was sincerely Catholic, had no mention of providence in its constitution, out of respect for the conviction of an important minority. He wanted to carry this tolerance for the minority point of view over to the international arena," which is why Chile "would not support the Dutch amendment" (A/C.3/SR.166/774). France, Australia, and the United Kingdom also did not go along with the idea of a religiously grounded UN declaration.

Beaufort did not share the view that controversial questions could not be settled by a vote. Linking his proposal to their common fight against authoritarianism, he asked his colleagues, "Was agreement really impossible between those who believed that human rights were inalienable and those who affirmed that man was only a means and that the State was an end in itself?" He continued, "Bitter experience in the recent past had shown the danger of allowing the monstrous materialistic conception of man as a mere tool in the service of the State" (A/C.3/SR.166/776). He withdrew his amendment when he saw that he did not have the votes.

> 2) *Whereas disregard and contempt for human rights have resulted in barbarous acts which have outraged the conscience of mankind, and the advent of a world in which human beings shall enjoy freedom of speech and belief and freedom from fear and want has been proclaimed as the highest aspiration of the common people.*

The use of the word "conscience" in this recital as well as in Article 1 tells us how the drafters thought people come to a knowledge of human rights. Generalizing their own feelings over the rest of humanity, they supposed that every human being would feel the same moral outrage when faced with or told about "barbarous acts" committed by Nazis, fascists, and other perpetrators of evil.

When this recital arrived at the Third Committee from the commission, it read as follows: "Whereas disregard and contempt for human rights resulted, before and during the Second World War, in barbarous acts which outraged the conscience of mankind and made it apparent that the fundamental freedoms were one of the supreme issues of the conflict." As you can see, the specific reference to World War II was deleted and US president Roosevelt's four freedoms were added.

Two war amendments called for opposite changes. Australia proposed that the reference to World War II be deleted, suggesting the opening terminology that we now have, which makes no reference to war but does mention "barbarous acts that have outraged the conscience of mankind," a barely hidden reference to Nazi practices (A/C.3/257). Going in the opposite direction, France proposed this text: "Whereas ignorance and contempt for human rights are one of the essential causes of human suffering; whereas particularly before and during the Second World War, Nazism and racialism engendered countless acts of barbarism which outraged the conscience of mankind" (A/C.3/339). Both nations sought to make their case. Australia wanted to delete the reference to World War II because it was too specific. The declaration, it felt, should "contain immutable principles" and not "give the impression that it was prompted by the particular ideas of one epoch" (A/C.3/SR.164/756). France responded that "when dealing with the body of the declaration, [it] had always advocated the removal of any controversial wording; but in the preamble it was absolutely essential to set down a protest against the horrors which had taken place before and during the Second World War out of which the United Nations had risen. Such a protest was the essential starting point for a declaration of human rights" (A/C.3/SR.165/760).

Belgium sided with Australia, arguing that "the deletion of the mention of the Second World War was logical because quite as many barbarous acts were committed in the First World War, so that there seemed to be no reason to speak of the former without mentioning the latter. . . . It might also be asked why allusions to fascism and totalitarianism had been omitted" from the French amendment (A/C.3/SR165/761). Eleanor Roosevelt of the United States said that while "she personally preferred the Australian draft . . . , she realized that a number of delegations strongly favoured express mention of the Second World War and her delegation was prepared to support the original text," which did have such a reference in it (ibid., 763).

Benigno Aquino of the Philippines agreed with the French position "that it was necessary to include a reference to the Second World War. Mankind had to be reminded of the fact that a few men, through the use of force, had attempted to eliminate the fundamental freedoms" (A/C.3/SR.165/766). He further proposed that "fascism" be added to the French proposal because the "doctrine was still as repugnant as it had ever been and was the basic cause of militarism which had attempted to destroy the whole of Europe and parts of the Orient. In certain parts of the world, fascists were still on the alert, awaiting an opportunity to seize control" (ibid.). Jorge Carrera Andrade of Ecuador wondered why the French amendment, "which condemned Nazism and racialism, was silent on other equally criminal systems, such as Italian fascism and Japanese militarism. As any list of such systems was incomplete, it would be preferable to abandon the idea of including one in the preamble" (ibid., 776).

I noted in the Preface that the declaration is the result of lots of cooperation. We see that happened here when both France and Australia withdrew their own amendments and proposed this joint one: "Whereas disregard and contempt for human rights have resulted in barbarous acts which have outraged the conscience of mankind," and "whereas the advent of a world in which human beings shall enjoy freedom of speech and belief and freedom from want and fear has been proclaimed as the highest aspiration of the common people" (A/C.3/383). Just before the final vote, the second "whereas" was replaced with the comma we have in our text. Like the first recital, this one was also adopted unanimously with twenty-seven votes for, none against, and eight abstentions (A/C.3/ SR.166/787).

France and Australia patched this text together from the UN Charter Preamble and from the American Federation of Labor submission to the Preamble Committee that had cited President Roosevelt's four freedoms (E/CN.4/129). On January 6, 1941, Roosevelt gave a speech referring to the four freedoms of speech and belief and from fear and want that are mentioned in the American Federation of Labor submission. These freedoms had gained great notoriety in both of the Americas. Roosevelt had been an ardent founder of the United Nations. He even proposed to the US Congress legislation that translated these freedoms into "a second bill of rights." All four of these freedoms find their echo throughout the UD, including workers' human rights sponsored by Latin American nations in the second half of the declaration.

In the Third Committee, the word "disregard" that we now have replaced René Cassin's earlier term "ignorance" and was carried over to the joint amendment. Alexei Pavlov of the USSR said that keeping "the word 'ignorance' would give the impression that the acts of the Germans and the Japanese were being excused because they did not know they were violating human rights" (A/C.3/SR.175/5). Chang of China agreed, explaining that it "was true that the Germans and Japanese were to blame for their contempt for human rights, but it could not be said that they had been ignorant of those rights" (ibid.).

3) *Whereas it is essential, if man is not to be compelled to have recourse, as a last resort, to rebellion against tyranny and oppression, that human rights should be protected by the rule of law,*

Historically the rights to petition and rebellion often go together in that where a government does not respond to petitions of its people, they are thought to have a right to rebel. The authors of the 1776 American Declaration of Independence complained that "in every stage of these Oppressions We Have Petitioned for Redress in the humblest terms: Our repeated Petitions have been answered only by repeated injury. A Prince, whose character is thus marked by every act which may define a Tyrant, is unfit to be ruler of a free People." In Article 15 of their 1789 declaration, the French people also asserted that "every community has a right to demand of all its agents an account of their conduct." Thomas Paine, who influenced both these texts, put the right to petition this way: "If a law be bad it is one thing to oppose the practice of it, but it is quite a different thing to expose its errors, to reason on its defects, and to show cause how it should be repealed, or why another ought to be substituted in its place" (*Rights of Man* [New York: Penguin, 1984], 155).

This third recital gives us only the right to rebellion, leaving out the right to petition. That one was much discussed but not included because the drafters could not agree on whether citizens of nations should be able to petition not just their own governments but also the United Nations for redress. The majority of drafters felt that the latter kind of international right to petition would encroach too much on a nation's autonomy or sovereignty.

Cuba and Chile at first wanted the right to rebellion more explicitly stated and submitted a text for this recital that told "individuals and peoples" that rebellion "would be their legitimate right as a last resort" (A.C.3/314/Rev.1/Add.1). "Mrs. Roosevelt (United States of America) criticized the dangerous character of the Cuban and Chilean proposals. In her opinion, the recognition in the declaration of human rights of the right to resist acts of tyranny and oppression would be tantamount to encouraging sedition, for such a provision could be interpreted as conferring a legal character on uprisings against a Government which was in no way tyrannical" (A/C.3/SR.164/749). The United Kingdom also felt this language "might be construed as an invitation to revolt, since it stressed the right to rebel" (A/C.3/SR.166/772). Chile responded that "there was nothing in the amendment in question to encourage rebellion against a really democratic regime based on universal suffrage and human rights" (ibid., 774). The Netherlands thought this amendment "was important and should be incorporated" (A/C.3/SR.165/768).

At the start of the 167th meeting, the chairperson explained that some amendments had been withdrawn, including the Cuban-Chilean one on the third recital. However, together with France, they had submitted this new, less explicit text on rebellion: "Whereas it is essential, if man is not to be compelled to fall back, as a last resort, on rebellion against tyranny and oppression, that human rights should be protected by a rule of law" (A/C.3/382/Rev.1). The idea here is that rebellion is a human right, but only as a last resort. Eleanor Roosevelt still objected because "it would be unwise to legalize the right to rebellion, lest the formula should be invoked by subversive groups wishing to attack or undermine genuine democratic Governments. Honest rebellion was permitted by the Declaration. Subversive action was quite a different matter . . ." (A/C.3/SR.165/763). Bolivia, Cuba, Chile, and Ecuador all spoke of the struggles their countries had had in "the conquest for freedom" (A/C.3/SR.166/773). Many more could say the same thing.

The question came down to how explicitly to state the right to rebellion. Just before the vote, Cuba made the point that "the words 'to fall back as a last resort' suggested that some sort of reluctant concession had been made, which was not true of the French text" that had used the word *recours*, which means "last resort" or "way out" (A/C.3/SR.167/885). Australia agreed that the "French text had a positive meaning which the English text did not have" (ibid.). This led the United States to propose that the phrase "to have recourse to rebellion, as a last resort," be used instead. The minutes then record that "it was so decided." It was also "agreed" that the United Kingdom's proposal to use "by *the* rule of law" instead of "by *a* rule of law" be adopted for this recital's text (ibid.). The vote of twenty-five in favor, one against, and eleven abstaining shows that by adopting the foregoing italicized text with these just mentioned changes, the majority preferred to state the right to rebellion somewhat modestly as a submerged right. Sweden was the only negative vote, and one wonders whether the abstaining nations (Pakistan, Peru, the Philippines, the United Kingdom, the United States, Venezuela, Belgium, Burma, Canada, China, and Denmark) did not think it was a real human right to begin with (ibid., 788). One reason could be that rebellion is often thought of not so much as a right of individuals but as of a collectivity or a whole people.

> 4) *Whereas it is essential to promote the development of friendly relations between nations,*

The next four recitals go back to and are based on specific clauses and articles in the United Nations Charter. We should keep in mind that the UN Charter is a legally binding convention that Member States sign upon joining and are legally bound to follow. These four recitals indicate that the drafters took these charter references to human rights seriously and saw the writing of the declaration as a way of following up on the pledges they made when signing the charter.

This reference in the fourth recital to the "development of friendly relations between nations" is taken from Article 1(2) of the charter, where the development of "friendly relations among nations based on respect for the principle of equal rights and self-determination of peoples" is given as one of the goals of the United Nations. It first occurred in a UK submission and was dropped but revived by the Soviet Union, which kept pushing for its use in the preamble (E/800). Twice rebuffed by the commission, it succeeded in the Third Committee, where, with the help of other communist nations, this "short and concise" recital was adopted in a vote of twenty-six for, eight against, and three abstaining. The negative vote might have been the result of Cold War tensions. It could also be that "the right to self-determination of peoples," which was part of the UN text from which this recital was lifted, was linked to the fight to liberate colonial peoples (for which see Article 2[b]). The negative votes came from the Netherlands, New Zealand, the United Kingdom, the United States, Venezuela, Canada, China, and Greece. Lebanon, the Philippines, and Afghanistan abstained.

5) *Whereas the peoples of the United Nations have in the Charter reaffirmed their faith in fundamental human rights, in the dignity and worth of the human person [and in the equal rights of men and women and] have determined to promote social progress and better standards of life in larger freedom,*

This recital comes straight out of the first paragraph of the UN Charter, but the version that came from the Third Session of the commission did not include the phrase I have placed in brackets. This omission was corrected at the level of the Third Committee when the Dominican Republic suggested that the charter phrase "and of equality of rights between men and women" be added to this recital (A/C.3/217/Corr.1). New Zealand made a similar suggestion, arguing that "omission of a reference to the equal rights of men and women . . . might be wrongly interpreted (A/C.3/SR.165/758). Lakshmi Menon of India said she would "whole-heartedly support" the Dominican amendment. She believed "the omission in the preamble of a statement to the effect that men and women were equal in rights could very easily be construed as permitting discriminatory measures by nations which did not believe in the equality of the sexes" (ibid., 764).

The vigorous defense of this insertion by women UD drafters calls to mind the career of Justice Ruth Bader Ginsburg of the United States Supreme Court, who passed away as this book was sent to the publisher. Minerva Bernardino explained that the Dominican Republic was persistent in its amendment "because it was aware that in certain countries the term 'everyone' did not necessarily mean every individual, regardless of sex. Certain countries did in fact recognize certain rights for everyone, but experience had shown that women did not enjoy them, as, for instance, voting rights. She thought it was necessary to state that principle explicitly, in order to pay tribute to the part which women had played in the cultural development of the world and to the heroism they had shown during the war" (A/C.3/SR.166/771). After Bernardino finished,

Eduardo Anze Matienzo, her colleague from Bolivia, paid her "tribute . . . for her admirable efforts in support of women's rights" (ibid., 773). Ann Newlands of New Zealand echoed what Menon of India had said, that the "principle of equal rights for men and women should be explicitly mentioned" (ibid., 779). The insertion of this clause regarding the equality of the sexes was done by roll-call vote of thirty-two for, two against, with three abstentions. The United States and China voted against, while the United Kingdom, Canada, and Ethiopia abstained.

> 6) *Whereas Member States have pledged themselves to achieve, in co-operation with the United Nations, the promotion of universal respect for and observance of human rights and fundamental freedoms,*

This sixth recital is also taken literally from the UN Charter, this time from Article 56, where we read that "all members pledge themselves to take joint and separate action in cooperation with the Organization for the achievement of the purposes set forth in Article 55." One of the purposes explicitly mentioned in Article 55 is the promotion of "universal respect for, and observance of, human rights and fundamental freedoms for all without distinction as to race, sex, language or religion." These four items make up the standard way in which the charter talks about nondiscrimination in "human rights and fundamental freedoms," which is another standard phrase of the charter. In my comments on Article 2[a], I tell the story of how this short charter list of nondiscrimination items was expanded to the much longer list of "race, color, sex, language, religion, political or other opinion, national or social origin, birth or other status."

The New Zealand draft proposal for the preamble (C.3/257) that contained this recital did not include our first three recitals. In fact, it proposed that those three be pulled from the lineup because, as its representative, A. M. Newlands, said, "they did not contain anything essential to an international declaration of fundamental rights and freedoms" (A/C.3/SR.164/758). My reader already knows how helpful the first three recitals are in understanding why the declaration was proclaimed. Australia also objected to deleting these three recitals because doing so was carrying the "virtue of brevity too far." As a result, the New Zealand proposal to pull the first three recitals out of the lineup was withdrawn and we have what we have. This means that the only changes made in the Third Committee to the preamble were ones to the received text, not substitutions for it.

> 7) *Whereas a common understanding of these rights and freedoms is of the greatest importance for the full realization of this pledge,*

This recital takes off from where the sixth recital stopped. An earlier draft under discussion in the Third Session of the commission stirred quite a philosophical controversy over the phrase I have put here in italics: "Whereas this [sixth recital] pledge can be fulfilled only through a common understanding of *the nature of* these rights and freedoms." The commission had borrowed this entire recital, including the italicized phrase, from the Lebanese and UK submissions for the preamble (E/CN.4/132/124). Since the Third Session of the commission sent this text on to the Third Committee and the General Assembly without the italicized phrase, I report on the deletion of this phrase.

This seventh recital takes away some of the philosophical depth that I argued the first recital gives to the idea of modern human rights, that they are inherent in and inalienable to the human person. What most drafters meant by "inherent" and "inalienable" was caught up in the commission's language of "a common understanding of the nature of these rights." Any drafter voting for this phraseology would presumably agree that it is the nature of human rights that they are inherent in and inalienable to the human person. But that is something no communist steeped in Marxist ideology could accept. For them and some others, human rights are human-made or society-created. They are not part of our moral DNA, as I suggested in commenting on the first two recitals. No vote was ever taken on this particular issue (the communists forgot to abstain on the first recital), but to me a close reading of the drafting stories I present in this book suggests that something like inherence and inalienability best explains the miracle of this UD adoption in the shadow of the Holocaust. I argue this case in detail in Johannes Morsink, *The Universal Declaration of Human Rights and the Holocaust: An Endangered Connection* (Washington, DC: Georgetown University Press, 2019).

Pavlov from the Soviet Union noted that "to make the Declaration on Human Rights dependent on the application of a common conception of the nature of rights and freedoms would destroy its very purpose. The Commission's discussions had clearly shown the divergences which existed between the members in the fields of philosophy and ideology; that difference of ideas had not prevented fruitful co-operation, because even though there had been disagreement on the nature of these rights, the Commission has, nevertheless, come to a satisfactory agreement as to their practical application." As presented, he said, "the wording seemed to require unity of thought and ideas which was impossible to achieve" (E/CN.4/SR.77/7).

Chairperson Roosevelt responded that "the realization of the purposes of the Declaration depended above all on a common understanding of the essential human rights and freedoms. If a common view of the nature of these rights and freedoms could not immediately be attained, then identity of views nevertheless remained the supreme aim to be sought. There had been disagreement in the Commission," she admitted, "but the decision of the majority had prevailed in the choice of articles, and the Declaration, as drafted, indicated as effectively as was possible at present the degree of agreement which had been reached" (E/CN.4/SR.77/7). China, the United States, Lebanon, and France all yielded fairly quickly.

First Chang noted that it made no sense to believe that, as the paragraph seemed to suggest, "the obligations assumed by members of the United Nations would not be binding should agreement on a common conception not be reached" (E/CN.4/SR.77/8). Right he was. In the seventy-five years since the declaration's adoption, even Western philosophers have not reached a common conception on the nature of what a human right is. To remove any ambiguity, Roosevelt proposed that the disputed phrase "the nature of" be deleted from the recital. Charles Habib Malik from Lebanon, who all along had been defending the Catholic natural law point of view, thought that even "without making that common conception [of human rights] *sine qua non* for international cooperation, the usefulness of such an identity of views could [still] be recognized," which is why he proposed simply saying, "Whereas this pledge could be best fulfilled through a common understanding of these rights and freedoms," joining Roosevelt in arguing for the deletion of the phrase "the nature of" (ibid., 8). Pavlov "nevertheless insisted on the deletion of paragraph 6 [=7]" of the preamble (ibid., 9).

Seeking to save the recital, the French delegation said that it would accept any text that "would satisfy [the] USSR representative and which would make it clear that the Commission has tried to find a common understanding and had succeeded in doing so" (E/CN.4/SR.77/9). But Geoffrey Wilson of the United Kingdom held out, arguing that "it should be emphasized in the Preamble that the Commission had achieved a remarkable degree of understanding and that the Declaration was the result of that identity of views" (ibid., 9). A subcommittee consisting of China, France, Lebanon, the United Kingdom, and the USSR was appointed. In a vote of thirteen for, none against, and one abstention (probably the USSR), it adopted the preamble's last recital as we now have it.

I again ask that the reader not skip the statement of purpose that comes next before we get to the individual articles. That statement explains the educational purpose both of the declaration and of this commentary on it. You will also find a helpful flowchart of the stages through which all the articles went on their way to final adoption. Vaguely knowing those stages will give the reader a sense of the plot for each article's drafting.

Operative Paragraph: Statement of Purpose

Now Therefore,
The General Assembly
Proclaims
The Universal Declaration of Human Rights

as a common standard of achievement for all peoples and all nations, to the end that every individual and every organ of society, keeping this Declaration constantly in mind, shall strive by teaching and education to promote respect for these rights and freedoms and by progressive measures, national and international, to secure their universal and effective recognition and observance, both among the peoples of Member States themselves and among the peoples of territories under their jurisdiction.

When this so-called operative paragraph (which I have called a statement of purpose) came up for adoption in the Third Committee, the Soviet Union proposed that it be offered to the world's nations as a recommendation instead of a proclamation. I italicized that word in this Soviet proposal: "The General Assembly *recommends* the following 'Declaration of Human Rights' to all States Members of the United Nations to be used at their discretion both in adopting appropriate legislative and other measures and in their systems of upbringing and education" (E/800). The drafters rejected this idea of the declaration being a "mere" recommendation, linked as it was by this Soviet proposal to an open espousal of discretion.

The chairperson Eleanor Roosevelt felt that "too much discretion would seriously impair the moral forcefulness of the declaration as a whole. The fact that the declaration would not be legally binding upon Governments made it all the more necessary that it would exercise upon them the greatest moral suasion" (A/C.3/SR.165/762). Also, this Soviet proposal directly addressed the Member States of the UN, and that went against the drafters' policy of not dealing directly with the obligations of states or governments. They wanted to save states' obligations for a later convention and for now keep the focus on just a declaration of human rights. However, the Soviet point about "upbringing and education" was well made.

A proclamation, which is what the declaration is, is more serious and—if it is to be adhered to—needs to be well prepared by the appropriate authority that makes it. As the reader will see, the UD drafters took their task very seriously. They did not serve simply in their individual capacities as experts or diplomats with special experiences. From December 1946 through December 1948 they attended hundreds of meetings and took thousands of votes, all on behalf of the countries they represented.

A proclamation or declaration cannot be undone by those to whom it is addressed, which in this case is the world's "peoples and nations." We know that these peoples and nations often fall short of this proclamation. They are often found not to be in compliance with it, but they cannot undo it. The same thing happens to us when we do not follow the president's proclamation of a certain day as a day of prayer or mourning or service. We can ignore it but not undo it. The UD drafters hoped that the world's peoples and nations would be inspired by this moral banner of a text that they would see floating over their intellectual landscapes and legal borders. That is in fact pretty much what happened in the first two decades after this proclamation was made. It was offered to them as a way to repair their nationalism, which in many places was obviously broken at that time, as it also is today.

In this proclamation, the peoples and nations of the world are addressed by the 1948 Third General Assembly of the United Nations, and only another future General Assembly meeting can undo or amend this proclamation, which—now that this text has worked its way into the deepest crevices of international law—is highly unlikely.

The Universal Declaration is very much a product not just of the peoples of the United Nations but also and especially of the United Nations as an international organization of Member States, which in 1948 counted just fifty-six. As I said, each of the many drafters the reader will encounter in this commentary represented his or her nation and government, in the same way that those who speak in today's Security Council speak and vote for their own nations. The UD drafters were official governmental delegates who represented and spoke for their nations and on behalf of their governments. I have therefore liberally referred to them either by their personal names or just by their country's name, as in "France said" or "Egypt proposed" or "Chile and Ethiopia joined forces." This way the reader will come to realize just how truly cooperative a project the Universal Declaration was on the international diplomatic level and not just personally among some eminent drafters.

By often just giving country positions or votes (leaving the delegates' names aside), I want to underscore what the president of the Third General Assembly, who was a Brazilian, said at midnight on December 10, 1948. He said that "the draft declaration did not reflect the particular point of view of any one people or any one group of peoples. Neither was it the expression of any one political doctrine or philosophical system. It was the result of intellectual and moral cooperation of a large number of nations; that explained its value and interest and also conferred upon it great moral authority" (A/PV.181/878). I dare my reader to go through this commentary and then not agree with what I just quoted the president of the 1948 General Assembly as saying, and not be inspired to work harder in the human rights trenches, now that you have seen the spirit of cooperation that made this invaluable text happen.

I need to point out the obvious fact that countries have changed a great deal since the 1940s, so that what a nation said then it might not say today. If you do not keep this crucial fact in mind, you will make some bad mistakes, for some of the changes are huge. Today's People's Republic of China was not established till 1949, one year after the declaration was adopted. This means that Peng-Chun Chang, who contributed a great deal, spoke on behalf of Chiang Kai-shek's fading government rather than express the wishes of the communist regime soon to be set up. Even when countries' names are the same now as then, their positions need no longer be what they were then. You will meet apartheid South Africa and not the post–Nelson Mandela one. While all of us will note many such big and small changes in countries whose histories we think we know, the point of this commentary is that the times are similar and the needed response just as great.

What the drafters had in mind was a declaration that was brief enough and written in plain enough language so that ordinary men and women the world over could understand it. I let my reader be the judge of whether they succeeded in that goal of reaching ordinary people and not just elites. As they say in this operative paragraph, they hoped this broader goal might be achieved if and when "every individual and every organ of society, keeping the Declaration constantly in mind, shall strive by teaching and education to promote respect for these rights and freedoms and by progressive measures, national and international, to secure their universal and effective recognition and observance." This aspirational language draws a great deal on submissions by the United Kingdom (E/CN.4/124) and Lebanon (E/CN.4/132) to the Preamble Committee of the Third Session of the commission.

It is obvious that the UD drafters wanted this text to become an educational tool on all levels of society, and that this education campaign would lead to later legal measures that over time would lead to "effective recognition and observance" of the rights it listed. They were not looking for a sudden human rights miracle that infused an instant reevaluation of values on a worldwide scale. Instead, they saw a lot of hard work ahead. I hope that by profusely citing the United Nations archives, I have opened up new avenues of research as to what nations in the late 1940s did or did not believe about human rights, and why.

Having taught numerous human rights courses, and having authored other books on this text, I confess to having had this declaration "constantly in mind" for some four decades. My hope is that this commentary meets its goal of being brief enough to be used as a teaching and research tool, a study guide on various educational levels, and a platform for progressive action.

Leonid Kaminsky of Byelorussia was disappointed in education being made the purpose of the declaration. He argued that this "operative part" of the declaration, "when seen in connection with the recitals, appeared to state that the main purpose of the declaration was merely to teach men to respect human rights and freedoms. While there was a vague reference to progressive measures, it contained no recommendation that progressive laws should be passed to ensure a common standard of achievement" (A/C.3/SR.165/765). Poland also asked whether "the work of two years by various bodies of the United Nations [was] to result merely in urging individuals and organs of society to strive by teaching and education" to promote respect for observance of human rights and freedoms (ibid., 761). The word "merely" overstates the case, for history shows that radical democratic, antiauthoritarian revolutions work best in nations where the public is familiar with liberal democratic values.

The history of what happened after the declaration was proclaimed shows these critics to have had too little faith in the idea of first proclaiming and inculcating the public with a moral standard and then later seeking to implement it, often incrementally. There can be no doubt that Kaminsky's call for "progressive measures" has been amply fulfilled since he made these remarks. By the end of the 1980s, nations around the world had, under auspices of the UN, adopted some 125 legally binding conventions that for their inspiration draw on one or several articles of the Universal Declaration.

Two of these international conventions are called covenants: the 1967 International Covenant on Economic, Social and Cultural Rights and the International Covenant on Civil and Political Rights of the same year. Between them, these two covenants implement the entire range of the Universal Declaration (except for Article 17 on property), which itself is not a legally binding convention as these two covenants are. Only nations can sign these human rights legal treaties. However, there are thousands of nongovernmental interest groups—such as Save the Children, the ACLU, and the Hunger Project—that claim moral backing in various articles of the Universal Declaration. Some of these groups lobby their governments to ratify (sign up to) specific treaties.

My readers can join any of these or other human rights interest groups and in that way fight back with human rights against all kinds of discriminatory practices, against terror, oppression, poverty, and different kinds of autocracy the world over. Today such organizations exist for almost every right mentioned in the declaration. I once bought my wife a bracelet from a company dedicated to implementing UD Article 22, about the human right to social security. The bracelet was made by artisans from recycled bomb material retrieved by peasant families in Laos from the secret war the United States waged there between 1964 and 1973.

When a nation joins one of these international conventions or treaties, it is legally obligated (depending on its own constitutional system) to follow through with measures of implementation. That accountability began when the nuclear session, or preparatory committee, decided that the UD drafters were to serve as representatives of their states or governments. It also shows in the fact that after signing on to the UN Convention Against Torture and Other Cruel, Inhuman or Degrading Treatment or Punishment, the United States followed up by passing the 1994 Federal Torture Act, which brought it in compliance with this convention. In 1990 the United States had passed its Americans with Disabilities Act (ADA), so after the adoption of the 2006 International Convention on the Rights of Persons with Disabilities, the United States included needed changes in its 2008 ADA Amendments Act, which brought it into compliance with this 2006 convention.

I wrote each of these birth stories on the different articles of the declaration so each could stand on its own without involving any of the rest. In this way even an interest in just one article can be satisfied by reading how that particular one got its shape. Since most of the articles went through eight of what I call construction stages, just this fact alone should give the reader an idea of how much effort the drafters went through to reach the finish line by December 10, 1948. All these construction or drafting stages are listed in the UN research guides (http://research.un.org/en/undhr), where the reader will find most of the citations in this book. After the reader knows to which drafting stage a citation belongs, he or she then needs to find the exact UN reference that I give after the citation.

Here are the eight stages with brief explanations.

Flowchart of the Debates

Stage One: **First Session of the Commission** (January 1947). Nations made general comments. Eleanor Roosevelt (United States) elected chair of this eighteen-member body. No text adopted.

Stage Two: **First Session of the Drafting Committee** (June 1947). Eight delegates discuss the UD text submitted by John Humphrey, the first director of human rights in the UN Secretariat. Revised by René Cassin, the delegate from France. Humphrey submits his survey of national constitutions that shows which nations have provisions pertinent to each of the proposed UD articles. First provisional text adopted.

Stage Three: **Working Group on the Declaration of Session Two of the Commission** (December 1947). Soviet Union is most cordial and cooperative. Productive session. New version adopted.

Stage Four: **Second Session of the Commission** (December 1947). Met in Geneva, Switzerland. Produced what is referred to as the "Geneva text" of the declaration. The document is getting quite long.

Stage Five: **Second Session of the Drafting Committee** (May 1948). Sometimes surprisingly important for finding solutions to drafting problems. UD draft submitted to UN Member States for comment.

Stage Six: **Third Session of the Commission** (May–June 1948). Very intent on making cuts in the received text. Crucial decision made to only seek adoption of an "international bill." Postponement of considerations of a legally binding covenant and of Measures of Implementation.

Stage Seven: **Third Committee Meetings** (of UN General Assembly) (Fall 1948). Most of the then fifty-six UN Member States eagerly take part in these "Great Debates." Because of this enlarged input, I often stress this stage in my stories. Title changed to "Universal Declaration of Human Rights." Malik from Lebanon in the chair.

Stage Eight: **Adoption Statements and Final Vote** (December 9 and 10, 1948). Third Session of the General Assembly. Herbert Evatt from Australia in the chair. Held in Paris, France.

In my notes the reader will encounter hundreds of documents as the UD text travels toward its final adoption. I mention one of them here. It is the "Documented Outline" of June 9 (E/CN.4/AC.1/3/Add.1) that I mentioned in Stage Two. In it Humphrey matched each of what became our thirty UD articles with provisions of the constitutions of Member States of the UN at that time. That means drafters could tell from this Humphrey survey how "popular" a certain proposed human right was in domestic constitutions before and into the 1940s. You might therefore say that the Universal Declaration was constructed "from the ground up." Humphrey's survey made the drafters comfortable with the idea of universalizing a certain right because they had seen it in the constitutions Humphrey had collected. It was up to them to find the universalizing phraseology, which, as you will see, was not an easy thing to do.

A second crucial, confusing result of the text's traveling through these different stages is that an article often changed its number in the lineup. What might be Article 5 at one stage might be Article 6 at another stage, or what was Article 2 at the start might be Article 29 at the end. I dealt with these changes in the lineup in two ways. If the number of the article is not part of one of my citations, I simply use the number that the article got at the very end, as in, "When Article 6 arrived at the Second Drafting Committee Session, four amendments were offered." That means that our Article 6 (on person before the law) received four amendments in the Second Session of the Drafting Committee, which is stage five in the flowchart. But when an article's number is part of one of my citations, I remain faithful to what was actually said, as in, "When Chairperson Roosevelt indicated that she did not agree with the wording of Article 5 [=6], Cassin responded . . ." Phraseology like this means that at that particular drafting stage (e.g., stage three or five or whatever), what became Article 6 in the end was at that point Article 5 in the lineup. All the articles underwent these kinds of number changes. They are the bane of any UD archival researcher.

The meetings and the debates in the Third General Assembly of 1948 make up the last of these eight construction stages. Fifty-six nations adopted the declaration at about midnight on December 10, 1948, in a vote of forty-eight for, zero against, and eight abstentions. On this December day the drafters took a great deal of time praising what they had done and explaining the eight abstentions. These abstentions came from South Africa, Saudi Arabia, and the communist block, which included the Soviet Union, the Byelorussian Socialist Republic, the Ukrainian Soviet Socialist Republic, Yugoslavia, Poland, and Czechoslovakia. The reader will see that many of these abstaining nations (except Czechoslovakia) participated in the drafting process. For different reasons, these abstainers were not satisfied with the final product and therefore abstained, but no nation voted against the declaration. It was adopted unanimously.

Evatt of Australia, the General Assembly chairperson, correctly predicted that "millions of men, women and children all over the world would turn to it for help, guidance and inspiration" (A/PV.181/934). Abdul Rahman of Syria noted that "civilization had progressed slowly through centuries of persecution and tyranny, until finally the present declaration had been drawn up." It was not, he said, "the work of a few representatives of the Assembly or in the Economic and Social Council; it was the achievement of generations of human beings who had worked towards that end. Now at least the peoples of the world would hear it proclaimed that their aim had been reached by the United Nations" (ibid., 922). You will see in these commentaries that the drafters often went beyond representing their own countries or generation and spoke up for humanity at large.

I need to make one more preliminary point. You do not have to read all these commentaries in one session or in the order I give them. Pick and choose as you go, and have a good read each time you check out one of them. I think you will find quite a few surprises.

Article 1
Born Free and Equal

> If God does not exist, everything is allowed.
> —Fyodor Dostoevsky
>
> Evolution has endowed us with ethical impulses.
> Do we know what to do with them?
> —Steven Pinker

All human beings are born free and equal in dignity and rights.
They are endowed with reason and conscience and should act
towards one another in a spirit of brotherhood.

As a warning to the reader that the drafting of the declaration was not a simple process, I need to begin with the observation that I think the opening phrase, "All human beings . . . ," though felicitous, is the result of a mistake in transmission. Until the Third Session of the commission, the text had read, "All men . . ." But in that session Belgium proposed it be changed to read, "All human beings . . ." However, the session instead adopted the UK-India amendment's phrasing of "All people, men and women . . ." At that point an unfortunate transmission error occurred because this vote was not passed on to the Third Committee. What that committee and later the General Assembly approved was the Belgian phrasing of "All human beings . . . ," which had not been officially adopted but had slipped in under the radar. Similarly, the women's lobby had gotten accepted "All people" for the opening phrase, but ended up with what we have. Luckily the same group did see to it that "in a spirit of brotherhood" replaced "like brothers" as the closing phrase of the article (E/CN.4/81). These and other changes led the Office of the UN High Commissioner for Human Rights to point out in its 2019 series of UD articles that "for its time the document is remarkably free of sexist language" (Art.1).

The first sentence of Article 1 reminds us of two Enlightenment-era terms ("inherent" and "inalienable") that the drafters used in the first recital of their preamble (see my discussion of the preamble). It is a virtual rewrite of the first sentence of the 1789 French declaration, which says that all "men are born, and always continue, free and equal in respect of their rights." The word "born" also reminds us of the first sentence of Rousseau's *Social Contract*, which he begins with the observation that "man is born free, yet everywhere he is in chains." The French delegate René Cassin (who wrote this Art.1 first sentence) told the 1948 General Assembly that "in common with the 1789 Declaration, the [Universal Declaration] was founded on the great principles of liberty, equality, and fraternity" (A/PV.180/865). The idea is that people are born with human rights, which is the source of their freedom and equality. These rights are part of their moral DNA and not the result of any kind of legislative or judicial procedures. After a vigorous debate and with a vote of twenty for, twelve against, and five abstentions, the Third Committee voted to keep the word "born" in the text (A/C.3/SR.99–124).

Lebanon proposed (A/C.3/235) replacing the words "are born" with "are" because it felt "there should be no implication that people though born equal, might lose that equality for any reason" (A/C.3/SR.98/98). Others worried that that loss might already have happened, as when the Soviet delegate theorized that the assertion "that all men are born free and equal represented a somewhat shaky basis for the declaration . . . [for] it was obvious that in the days of feudalism men had not been born free and equal." He therefore "laid emphasis on the fact that equality of rights before the law was determined not by the fact of birth but by the social structure of the state which had to promulgate laws to ensure that equality" (ibid., 110). Lebanon was a proponent of Catholic natural law ideas and not friendly to this Soviet legal positivist stance. When it saw where its proposal would lead, it withdrew its own amendment in order to support a Chinese one (A/C.3/236) that the word "born" be deleted from the first sentence. But as I said, the Third Committee wanted to keep that word in.

Many of Alexei Pavlov's colleagues did not see "born free and equal" as a legal statement, for that would involve them in discussions about legal implementation by states, which issue they had a policy of avoiding. They looked on this birth as a moral rider to people's physical births. Most did not say exactly when this moral rider attached itself to the physical process, though some Latin nations were willing to answer that by saying it happened at conception. Mexico thought "a human being's right to freedom and equality began from the moment of his conception and continued after his [physical] birth" (A/C.3/SR.99/121). The Venezuelan constitution also "guaranteed the protection of the child from its conception until its development had been completed" (ibid., 122). No roll-call vote was taken, so it is hard to say which way these nations voted on the word "born," whether to keep the text transcendent to national legal systems with that word in it or hold out for the moment of conception by deleting the word.

An Iraqi amendment captured this ambiguity by proposing that "all men *should* be free and equal in dignity and worth, and should be entitled to similar treatment and equal opportunities" (A/C.3/237). This put the entire article on an ethical plane, which is what China had also suggested be done. Explaining his country's amendment, Minochehe Masani Abadi said he felt "that the authors of the article had apparently been carried away by its emotional content; it was reminiscent of Rousseau and of the French revolution; [but] it was lacking in both clarity and originality" (A/C.3/SR.96/100). The article should make a statement either of fact or of rights, in which case the word "should" would be appropriate.

In the ensuing discussion it was repeatedly pointed out that though people are often not born into equal circumstances, they do have a deeper moral equality and that the word "should" failed to capture that deeper shared human dignity. For instance, the Egyptian delegate thought that "the Iraqi amendment weakened [Article] 1 . . . which should set forth man's inherent right to freedom and equality" (A/C.3/SR.99/118). His country had proposed a recital for the preamble that said that "the fundamental rights of man are not derived from his status as a national of a certain State, but constitute inherent attributes of his person" (A/C.3/264). At this point the Iraqi amendment was withdrawn.

Most drafters understood that the claim that people "are born free and equal in dignity and rights" was in no way meant to deny that gross inequalities existed everywhere. It was against the background of these obvious inequalities that they wanted to assert certain moral rights that are inherent in the human person. Syria wanted to retain the word "born" in order to "exclude the idea of hereditary slavery" (A/C.3/SR.99/118). The Lebanese and Chinese delegations that had first proposed deletion of the word "born" were themselves adherents of this inherence view. In the later discussion on the human right to asylum, Lebanon called this right "part of the birthright of man" and said that this right to asylum was one of those that were "inherent in the human person" (A/C.3/SR.121/335–36). And right after the word "born" was kept in the text, Lebanon (supported by China) suggested that in that case "and remain" should be added because "it would be dangerous to leave the words 'are born' without adding 'and remain,' as it would imply that human beings were born free and equal, but later, for various economic, social and political reasons ceased to be" (A/C.3/SR.99/124).

That addition was never voted on. Eleanor Roosevelt of the United States objected to it because "it was obviously not true that human beings always remained free and equal in dignity and rights" (ibid.). To which observation Cassin of France responded that "the [Third] Committee was not acting as a national parliament but as representative of the human community and in that capacity was competent to proclaim such an ideal" (ibid.). France had also calmed the waters earlier by saying that the drafters of the French bill of 1789 also had known that there were inequalities everywhere, but they had "wanted to affirm their belief in man's inherent right to equality and freedom" (A/C.3/SR.99/116). As I said, "and remain" was never voted on, but the moral rider suggested by the word "born" was kept in the text by a sizable majority.

In the Working Group of the Second Session of the commission, the chair asked France and the Philippines to come up with a joint proposal for the second sentence of Article 1. This is what they proposed: "They are endowed by nature with reason and conscience and should act towards one another like brothers" (E/CN.4/AC.2/SR.9). Led by Bodil Begtrup, its chairperson, the women's lobby had no trouble replacing the word "brothers" with our "in a spirit of brotherhood." But the phrase "by nature" was not so easily dealt with. In the Third Committee Brazil proposed to start the second sentence this way: "Created in the image and likeness of God, they are endowed with reason and conscience" (A/C.3/243). The Brazilian delegate said that his amendment "was simply intended to express the religious sentiments of the Brazilian people," and that "he felt sure [it] would be welcomed by an overwhelming majority of the peoples of the world" (A/C.3/SR.95/91). Argentina supported the amendment, arguing that the idea of men "being created in the image and likeness of God" was a belief that "all men held in common" (A/C.3/SR.98/109). Bolivia did not agree with the Soviet Union that no reference should be made to God because many countries had a separation of church and state: "Even in the USSR, where an attempt had been made to abolish all idea of God, freedom of worship had been restored. The common factor in mankind and the most realistic basis for human understanding was the belief in a Supreme Being and that belief should therefore be mentioned in the Declaration of Human Rights" (ibid., 113).

The Brazilians wanted to combat a materialistic view of human nature on which to base belief in human rights. One can interpret that religious stance as taking Dostoevsky's side when he is supposed to have suggested that "if God does not exist, everything is permissible," meaning theistic belief is necessary to ground moral values. I devoted an entire book to this question, defending the opening citation from Steven Pinker with which I began this essay (see Johannes Morsink, *The Universal Declaration and the Challenge of Religion* [Columbia: University of Missouri Press, 2017]). My point there is that all the world's major religious traditions contain a strand according to which people have independent access to the basic truths of morality, such as are found in the UD. That is why the UD drafters—many of whom were people of faith—were willing to approve a secular but benign declaration. Article 18 shows that the declaration is in no way an antireligious document. The drafters just did not think this kind of foundational question should be settled by voting on it.

I noted earlier that the phrase "by nature" had first been introduced in the Working Group of the Second Session. When that phrase arrived in the full Second Session of the commission, Alexandre Bogomolov of the USSR took it to be a reference to "the ideas of the materialistic French philosophers of the eighteenth century" (A/CN.4/SR.34–35). Belgium pointed to Rousseau as an exception, but the image that "nature" stood for materialism took hold, so that now with the Brazilian proposal in the Third Committee the drafters were asked to choose between basing these rights on God (or spirit) or on nature (or matter). Peng-Chun Chang from China did not see any benefit in his colleagues debating once again the nature of man. As he saw it, "the concept of God laid particular stress on the human, as opposed to the animal, part of man's nature" (A/C.4/SR.98/114). He therefore suggested that the phrase "by nature" be deleted "in the hope that the Brazilian delegation would be willing to withdraw its amendment and so spare the members of the Committee the task of deciding by vote on a principle which was in fact beyond the capacity of human judgment" (ibid., 114). That is exactly what happened. The phrase was taken out and the amendment withdrawn.

Article 2a
Nondiscrimination

No two leaves are alike, and yet there is no antagonism
between them or between the branches on which they grow.
   —Mohandas Gandhi

Throughout history, demagogues have used state power to
target minority communities and political enemies, often
culminating in state violence. Today, we face that threat in
our own country, where the president of the United States
is using the influence of our highest office to mount racist
attacks on communities across the land.
   —Ilhan Omar (US congresswoman from Minnesota,
   July 26, 2019)

---

[a] *Everyone is entitled to all the rights and freedoms set forth in this
Declaration, without distinction of any kind, such as race, color,
sex, language, religion, political or other opinion, national or social
origin, birth or other status.*

The Charter of the United Nations mentions "human rights and fundamental freedoms" seven times, but it never gives us any specifics. Several
times it speaks of these rights and freedoms negatively, as when it pro-
hibits discrimination among peoples on the basis of "race, sex, language
or religion." Articles 2 and 7 of the UD are an elaboration of this charter
principle of nondiscrimination, which is why they for a long time used to
be treated as one article. I explain their separation when we get to Article 7. Here I tell the story of the first half of Article 2, which is the only
article to which I devote two stories.
   The long nondiscrimination list of Article 2[a]—"such as race, *colour,*
sex, language, religion, *political or other opinion, national or social origin,
property, birth or other status*"—is a bold expansion of the four charter
items of "race, sex, language or religion." Much of this expansion happened in the Sub-commission on the Prevention of Discrimination and
the Protection of Minorities, to which the UD drafters had sent their
text for advice. The title of this subcommission speaks to my opening citations about race relations in the United States because the drafters saw
the protection of minority rights and the prevention of discrimination as
intertwining causes. They felt that banning discrimination in the full

range of UD human rights was the best way to protect the rights of members of minority groups. This belief ended up being the main reason why the drafters did not include a specific article on the rights of members of minority groups. Opponents of such an article (for which see UD 27) held that Article 2 had done a good job protecting members of minority groups.

The UD drafters took the UN Charter items of "race, sex, language or religion" for granted and went on from there. Even so, the women's lobby took a great deal of *sexist* language out of the UD text, *religion* got its own article (Article 18), and *race* elicited a discussion about *color*. As to *language* rights, unfortunately there are only vague hints of those in the text when it speaks of a "fair . . . hearing" in Article 10 and of "all the guarantees necessary for his defense" in Article 11. For us the question is why the drafters felt the need to go beyond these four UN Charter items. I briefly comment on the newly added, italicized items in the UD 2 list quoted in the previous paragraph.

Color. Since color is the most obvious and frequently used physiological characteristic used to draw invidious distinctions between people, it is no accident that the strongest proponents of this addition to the UD list were countries like India, Lebanon, and the Philippines with large minority groups. Note that none of these are North Atlantic nations.

John Humphrey's constitutional research (E/CN.4/AC.1/Add.1) had shown that the Cuban (Art.20), Guatemalan (Art.21), and US (Fifteenth Amendment) constitutions all included the term "color." Pointing out that the American Federation of Labor "had thought fit . . . to refer explicitly to colour as well as race in connection with discrimination," M. R. Masani, the expert on the previously mentioned subcommission from India, proposed an amendment to do just that for UD Article 2 (E/CN.4/Sub.2/SR.4/2). His argument was that "race and colour were two conceptions that did not necessarily cover one another" (ibid., 3). Chairperson W. M. J. McNamara from Australia also "urged that if there was the slightest doubt it was better to add the word 'colour' than risk leaving out certain groups" (ibid., 3). French expert Samuel Spanien supported the idea because "the Sub-Commission could not embark on ethnological research" and "there was no scientific definition of the word 'race'" to begin with (ibid.). The Haitian, US, and Belgian experts disagreed. They all felt that adding "colour" at this time would cause problems because UN-related organizations like the International Labour Organization, the World Health Organization, and the United Nations Educational, Scientific and Cultural Organization had been using the standard four charter items. If "colour" was now added. those related texts would need to be revised and "the whole Charter would need to be revised" (ibid.). Supported by France, Iranian expert Rezazada Shafaq argued that "since there was no precise scientific definition of 'race,' the word had to be used in a general sense, which included the idea of 'colour'" (ibid., 3–4). At this point the Chinese expert "announced his readiness to withdraw his first statement" that under current usage race meant "colour" and that he would accept the idea of adding color (ibid., 4). Seeing that not all the experts agreed, the chair ruled that a note stating that "the term 'race' includes the idea of 'colour' be added to the text" that was sent to the Human Rights Commission (ibid., 5).

In the Second Session of the Human Rights Commission, the campaign to add "colour" was picked up by Masani's colleague Hansa Mehta. She pointed out that in the text of the legal covenant that the UD drafters were also writing, the word "colour" did follow "race," so why not in the declaration's text as well? She herself "understood the word 'race' to include 'colour,' but if there was any doubt on the subject, she felt that the word colour should be inserted in the Declaration" (E/CN.4/SR.34/10). She received strong support from the Lebanese and Philippine delegates. The Indian amendment to add the term "colour" to the nondiscrimination list of UD 2[a] was adopted by ten votes to none, with six abstentions (E/CN.4/SR.35/5).

Political or other opinion. The addition of this item was also initiated by Masani, the Indian expert on the *subcommission.* The Indian government had already gone on record in support of the principle that "every human being has the right of equality, without distinction of race, sex, language, religion, nationality or political belief" (E/CN.4/AC.1/3/Add.1/360). In line with this principle, Masani proposed "the addition of the words 'political opinion' after the word 'religion'" (E/CN.4/Sub.2/SR.4/5). This proposed addition elicited two kinds of objections.

One was that since "political opinion" was at this time covered later in UD Article 19, there was no need to add it to Article 2(1)'s list. On these grounds, Chairperson E. E. Ekstrand from Sweden "questioned the necessity for this addition" (E/CN.4/Sub.2/SR.4/5). E. Monroe from the United Kingdom was ready to support the addition "in view of the importance of matters of political opinion in case of minorities" (ibid.) Her point was well made because 2(1)'s list must be read into all the other articles to see its effectiveness and not just into UD 19. Herard Roy of Haiti agreed because "religion" was on the list but was also mentioned in Article 18. To reconcile these different views, McNamara from Australia proposed that "or other opinion" be added to the term "political," making the text applicable to "any other opinion" as well (ibid., 7). Spanien of France pointed out that there was a "gap in the Charter which ought to be filled" and therefore supported the Masani proposal (ibid., 6).

A second objection to the addition of "political opinion" came from USSR expert A. P. Borisov, who asked, "If the Sub-Commission accepted these proposals unreservedly, would the terms 'political or other opinion' also cover the political opinion of Nazis or Fascists concerning, for instance, the superiority of the white race over the black?" (E/CN.4/Sub.2/SR.4/8). J. Daniels from the United States "agreed with Mr. Borisov, that the expression 'or political opinion' involved a certain danger. But experience has shown that any restriction imposed in this sphere was a blow to human freedom" (ibid., 9). Shafaq from Iran answered Borisov by pointing out "that the Nazi and Fascist movements were not purely racial in character, since they brought one section of the white race into conflict with another, that is the Aryan and the Semitic. He added that the Nazi movement had been finally condemned, and it seemed futile to reopen the question" (ibid., 10). When Masani called for a vote, the phrase "political or other opinion" was accepted for insertion in the list of nondiscrimination items (by ten votes with one abstention) and sent on to the Second Session of the Human Rights Commission.

There Alexei Pavlov of the USSR tried once more to delete the item "political or other opinion" from the list. The attempt failed when both the Belgian and British delegates objected. Belgium said the substitute list was "unacceptable" because "there was no mention [in it] of political opinion" (E/CN.4/SR.35/3). And the United Kingdom would vote against the Soviet amendment "because it did not protect the individual against discrimination on grounds of his political opinion . . . [and] a one-party Government would not be obliged to take measures to safeguard the freedom of those professing a different political opinion from its own" (ibid.). The Soviet Union again used the subterfuge of Nazi "political opinion which tolerated not only the advocacy of racial or national hatred, but also the actions rising therefrom" (ibid., 4). When Hernan Santa Cruz from Chile asked whether an individual could be prosecuted for his political opinion, Pavlov repeated that he was focused on "propaganda and actions based on national and racial hatred" (ibid.). Other commission members did not accept this Soviet subterfuge and rejected the proposed substitute list by ten to four votes with three abstentions (ibid., 5).

Property status, national or social origin. In the same *subcommission,* the USSR proposed the following text for what was then Article 6 (but really an early combination of UD 2 and 7): "All people are equal before the law and shall enjoy equal rights in the economic, cultural, social and political life irrespective of their race, sex, language, religion, *property status, national or social origin*" (E/CN.4/Sub.2/21). Here you have the origin of three more (italicized) items on UD 2(1)'s nondiscrimination list. The problem was that this list had already been changed by the two Masani proposals discussed earlier, which had first added "colour" and then also "political or other opinion" to the list. This led to a very diffi-cult procedural discussion that I will spare my reader. The result was that, by nine to one with one abstention, the *subcommission* adopted just these three new items, "property status, national or social origin," for inclusion in UD 2's list.

When Spanien of France suggested using just the word "origin" and deleting the adjectives "national" and "social," Borisov of the USSR re-sponded with the observation that "in his opinion 'origin' did not neces-sarily include 'national origin.' The U.S.S.R. for example had various nationalities of the same origin" (E/CN.4/Sub.2/SR.5/7). This did not interfere with being a Soviet citizen because later on Borisov noted that it was "in the interest of countries where people of different national ori-gins lived together under the same government that the words 'national origin' should be specifically mentioned" (ibid., 9). I think Borisov was referring to peoples from Tajikistan, Azerbaijan, Georgia, Byelorussia, Lithuania, Latvia, Estonia, Moldova, and Armenia, all of whom Lenin had made part of the Soviet State in 1922. It would seem that Borisov had this quilt of Soviet peoples in mind when he vigorously defended his proposed addition of "national or social." We might compare it to what today in the United States is meant by "hyphenated Americans," which includes millions of African Americans, some Dutch Americans, and not a few Polish Americans, right down the list of immigrants and their fore-bears, all of whom have different national origins but the same citizen-ship. Borisov said he had "no wish for aliens to be given the right to vote in a foreign country, but he thought the rights of national groups, living as citizens in a country, should be protected" (ibid., 10).

When Roy from Haiti pointed out that in many countries there was a difference between native and naturalized citizens (E/CN.4/Sub.2/SR.6/4), Borisov responded that "within the same nationality there could be different origins. . . . This meant that any citizen of the Soviet Union, were he Jew, Negro, Georgian, Caucasian, etc. could become a member or the President of the Supreme Council. The social ranks to be found within every country should not stand in the way of equality of rights. He asked whether in the United States a Negro, a Jew, or a naturalized Mexi-can could become President. If there were any discrimination in that field, there could be no equality of rights" (ibid., 6). The phrase "prop-erty status, national or social origin" was adopted in the subcommission with six votes and five abstentions and sent on to the Human Rights Commission (ibid., 14). The entire list of 2(1), "Everyone is entitled to all the rights and freedoms set forth in this Declaration without distinc-tion such as race, sex, language, religion, political or other opinion, property status, or national or social origin," was adopted by nine votes to one with one abstention and passed on to the Commission of Human Rights as advice (ibid., 15). The commission took the advice and adopted this text.

Birth or other status. At one point in the Third Committee, Alan S. Watt from Australia said he "agreed with the Cuban representative that it might be dangerous to insert the word 'birth' in article 2. Article 1 stated that all men were born equal; it was now suggested that article 2 should state that all men were not born equal" (A/C.3/SR.101/139). My report shows that here in Article 2[a] the term has a social-economic meaning that complements and strengthens the moral and philosophical meaning it has in Article 1.

In the Third Session of the commission, Michael Klekovkin from the Ukrainian Socialist Republic sought to insert the Russian concept of *soslovie* (the approximate meaning of which is "class or social structure") after the words "property status" in the list of Article 2[a] quoted a couple of paragraphs above. He wanted to draw attention to differences in class and social status (E/CN.4/SR.52/5). This led the United Kingdom to suggest deleting the word "property," leaving the word "status" all by itself. Pavlov from the USSR wanted to keep the term "property" since "it was most important that rich and poor should have the same rights. The Ukrainian amendment was directed against feudal class privileges which were generally determined by birth rather than wealth" (ibid.) At that point Ukraine accepted China's proposal to insert the words "or other" between the terms "property" and "status." The insertion met with unanimous approval (ibid., 6). It opened the door to a social-economic interpretation of the term "birth," as is shown by a later slap on the wrist of the subcommittee on style.

When the Third Committee's subcommittee on style rearranged the items on the list and moved "birth" from its social and economic context at the end to the middle of the list right after "religion" and before "national or social origin," it was rebuffed and "birth" was moved back to its end position. While France, China, and Cuba all were satisfied that the forward move had been the right one, Bogomolov from the USSR was not pleased. He "recalled that when the article had been studied in the Third Committee he had declared himself opposed to the use of the word 'birth,' to which he preferred the word 'estate' [A/C.3/SR.101/137]. Since certain delegations had not wished that expression to be used, though it was rich in meaning both historically and politically, he had agreed to accept the word 'birth' on condition that it should be in its proper place in the Third Committee's text, namely, following considerations of a social character" (A/C.3/SR.175/851). Supported by Karim Azkoul from Lebanon, who also felt the subcommittee had overstepped its mandate, Bogomolov repeated that "it should not be forgotten that the declaration of human rights should also apply to countries which had not yet evolved as fully as had France and the USSR, and that there were still backward countries, in some of which castes and privileges attached to estates still existed" (ibid., 852). That sense of birth was gutted by having it appear in the earlier context of race, sex, language, and religion and not in the vicinity of the later social and economic items, to which place it was restored.

Article 2b
Colonialism and Systemic Racism

Colonialism hardly ever exploits the whole of a country. It contents itself with bringing to light the natural resources, which it extracts, and exports to meet the needs of the mother country's industries, thereby allowing certain sectors of the colony to become relatively rich. But the rest of the colony follows its path of under-development and poverty, or at all events sinks into it more deeply.

   —Frantz Fanon, *The Wretched of the Earth*

racism (noun), 2a: the systemic oppression of a racial group to the social, economic, and political advantage of another, *specifically* WHITE SUPREMACY.

   —*Miriam-Webster's Dictionary* online

---

[b] *Furthermore, no distinction shall be made on the basis of the political, jurisprudential or international status of the country or territory to which a person belongs, whether it be independent, trust, non-self-governing or under any other limitation of sovereignty.*

There is a connection between the colonialism that Frantz Fanon talks about in the epigraph and the "institutional" or "systemic racism" that has been in the news since the killing of George Floyd in Minneapolis, Minnesota, in 2020. Colonialism is a prime example of institutional or systemic racism. Former colonial powers and their friends, of whom the United States is one, are now called on by the Black Lives Matter movement to treat all migrants of the colonized world as equal human beings and value their cultural traditions as much as the Eurocentric one that has held sway until now. The presence of statues, street names, school curricula, and museum exhibits that go back to that period of their histories must be reevaluated. The irony of this piece of drafting history is that only now, seventy-two years later, former metropolitan powers and their friends—who thought they were done with the ideology of white supremacy when they adopted this second paragraph of UD Article 2— are forced to face up to the fact that that same ideology of white supremacy has been operating on their metropolitan home territories in ways they have failed to address all these many years.

I therefore invite my readers to read between the lines of these debates about colonialism and detect a deeper systemic racism wherever it can be found, which is almost everywhere, even in the nations that joined the United Nations as a result of the success of this anticolonialism fight in the 1940s. When this 2b story reaches its Third Committee stage, I will make one of those between-the-lines observations about the Netherlands, my country of birth.

Between 1945 and 1975 United Nations membership rose from 51 Member States to 144 largely because of the dismemberment of what in the 1940s were still the colonial empires of mostly European Member States of the United Nations. That process of dismemberment was just starting when the declaration was being written and the drafters devoted the second paragraph of Article 2 to that issue. They knew that the nondiscrimination measures of Article 2's first paragraph were not enough and that they had to also address the question of the human rights of the enslaved peoples living in the colonial empires of these mostly European states.

In 1914 Lenin calculated that "more than half the world's population lived in colonies, which together covered ¾ of the world's territory" (*Imperialism: The Highest Stage of Capitalism*, 76), a calculation that was still roughly correct in the late 1940s when the UD was crafted. This nonfree half lived in colonies governed by metropolitan powers or in territories that were held in trust for the United Nations. They therefore had no direct representatives at the UD drafting table, around which only independent states were sitting. As firm believers in the principle of nondiscrimination, the communist delegations took it upon themselves to bring the question of the colonies out in the open. The second paragraph of Article 2 is the result of that effort. I discuss it in this separate essay because, as you will see, it is not a normal second paragraph.

In September 1947 Andrei Zhdanov, Stalin's heir apparent, gave a key speech, "The International Situation," at the founding of the Cominform, the Communist Information Bureau, in Poland. He asserted that there was "a crisis of the colonial system" and that "the peoples of the colonies no longer wished to live in the old way. The ruling classes of the metropolitan countries can no longer govern the colonies on the old lines." The impact of Zhdanov's speech was immediately felt in the working groups of the Second Session of the Commission on Human Rights, which met in Geneva in December 1947.

When the requirements for the right to participation in government of UD Article 21 were being discussed, the Soviet and Byelorussian delegates cited Articles 73 and 76 of the United Nations Charter about the responsibilities of the metropolitan powers over their colonies and the trust territories under their jurisdiction. The United Kingdom responded that "some of the western democratic procedures" were not recognized by "some of the British African dependencies . . . their forms of native government being based on old-established customs with which it was the policy of his government to interfere as little as possible" (E/CN.4/AC.2/SR.7/8).

The matter came to a full-blown debate in the Third Session of the commission, which met in May and June 1948. You will recall that the operative paragraph (Statement of Purpose) of the declaration ends with the demand that human rights be secured for "the people of the Member States themselves and among the peoples of territories under their jurisdiction." The "peoples of territories under their jurisdiction" obliquely refers to the colonies and was added upon the recommendation of Egypt. The Soviet Union had submitted a much longer amendment to correct what it saw as a mistake of the Sub-committee on the Preamble because it made no reference to "trust and non-self-governing territories." The United Kingdom objected to the Soviet version because of the "apparent discrimination made in the USSR text by especially mentioning the trust and non-self-governing territories" (E/CN.4/SR.77/12). France also objected to any suggestion that "the populations of these territories did not enjoy the essential rights and freedoms on an equal footing with the populations of the metropolitan territories" (ibid., 13). To avoid the longer Soviet version that made explicit mention of these non-self-governing and trust territories, the Egyptian proposal that spoke only of "the peoples and territories under their jurisdiction" was adopted. In the next meeting, a Chinese proposal to insert "for all peoples" before "all nations" in the same operative paragraph was also adopted to cast the human rights net over all peoples, including those living in the colonies.

Because Tito (dictator of Yugoslavia) and Stalin (dictator of the Soviet Union) had just split, the communist forces in the Third Committee did not synchronize their efforts. They proposed separate amendments to add an article on the colonies to the declaration. The Soviet version was the longer of the two, which is probably why this shorter Yugoslav article was adopted in a vote of sixteen to fourteen with seven abstentions: "The rights proclaimed in this declaration also apply to any person belonging to the population of Trust and Non-Self-Governing Territories" (A/C.3/307/Rev.1/Add.1). The fourteen nations voting against this insertion were mostly the metropolitan powers and their allies: Australia, Belgium, Canada, Chile, China, Costa Rica, the Dominican Republic, France, Honduras, the Netherlands, Paraguay, Sweden, the United Kingdom, and the United States. The seven abstentions are notable for including so many Latin American nations: Argentina, Brazil, Denmark, Ecuador, Greece, Uruguay, and Venezuela.

I was born in the Netherlands, and Piet Hagen, a high school acquaintance of mine, wrote a two-volume account of the Dutch colonial regime in Indonesia (*Koloniale oorlogen in Indonesia: Vijf eeuwen verzet tegen vreemde overheersing*) that at the time of this vote was just starting to fold. He told me that throughout its history, the Dutch clearly practiced their version of systemic or institutional racism as recently defined by *Merriam-Webster's Dictionary* and cited at the start of the discussion of Article2[b]. I invite my reader to make similar inquiries about the hypocrisy of any of the other twenty countries in this coalition of deniers of systemic racism in this as well as in the other votes on Article 2[b] that follow.

As a rationale, all these nations shared the idea that it was unwise to mention special cases of discrimination for fear that other possible exceptions that were not singled out would avoid judgment. Following Greece, Belgium made that point when it argued that a more general language would catch the anomaly of "territories with a special juridical status . . . namely of Tangier and Trieste currently and Jerusalem in the future." It wanted to avoid "the danger of excluding a single human being from enjoying the rights and freedoms to be established in the declaration" (A/C.3/SR.176/858–59).

One of the clearest statements on behalf of the colonial peoples and the inclusion of the separate article came from New Zealand, which held Western Samoa in trust for the UN. Ann Newlands said she felt that "all delegations would probably agree in principle that the human conscience has progressed so far as to find oppression of colonial peoples intolerable" (A/C.3/SR.173/741). To the nations that argued that a general statement about discrimination as we find in UD 2[a] was good enough, she responded that the general principle had been repeatedly declared, "but it had not always been applied in colonial territories" (ibid.). To avoid all possible misunderstanding, a separate article was needed since "the rights of the colonial peoples should receive the same consideration as those of others, if the Declaration was to avoid the appearance of making discriminations." Delegations opposed to the separate article "had little idea," she said, "of the feeling of exasperation and despair generated in peoples living under colonial regimes" (ibid.).

This disagreement turned into a real fight when the text of the declaration came back from the Sub-committee on Style and Order. The members of that committee (Australia, Belgium, China, Ecuador, France, Lebanon, Poland, the USSR, the United Kingdom, and the United States) had been charged to examine the text "solely from the standpoint of arrangement, consistency, uniformity and style." However, they accepted a Cuban proposal to replace the already accepted independent Yugoslav article on the colonies with this additional second paragraph to Article 2: "Furthermore, no distinction shall be made on the basis of the political status of the country to which a person belongs" (A/C.3/400/Rev.1/Annex A). Not only had the charter language of "Non-Self-Governing and Trust Territories" been dropped for the less specific phrase "political status of the country," the colonies were in effect demoted from having their own article to being indirectly mentioned in a second paragraph on nondiscrimination. In their report the members of the subcommittee admitted that Ecuador, Poland, and the USSR had objected to this demotion (A/C.3/400/Rev.1/3). These countries felt that the subcommittee had exceeded its terms of reference.

Third Committee chair, Charles Habib Malik from Lebanon, agreed that the subcommittee "had gone beyond its terms of reference" and so ruled (A/C.3/SR.176/861). When the Cuban delegation appealed that ruling, the chair was upheld and the Yugoslav article reinserted by a vote of twenty-nine to seven with nine abstentions (ibid., 862).

In the Third Committee's general debate before it passed the UD on to the General Assembly, Yugoslavia proposed the following additional article 3[c]: "The rights proclaimed in this declaration also apply to any person belonging to the population of Trust and Non-Self-Governing Territories" (A/C.3/307/Rev.1/Add.1). Its representative, Ljuba Radevanovic, argued that the UD "should reflect the conscience of the times. The fundamental human rights therein declared should be applicable to every person, including all persons belonging to the population of Trust and Non-Self-Governing Territories. All delegations would probably agree in principle that the human conscience had progressed so far as to find oppression of colonial peoples intolerable. The declaration could not in itself alter existing conditions, but it could and should proclaim that the principle of human dignity applied to the populations of Trust and Non-Self-Governing Territories" (A/C.3/SR163/741). This Yugoslav provision was adopted in a sixteen-to-fourteen vote with seven abstentions and passed onto the General Assembly as a separate, additional Article 3 (ibid., 746). Support had come from the communist bloc over the opposition from the colonial powers. Stephen P. Demchenko from the USSR had drawn his colleagues "to the two different attitudes that had been expressed during the debate. On the one hand, there was the point of view of the colonial Powers, who, not surprisingly, objected to the adoption of the Yugoslav proposal, On the other hand, several representatives had demanded equal rights for all the peoples of the world, among them representatives of countries that had experienced the colonial yoke. The declaration indicated that human rights should be enjoyed by all the peoples of the world. For some reason, the representatives of the colonial Powers had argued that the insertion of the Yugoslav proposal would weaken the declaration. The French and Belgian representatives had asked why it was necessary to include a special reference to the Trust and Non-Self-Governing Territories. It was necessary because it was in those areas of the world that people were not allowed to exercise their rights to equal pay for equal work, to education, and so on (ibid., 745).

In a bold, unprecedented move in the General Assembly, the United Kingdom proposed that the Yugoslav-inspired Article 3 on human rights in the colonies be dropped and replaced with what we now have as the second paragraph of Article 2 (A/778/Rev.1). No roll-call vote was taken, but we can see the impact of the Cold War that until then had been kept out of the proceedings. This is what the United Kingdom said:

Although the general view was that it was too late to modify the text of the draft declaration, the United Kingdom delegation nevertheless proposed an amendment (A/778/Rev.1) to [Yugoslav-sponsored] article 3. That article contained one of the most serious blemishes in a declaration which included certain passages that doubtless could have been better drafted, but which the United Kingdom delegation and the majority of the Assembly were prepared to accept.

Article 2 laid down that every individual was entitled to the rights and freedoms proclaimed in the declaration, without distinction of any kind. If article 2 had any meaning and if its terms were sufficiently precise and enumerated sufficiently clearly the distinctions to be outlawed, there was no reason to add an article 3 stipulating that those rights applied to the inhabitants of the Trust and Non-Self-Governing Territories.

The United Kingdom had been accused in the Third Committee of wishing to delete article 3, so that it should not have to respect the rights in its colonial territories. As the Assembly was aware, there was no justification whatsoever for making a statement of that kind. If that were the case, the United Kingdom would not have accepted article 2. (A/PV.181/883)

As I said, the USSR and Yugoslavia did not strategize together. Soviet delegate Andrei Vishinski (known for his role in the infamous Stalin show trials) attacked the Yugoslav article (UD 3) as "still less satisfactory" than the already highly defective article on nondiscrimination (UD 2(a)) because neither contained a reference to "the right of nations to self-determination," which had become the hallmark of the Soviet campaign to end colonialism (A/PV.183/926). However, by not supporting their Yugoslav comrades, the Soviet Union—which controlled other communist delegations, but not Yugoslavia—helped the British demotion proposal succeed.

The vote in the General Assembly to demote the colonies from having their own article to becoming the second paragraph of Article 2 came in at twenty-nine for, seventeen against, and ten abstentions (A/PV.183/932). The symbolism of this vote is crucial, for in law as in poetry, separate spaces and lines matter a great deal.

Article 3
Life, Liberty, and Security of Person

All mankind . . . being all equal and independent, no one
ought to harm another in his life, health, liberty or
possessions.
  —John Locke

In the years 1893 and 1923, the number of lynchings per
year exceeded two hundred; as late as 1945 and 1946, more
than several dozen barbaric lynchings had taken place. It
was against such criminal acts that some provision had to be
included in article 3 [of the declaration].
  —Soviet delegate to UD drafters in 1948

Everyone has the right to life, liberty and security of person.

Alexei Pavlov, the Soviet delegate I quote in the epigraph, was addressing his colleagues on the Commission on Human Rights that drew up
the Universal Declaration. Eleanor Roosevelt was the chair, and Pavlov
aimed his ire at her country. What was she to say? President Franklin
Roosevelt had just received a report from which Pavlov was quoting. As
you see, the standard topics of the death penalty and abortion were not
the only issues raised by this first UD article that lists specific human
rights. These three rights to "life, liberty and security of person" are the
first ones from a long list, and the UD drafters wanted to make sure that
the first impression they gave to the world would be a good one, like you
want your front door mat to look nice. The text speaks of "security of
person," which to the drafters ended up meaning far more than what we
mean today when people install an alarm system in their houses to protect
their "personal security." Latin American drafters heard in the phrase
"security of person" a prelude to the social and economic rights of the
second half of the declaration. They wanted to make the mat more wel-
coming, but, though close, they failed.

  John Humphrey's first submission on the right to life went like this:
"Everyone has the right to life. This right can be denied only to persons
who have been convicted under general law of some crime to which the
death penalty is attached" (E/CN.4/21/9). Unlike today, when roughly
two-thirds of the world's 195 countries have abolished the death penalty,
Humphrey found only two constitutions (Ecuador and Uruguay) of the

twenty-six he paired with this Article 3 that seemed to have completely done away with it. So when he wrote his first draft, he was following the data. This is what the constitutions of Bolivia (Art.25, 1938), Brazil (Art.141, 1946), Greece (Art.18, 1911), the United States (Fifth Amendment, 1787), and many other nations told his survey (E/CN.4/AC.1/3/Add.1).

When this Article 3 was read in the First Drafting Committee Session, Chairperson Roosevelt "remarked that she understood that there was a movement underway in some States to wipe out the death penalty completely" (E/CN.4/AC.1/SR.2/10). René Cassin of France observed that "if the principle of universal abolition of the death penalty could be adopted it should not impose a strict obligation on States which wished to maintain the death penalty" (ibid.). Hernan Santa Cruz from Chile responded that his country's submission did both; it established the right to life and also noted that the state had "a duty to watch over the implementation of the right" (ibid.). He added that Chile's submission was more complete in that it also "referred to the life of any being, born or unborn" (ibid.). This placed the two controversial issues of the death penalty and abortion on the UD drafting table. However, neither ended up in the final text.

Peng-Chun Chang of China said "that more thought should be put into the definition of the word 'life'—was it intended to mean mere physical existence or did it imply something more than that?" (E/CN.4/AC.1/SR.3/12). Cassin—who had had a Gestapo arrest warrant posted on his Paris apartment door—responded that "the term 'right to life' referred to physical life and only to physical life. He pointed out that this distinction might not appear obvious at first glance but that recently the world had known of instances where certain persons felt they had the right to destroy life" (ibid.). But he "agreed that it was possible to group together everything having to do with life, physical inviolability, and liberty and personal liberty as one unified subject" (E/CN.4/AC.1/SR.8/4), as we also see John Locke doing in the opening citation. Since Cassin had been given the task of doing the rewrites, he could implement his own suggestion, and from that point on the article simply stated that "everyone has the right to life, to personal liberty and to personal security." This simple three-term text was passed on to the Second Session of the commission, where different working groups kept the issues of the death penalty and abortion out of the UD text.

In the Working Group on the Declaration, the International Federation of Christian Trade Unions pointed out that in Article 3 "the right to life was affirmed without any specification of the biological moment when human life began. The majority of laws included measures protecting life born or conceived" (E/CN.4/AC.2/SR.3/7). Bodil Begtrup from the Commission on the Status of Women pointed out that "Vanistendael's [of the International Federation of Christian Trade Unions] proposal could not be reconciled with the provisions of certain advanced legislations which in certain cases provided for the right to abortion" (ibid., 8). The chairperson of the group put the received three-term text of Article 3 (that did not mention abortion) up for a vote, and it passed seven to four with two abstentions (ibid.). Abortion continued to be discussed as an option for the convention text, where in the end it also failed.

In the Second Session, just before the vote on this three-term Article 3, Uruguay proposed this long addition: "The death penalty shall never be applied to political offenders. With regard to criminal offenders it shall only be applied after sentence rendered under existing laws after a trial with the necessary guarantees for a just sentence" (E/CN.4/SR.35/13). By a vote of nine to three with five abstentions, this death penalty paragraph was rejected and all of Article 3 was reaffirmed unanimously. However, the Working Group on the Convention did adopt a provision for the death penalty in its own Article 4: "It shall be unlawful to deprive any person of his life save in the execution of the sentence of a court following his conviction of a crime for which this penalty is provided by law" (E/CN.4/56/6). This means that Humphrey's death penalty clause made it into the convention but not into the Universal Declaration.

The Second Session of the Drafting Committee and Third Session of the commission adopted Article 3 ("Everyone has the right to life, to personal liberty and to personal security") unanimously. This brings us to the Third Committee, which, because it had representatives on it from all fifty-six Member States, was always a scene of interesting amendments. I highlight the two that received the most discussion.

The Soviet Union's proposed text for Article 3 read like this: "Everyone has the right to life. The State should ensure the protection of each individual against criminal attempts on his person. It should also ensure conditions that obviate the danger of death by hunger and exhaustion. The death penalty should be abolished in time of peace" (A/C.3/265). Pavlov defended this proposal with a hard-hitting opening speech. He "drew attention to the practice of lynching which was still being carried on in the United States and referred to a document put forward by the National Association for the Advancement of Colored People. Between 1893 and 1923, as noted in the epigraph to this article, the number of lynchings per year exceeded two hundred, and several dozen had taken place as recently as 1946 (A/C.3/SR.102/142). He also pointed out that more than fifteen million Indians had died of starvation in the last quarter of the nineteenth century. While in 1931 in India life expectancy was 26.9, that in England and Wales was 60 years. One could not blame climate conditions for these differences because the "mortality figures for Indians as compared with Europeans in India, proved that those conditions were the result of the practices of colonial administration" (ibid.).

Cold War rhetoric like this broke the rule that nations were not to comment negatively on each other's internal affairs. Roosevelt responded that she "very much deplored the fact that there were some cases of lynching in her country, but such a practice was exceptional and clearly in violation of law. She regretted that the USSR representative had chosen to repeat again the attack he had made against the United States, in spite of the plea she [as chair] had made for a different spirit among members of the Committee" (A/C.3/SR.102/147).

Christopher Mayhew of the United Kingdom responded,

The Soviet Union claiming to be the only country qualified to speak on behalf of democracy, had erected within its borders a system which made slaves of millions of human beings. Such a phenomenon was unprecedented in history. Since 1930 the world had felt concern about the existence of forced labour in the USSR. But at the time it had been viewed as a normal phenomenon, the inevitable result of a vast social experiment. . . . The most conservative estimate reached after a perusal of Soviet publications placed the number of prisoners in the USSR at 1,830,000; non-Soviet estimates placed that number at several million. Furthermore, tragic reports of the conditions prevailing in the detention camps of the Union came from prisoners who had escaped from those camps. . . . It was patent that the [world's] anxiety was justified, and that was why the United Kingdom could not allow Soviet propaganda to attack, as it was doing, the freedom of democratic peoples and their way of life. (A/C.3/SR.103/160–61).

At this point the debate was closed and the whole of the Soviet amendment except for the first sentence ("Everyone has the right to life.") was rejected by a large majority of drafters.

Also in the Third Committee, Mexico proposed to add this second paragraph to the three-term article: "The right to maintenance, heath, education and work, is considered essential in order to obtain an increase in the standard of living of the individual, as well as secure full existence of social justice and the full development of the human being" (A/C.3/266). Clearly, Mexico wanted to pull what is in Articles 15–27 forward to Article 3. Many other nations felt the same way; Uruguay, Cuba, and Lebanon proposed this joint amendment as a replacement for the three-term text (I placed the additions in italics): "Everyone has the right to life, *honour*, liberty, *physical integrity*, and to *legal, economic and social security, which is necessary to the full development of the human personality*" (A/C.3/274). Azkoul of Lebanon cut to the heart of the matter when he said that the first three articles were extremely important, as they gave a summary of the rights which were defined fully in the rest of the declaration. It was very important that the preliminary enumeration of rights in the first three articles should be complete. In the draft under discussion, the declaration did not include any mention of economic or social rights or of the right to freedom of thought. His delegation had therefore suggested the wording "full development of his personality" (A/C.3/260) to cover that omission (A/C.3/SR.102/144). The votes I record show why "personal security" became the wider "security of person" as Locke also understood it.

"Honour" rejected. Uruguay "thought that mention should be made of the right to honour, so that actions which might lower human dignity or prejudice the self-respect of the individual would be explicitly condemned" (A/C.3/SR.102/145). After the United States, Panama, and Cuba maintained that "honor" was not really a right but a sentiment, Uruguay agreed that "honour was not in itself a right, but . . . maintained that life was not a right either. What was meant was that man had a right to the protection of his life and to the protection of his honour." It added that the specific mention of the right to honor "would be particularly welcomed by Jews and by all who had suffered indignities at the hands of the Nazis" (A/C.3/SR.105/173). In a remarkably close roll-call vote, the inclusion of a right to honor in the joint amendment was rejected by a vote of twenty to nineteen with nine abstentions (A/C.3/SR.107/187).

"Physical integrity" rejected. The phrase "physical integrity" was thought by some to be part of the right to "security of person," which is why they may have voted against including it while keeping "physical security." Cuba argued that its desire to see "integrity of person" included as a separate right "had been prompted by the terrible events which had taken place during the war, when human beings had been used for surgical experiments. He, therefore, felt that the inclusion of the words 'integrity of person' was essential to complete the enumeration of fundamental human rights" (A/C.3/SR.102/145). France basically thought "that any additions to Article 3 would weaken it" (ibid.). The Dutch had thought of proposing "the addition of 'bodily integrity' after the word 'life'" but felt that the idea was covered by the Cuban amendment (A/C.3/224), which included "security and integrity of person" and had been merged into the joint amendment. "The inclusion of the principle of security and integrity of person was necessary, for even though the idea was to be found in the second paragraph of the preamble and in the second sentence of article 4 [=5], that right, which had been so barbarously violated by the Nazis before and during the Second World War, should be emphasized by being placed in the general statement of principle in article 3" (A/C.3/SR.102/148). Australia felt the joint amendment was "superfluous" because "dignity" was mentioned in Article 1 (A/C.3/SR.103/152). The representative of Uruguay noted that "the right to physical integrity of the individual was particularly important to his delegation because with honour it was one of the "vital rights" that needed to be included in ar-

ticle 3" (ibid.). "Analyzing the terms of article 3, Perez Cisneros stated that he was not in agreement with certain representatives who felt that the idea of 'physical integrity' of the individual was included in the words 'security of person' which appeared in that article. The idea of physical integrity should be clearly expressed and the Cuban delegation requested a separate vote on its insertion" (A/C.3/SR.104/164). That is exactly what the chairperson did. The vote on the insertion of "physical integrity" after the word "liberty" in the commission's text was a close rejection of nineteen to seventeen with twelve abstentions (A/C.3/SR.107/188). Earlier the Philippines had suggested that the Third Committee go on record as stating that "the words 'security of person' include the notion of physical integrity" (ibid., 181). The chairperson would not go along with that and the close rejection took place. Before the meeting rose, the Philippines pointed out that it had voted for Article 3 "on the understanding" that "security of person" included "physical integrity" (ibid., 194).

The phrase "and to legal, economic and social security, which is necessary to the full development of the human personality" was the last part of the joint amendment proposed by Cuba, Uruguay, and Lebanon. Many delegations felt that Article 3, being the first article dealing with specific rights, should have in it a reference to the social and economic rights that were to follow.

China did not agree with pulling the second half of the UD forward into Article 3. It bemoaned the fact that the Third Committee had "not studied the structure of the Declaration as a whole. . . . Articles 1, 2 and 3 expressed the three main ideas of the eighteenth century philosophy; article 1 expressed the idea of fraternity, article 2 that of equality, and article 3 that of liberty. . . . Article 3 set forth a basic principle, which was then defined and clarified in the nine following articles. . . . Article 20 [=22], like article 3, expressed a general idea which was explained and developed in the following articles. . . . The joint amendment . . . especially its second part was not in harmony with that structure" (A/C.3/SR103/154). Pedro de Alba of Mexico took exception to the Chinese delegate's view that the structure of the declaration made the joint amendment superfluous because the amendment "spoke of social rights, which, in his opinion, it was indispensable to mention at the beginning of the declaration" (A/C.3/SR.104/162).

Guy Perez Cisneros of Cuba, as one of the sponsors of the phrase now under discussion, also wanted to see the later rights mentioned in this early Article 3. He spoke at length about US president Franklin Roosevelt's four freedoms of speech and expression and from fear and want. These were "new freedoms," he said, that were characteristic of the twentieth century and "that should be inscribed on 'the frontispiece' of the document," which led him to hold up the joint amendment as the embodiment or application of "those four fundamental freedoms" (ibid., 164). "His insistence on the need for adopting that [joint] amendment could be ascribed," he said, "to the fact that he hoped that the new declaration of human rights would not be a slavish repetition of the 1789 declaration but would present a statement of the most lofty ideals of the current century" (ibid.).

I already indicated that the additions of "honour" and "physical security" were turned down. Then the chair called for a vote on the last phrase in the joint amendment: "and to the economic, social, and other conditions necessary to the full development of the human personality." Yet again, the rejection came in a close vote of twenty for, twenty-one against, and seven abstentions (A/C.3/SR.107/188). Especially this last vote shows the reader how divided the UN members were about the human rights message they wanted to send into the world. Those voting against pulling the social and economic rights forward were France, Greece, India, Luxembourg, the Netherlands, New Zealand, Norway, Panama, the Philippines, Siam, Sweden, Syria, Turkey, the Union of South Africa, the United Kingdom, the United States, Australia, Belgium, Canada, China, and Denmark. Voting in favor of mentioning the social and economic human rights in Article 3 were Haiti, Lebanon, Mexico, Pakistan, Peru, Poland, the Ukrainian Soviet Socialist Republic, the USSR, Uruguay, Venezuela, Yemen, Yugoslavia, Argentina, the Byelorussian Soviet Socialist Republic, Chile, Costa Rica, Cuba, Czechoslovakia, the Dominican Republic, and Ecuador. The abstainers were Egypt, Ethiopia, Guatemala, Honduras, Saudi Arabia, Brazil, and Burma (ibid.).

After this, "Everyone has the right to life" was adopted by a unanimous vote of forty-seven to zero with two abstentions, and the rights to "liberty and security of person" by a similar unanimous vote of forty-seven to zero with four abstentions (A/C.3/SR.107/191). The whole of Article 3 was adopted by a similar unanimous vote of thirty-six to zero with twelve abstentions. All these were roll-call votes.

I recorded all these close votes on Article 3 and its amendments to caution the reader about what the drafters had in mind with the three rights (to life, liberty, and security of person) in this article. As the first three rights to be listed, they were hotly debated in the Third Committee. While in the first six drafting stages only eighteen nations had been involved, in the Third Committee all fifty-six UN Member States had their say. Many of the additional delegates were from Latin American nations with democratic socialist inclinations that wanted to put their stamp on this early Article 3 in the same way they later put it on the second half of the document. That did not make them vote in a block, but it did make them leery of too heavy an emphasis on just eighteenth-century Enlightenment rights. They agreed with the communists in wanting to see the newer social and economic rights that had gained credibility in the nineteenth and twentieth centuries mentioned up front in the declaration. The joint amendment embodied the fight to make that happen. It did not succeed, but the debates and the closeness of the votes put my readers on notice to be careful about claiming to know just why a certain article has the shape it has.

Article 4
Freedom from Slavery

Whenever I hear anyone arguing for slavery, I feel a strong impulse to see it tried on him.

—Abraham Lincoln

No one shall be held in slavery or servitude; slavery and the slave trade shall be prohibited in all their forms.

This article does not just forbid slavery. That stark reference might have reminded us of how Romans manned their warships and Americans in the South their large plantations. The article also forbids "servitude" and then, to make doubly sure all bases are covered, it also forbids both practices "in all their forms." It took the commission quite a bit of effort to settle on the simple text that we have.

The very first draft of the article in the First Drafting Session read like this: "Slavery and compulsory labour are inconsistent with the dignity of man and therefore prohibited by this Bill of Rights. But a man may be required to perform his just share of any public service that is equally incumbent upon all, and his right to a livelihood is conditioned by his duty to work. Involuntary servitude may also be imposed as part of a punishment by a court of law" (E/CN.4/AC.1/11/12). John Humphrey had gleaned these items from his survey of constitutions. Many of them forbade "slavery" itself outright: Afghanistan, Argentina, Bolivia, Chile, Colombia, Costa Rica, El Salvador, Greece, Liberia, Mexico, and the United States. Others used or added the phrase "involuntary servitude" (E/CN.4/AC.1/3/Add.1). Quite a few countries also wanted to combat the trade in slaves by saying things like, "In Chile there are no slaves and he who sets foot upon its territory becomes free" (Art.10). Several countries made an exception for military service, which can be seen as a kind of "involuntary servitude." Humphrey captured this with the requirement of a man "to perform his just share of any public service that is equally incumbent upon all." Humphrey's last sentence refers to the many countries that in the 1940s and today require some prisoners to work as part of their sentence.

None of this was very controversial except for Humphrey's additional socialist point that a man's "right to a livelihood is conditioned by his duty to work." The Universal Declaration contains the human right to work in Article 23, but that is not matched by any kind of duty to work.

Maybe Humphrey was inspired by two communist constitutions. According to its 1936 Constitution, in the Soviet Union "work is a duty and a matter of honour for every able-bodied citizen in accordance with the principle 'He, who does not work, shall not eat'" (Art.12). Similarly, in the Yugoslav Constitution of 1945 we read that "it is a duty of every citizen to work according to this abilities; he who does not contribute to the community cannot receive from it" (Art.32).

The United States pointed out that the second sentence of Humphrey's text ("[a man's] right to a livelihood is conditioned by his duty to work") "might lead to all kinds of injustices" and proposed this alternate text: "No one shall be held in slavery nor be required to perform compulsory labour in any form other than public service equally incumbent by law upon all" (E/CN.4/AC.1/SR.8/6). Ralph L. Harry of Australia liked this text better than Humphrey's text because he "thought the concept of the right to a livelihood conditioned by the duty to work, should not be stressed in this article which dealt with the exploitation of man by man" (E/CN.4/AC.1/SR.4/3). China also preferred the US draft. From this stage on, the text simply stated that "slavery, which is inconsistent with the dignity of man, is prohibited in all its forms," the last clause having been suggested by France and the United States.

During a Working Group of the Second Session of the commission, voices were raised for expanding the text. Afanasi Stepanenko from Byelorussia said slavery should be "prohibited by law," for it existed "not only in colonial territories but also in certain democratic states, as had been emphasized in the Report on civic rights in the United States drawn up on President Truman's request" (E/CN.4/AC.2/SR.4/2). Eleanor Roosevelt responded that "even if certain civic rights had not yet been granted to all, nevertheless slavery was non-existent" (ibid., 3). Uralova, the rapporteur of the Commission on the Status of Women, wanted to add "the prohibition of traffic in women," and France asked that a ban on "forced labour" be added (ibid.). The only change accepted by the group was the Byelorussian one when it unanimously adopted this text: "Slavery in all its forms, being inconsistent with the dignity of man, shall be prohibited by law" (ibid., 5).

In the full Second Session the clause between commas ("being inconsistent with the dignity of man") was taken out because the United Kingdom and China felt it was not "appropriate" since this kind of observation might be added to most articles in the declaration. The text "Slavery is prohibited in all its forms" was sent to the Third Session, where it was replaced by a proposal from the United Kingdom and India stating, "No one shall be held in slavery or involuntary servitude," that was adopted in a vote of nine for, three against, and three abstaining (E/CN.4/SR.53/5). From there it went to stage seven of the drafting process as I depict it in my "statement of purpose." Two changes were made in this penultimate stage.

First, in the Third Committee the word "involuntary" was taken out after Costa Rica pointed out that "the adjective 'involuntary,' used in [the] English [text], was not to be found in the French text," to which France responded that "the word *servitude* alone seemed to be the only way of expressing precisely what article 4 should state" (A/C.3/PV.109/212). India wanted to retain the word because there it was used "to describe a particular type of military or labour contract" (A/C.3/PV.110/216). Amid some clamor to have a subcommittee appointed to fix the text, René Cassin of France again pointed out that "the Commission of Human Rights had thought it necessary to include some wording which would cover indirect and concealed forms of slavery. The word 'servitude' had been used to cover such aspects as the way in which the Nazis had treated their prisoners of war and the traffic in women and children, for in French the expression '*servitude volontaire*' did not have any meaning" (ibid., 217). The vote to delete the term "involuntary" from the English text was seventeen to fifteen with four abstentions (ibid., 222).

Second, the Soviet Union proposed to add, "Slavery and the slave trade are prohibited in all their aspects; and all violations of this principle, whether they be of an overt or clandestine nature, must be punished according to law" (E/800). Alexei Pavlov told his colleagues that his country wanted to "strengthen and clarify the text" (A/C.3/PV.110/214). He then gave a long explanation. "Certain representatives had already pointed out," he said, "that slavery was not a thing of the past and according to a letter he had received from an anti-slavery organization, forms of it still existed in Africa, Asia, and parts of America" (ibid., 215).

He reminded the Committee that in a speech on the American Constitution, Jefferson had recommended the abolition of slavery. Congress, unfortunately, had refused to accept this point of view. It had been stated that eight million people were living in slavery. Even if that figure were not correct, the practice existed and it was for the United Nations to guarantee the freedoms set forth in the first articles. The USSR delegation also wanted to include a provision stating that violations were punishable by law. It was a crime to treat a human being as an inanimate object. It was also a crime to carry on clandestine activities or to indulge in such crude practices as existed under the peonage system in parts of Latin America. (Ibid.)

Pavlov's point that slavery and the slave trade were "a problem which merited the United Nations' most careful attention" (A/C.3/PV.110/215) is still true today. According to the Walk Free Foundation, there were in 2016 forty-six million enslaved people worldwide. These modern forms of slavery include human trafficking, forced labor, bondage from indebtedness, forced or servile marriage, and commercial sexual exploitation. Eighteen million were said to be in India.

The first sentence of the Soviet amendment, "Slavery and the slave trade shall be prohibited," was adopted twenty-two to seventeen, with three abstentions (A/C.3/PV.110/221). Stephen Demchenko from the Ukraine (Soviet Socialist Republic) supported the insertion because "it could not be denied that the slave trade still existed and that slavery had been reintroduced by the Nazi regime, and [that] it was therefore essential to include a specific prohibition of slavery in the declaration" (ibid., 219). Poland, France, Venezuela, and Yugoslavia also spoke up before voting to include it. The majority view was probably also helped by a 368-page report that the Commission on Human Rights had received in May 1948 from the War Crimes Commission that had prepared the charges for the Nazis who stood trial at Nuremberg. Humphrey brought this report (E/CN.4/29), which had been specifically prepared to help them in their task, to the attention of the UD drafters (E/CN.4/SR.27/3).

This report told the drafters that "from the occupied territories whole populations were deported to Germany for the purposes of slave labor upon defense works, armament production and similar tasks connected with the war effort" (E/CN.4/W.19/48). Cassin may well have been thinking of the astounding details of this report when he defended the prohibition of slavery and servitude "in all their forms" because "there were attenuated forms of slavery which were vigorous in practice: for instance, the status of persons who were deported to Germany was certainly worse than that of ancient slaves" (E/CN.4/AC.1/SR.13/2).

Reading this birth story of UD 4, each reader will have in mind his or her own contemporary slavery or servitude example. There are plenty of them. With a lifelong interest in the law of the sea and eating a lot of fish, I was drawn to slavery on the world's oceans, particularly in the South China Sea, where a recent *New York Times* article told me that "unscrupulous captains buy and sell the men and boys like chattel" (September 15, 2019, BR9). I checked the Global Slavery Index and found that fish is the third-largest import product into G20 countries (to the tune of $12.9 billion) that has attached to it the risk of being processed by slaves. Am I obligated to find out where the fish I eat was caught and under what conditions? What about the shirt I wear and the laptop used to write this book?

Article 5
Torture and Relativism

The healthy man does not torture others—generally it is the tortured who turn into torturers.

—Carl Jung

No one shall be subjected to torture or to cruel, inhuman or degrading treatment or punishment.

This UD article is carried forward into the 1984 UN Convention of Torture, which tells us in its Article 2(2) that "no exceptional circumstances whatsoever, whether a state of war or a threat of war, internal political instability or any other public emergency, may be invoked as a justification for torture." No fewer than 166 nations have ratified this convention, and few, if any, will openly admit to practicing torture or other cruel or inhuman acts on their citizens or aliens.

Some twenty constitutions in John Humphrey's survey forbade "torture." Some mentioned "the rack," "whipping," "flogging," "beating with sticks," "deportation," "mutilation," "infamy," "branding," "bodily mistreatment," and many more contemporary types of punishments. Humphrey summarized all of this in his Article 4, saying that "no one shall be subjected to torture, or any unusual punishment or indignity" (E/CN.4/AC.1/SR.3/2). On the day I began a draft on this article, I heard in the news that the US Supreme Court had decided that giving life in prison without parole to a teenager for a first capital offense was the kind of "cruel and unusual punishment" that is forbidden by the Eighth amendment to the United States Constitution, which says, "Excessive bail shall not be required, nor excessive fines imposed, nor cruel and unusual punishments inflicted."

When the chairperson read Humphrey's Article 4 to have it approved in the First Drafting Committee Session, René Cassin of France immediately reacted. He thought the word "indignity" was shocking in its weakness, as did Hernan Santa Cruz of Chile. Adding that the word "torture" needed to be defined against the background of questions like, "Do some humans have the right to expose others to medical experiments and do any have the right to inflict suffering upon other human beings without their consent, even for ends that may appear good?" Ralph L. Harry of Australia also wanted the issue of "physical torture" addressed. Reaching for a "more careful definition," Charles Habib Malik of Lebanon wondered "whether forced labour, unemployment or dental pain might be considered torture. He also found the phrasing 'no one' and 'every one' objectionable and suggested that either 'person' or 'human being' be used instead" (E/CN.4/AC.1/SR.3/13).

In the Second Session of the commission, Belgium suggested the wording we now have: "No one shall be subjected to torture or to cruel, inhuman or degrading treatment or punishment" (E/CN.4/SR.54/15–16). For most of its history, this article was teamed with slavery in one text, our UD 4. When in the Third Committee Cuba (A/C.3/224) and Uruguay (A/C.3.268) wanted to see it moved to what became UD 11 (on the presumption of innocence), they failed and, "with no prejudice to the order of the parts," the whole of UD 4 was unanimously adopted (A/C.3/PV.11/229). On November 30, 1948, the Third Committee set up a subcommittee "to examine the totality of the declaration of human rights . . . solely from the standpoint of arrangement, consistency, uniformity and style and to submit proposals to the Third Committee thereon" (A/C.3/400/Rev.1/120). This subcommittee split UD 4 into 4a on slavery and 4b on torture. The Third Committee accepted this split and gave the right not to be tortured its own status as Article 5. Together with other changes that were made at this time, that gives us the thirty articles we have.

At the time the Universal Declaration was being written, a group of the same people was also preparing a legally binding convention that in many ways overlapped with the text of the declaration, except that the convention text was far more detailed. That other text did not get finished in the 1940s, but I relate one of the overlaps because it raises the question of moral relativism that has always dogged the UD. Article 6 of this legal convention contained this wording: "No person shall be subjected to torture or to cruel or inhuman punishment or to cruel or inhuman indignity" (E/600/B).

When the Member States of the United Nations were given a chance to respond to this convention article on torture, not many responded, but South Africa said that the phrase "cruel or inhuman dignity" was "somewhat vague" (E/CN.4/85/62). It went on to elaborate on the relativism of these moral values to the place and time of their birth: "The standards of cruelty, inhumanity, and dignity vary according to the times, places and circumstances. . . . Whether or not [a punishment] is regarded as clearly excessive in a particular community depends upon the protective needs and general concepts of justice prevailing in that community. It is not so very long ago that hanging was not considered a cruel and inhuman punishment for a petty theft. Today there are an increasing number of humanitarians who regard corporeal punishment and solitary confinement on a spare diet, for whatever offense, as too inhuman to be tolerated" (ibid).

Regarding the phrase "cruel and inhuman indignities," the United Nations would, according to South Africa, "soon have to deal with alleged mental cruelties and will in any case be faced with divergent national and personal notions, prejudices and susceptibilities, which determine the sense of dignity" (E/CN.4/85/62). For these reasons South Africa wanted to see the phrase "or to cruel and inhuman indignity" deleted from the convention (ibid.). The abuses against which these words were aimed were not clearly spelled out. To those who held up Nazi practices as the target of this article, South Africa's delegate responded that "degradation of the nature practiced in Buchenwald and Treblinka" were covered in Articles 5 and 9 of the convention, where the rights to life and liberty were spelled out (ibid.). After objections by France and the United Kingdom were dealt with, the majority agreed that the English text of Covenant Article 7 would read as follows: "No one shall be subjected to torture or to cruel or inhuman punishment or to cruel or inhuman dignity" (E/CN.4/AC.1/SR.30/4).

Malik of Lebanon did not object to the South African position with abstract argumentation, though as a Catholic natural law philosopher he might well have done that. Instead he stuck to the need to explicitly condemn what had happened in the Nazi camps. What he said reminds us of the second recital of the UD preamble (which was not yet written), which speaks of the "conscience of mankind" being "shocked" by the Nazi horrors. Malik felt "the time had come to explain to the world what was meant by torture, inhuman punishment and inhuman indignity. The basic idea was to explain in an international instrument that the conscience of mankind had been shocked by inhuman acts in Nazi Germany, and therefore a positive and condemnatory article was needed. Considering what had happened in Germany he felt it was better to err on the side of vagueness than on the side of legal accuracy" (E/CN.4/AC.1/SR.23/3). The word "dignity," he said, "was found in the Preamble of the Charter of the United Nations, which was the creation of Field Marshall Smuts of the Union of South Africa. It would be better to run the risk of being vague than of being too particular, and considering the reaction of mankind to the barbarous activities of the Nazis, he felt that these expressions should be included in the Article" (ibid.).

Examples of barbarous Nazi activities would be what Johann Kremer did when he saw an Auschwitz inmate with what to him was an interesting cranial shape. "He would order that prisoner photographed and injected with [fatal] phenol for his collection of fresh corpse samples of liver and other organs" (Robert Jay Lifton, *The Nazi Doctors: Medical Killing and the Psychology of Genocide* [Basic Books 1988], 292). His colleague Friedrich Entress "would infect prisoners with typhus to make medical observations" (ibid., 262). At the Natzweiler camp, "anthropological" research was done. For museum purposes, very exact measurements of women were taken. After that they were gassed and their skeletons put on display.

I mention this legal convention episode because the South African objection was not totally unreasonable, not just to this Article 7 of the convention and to Article 5 of the declaration, but also to the entire project of presenting a declaration of human rights that is to serve as "a standard of achievement for all peoples and nations." Reading this commentary, my reader must make up his or her own mind on whether human beings have moral human rights that are inherent in their persons, the enjoyment of which all societies must strive to attain and make real. I present my accounts of how the UD articles got written as background reading for watching BBC footage of a film taken when the camps were liberated; for watching any atrocity footage; or for just thinking about similarly shocking events happening in faraway places or closer to home, perhaps even at home.

Article 6
Person Before the Law

All persons born or naturalized in the United States, and
subject to the jurisdiction thereof, are citizens of the United
States and of the State wherein they reside. No state shall
make or enforce any law which shall abridge the privileges
or immunities of citizens of the United States; nor shall any
State deprive any person of life, liberty, or property, without
due process of law; nor deny to any person within its jurisdiction the equal protection of the laws.

    —Fourteenth Amendment, US Constitution

---

*Everyone has the right to recognition everywhere as a person before
the law.*

Throughout, René Cassin, the French delegate to the drafting process,
maintained that this "was one of the most important texts of the Declaration, on a national as well as an international level. On the national level
it meant that every citizen had the right of access to justice. On the international level it meant improving the position of foreigners in this respect"
(E/CN.4/AC.1/SR.13/16). How would you compare the Fourteenth
Amendment to Cassin's claim or to the text of this UD article?

When the declaration was being written, the United Nations had only
two working languages, English and French. This meant that the drafters had to agree on two versions of each article, one in English and one
in French. The French text of Article 6 read like this: "Chacun a le droit
a la reconnaissance en tous lieux de sa personnalite juridique." John
Humphrey, the first director of the Human Rights Division in the UN
Secretariat, who was from bilingual Quebec, had drafted a two-sentence
article. First, he gave the English equivalent ("Everyone has the right to
a legal personality") of the just-cited French sentence. However, he left
out the "en tous lieux," which means "in all places" or "everywhere," that
had been in the French text. When Cassin was asked to rewrite Humphrey's list, he inserted this "everywhere" into the English text, where it
stayed till the end.

When Chairperson Eleanor Roosevelt said she "did not think that the
word 'everywhere' was of great importance" (E/CN.4/AC.1/SR.37/3),
Cassin responded in a way that speaks to us in the twenty-first century:
"Here was a difficult problem, left unsolved by the declaration, namely,

the status of individuals living on foreign soil. There was not a single country which did not discriminate to some extent between its own subjects and aliens. The rights of aliens in respect of the countries in which they lived should therefore be defined more closely. The Draft Declaration should guarantee them a minimum of fundamental rights" (ibid.) The reference to "a minimum of fundamental rights" shows that the drafters had difficulty keeping Article 6 separated from other legal human rights like the ones on equality before the law (UD 7) and especially on possession of fundamental civil rights (UD 8).

In extant constitutions, these two ideas of possessing a legal personality and possessing civil rights were often merged, which is why the constitutions of two countries (Belgium and Greece) came at the concept in a negative way, with Belgium's stating that "total deprivation of civil rights (mort civil) is abolished and shall not be re-established" (Art.13) and Greece's Article 18 stating that "civil death is abolished" (E/CN.4/AC.1/3/Add.1). Humphrey also had a second sentence: "No one shall be restricted in the exercise of his civil rights except for reasons based on age or mental condition or as punishment for a criminal offence" (E/CN.4/AC.1/SR.11/16). That extra explanatory sentence did not quiet misgivings expressed in the First Drafting Session about what a "legal" or "juridical personality" meant. Opponents of the article argued that the concept of a "legal personality" that Humphrey had used did not exist in English legal systems. Vladimir M. Koretsky of the USSR felt that the concept "introduced a complicated juridical concept" (E/CN.4/AC.1/SR.13/14), while Roosevelt of the United States and Peng-Chun Chang of China thought it "to be too technical for the common man" (ibid., 15). Cassin responded by defining the idea positively as being the ability "to be a bearer of rights, obligations and responsibilities" (ibid., 14), which brought about the linkage with UD 10 about everyone being a possessor of fundamental rights. He and Roosevelt came to an understanding that he would accept the simpler language of "Everyone has a right to a status in law" and she would accept adding "and to the enjoyment of civil rights," thus combining UD 6 and UD 10 (E/CN.4/AC.1/SR.13/14). But that combination did not last because the report from the First Drafting Session to the Second Session of the commission contained two articles, one that became our UD 6, "Everyone has the right to a legal personality," and one that became our UD 10, on possession of fundamental human rights (E/CN.4/95).

When, in the Second Drafting Session, Roosevelt admitted "that she was not quite certain of the meaning of this article," Cassin responded that this provision was directed "against modern forms of slavery" (E/CN.4/AC.1/SR.37/5). He stated, "There would have been no need to reaffirm that a human being could not constitute the property of another human being, had not certain heads of state such as Hitler sought in the last ten years to revive the ancient idea that an individual considered as a slave had no right to marry, to be a creditor or to own property" (ibid., 3).

In the Third Session the United Kingdom, India, and China all proposed the deletion of this Article 6. The United States said it would vote against retaining the article because "its wording was ambiguous" and the idea in it was covered by Article 3, which subsequently became our two articles on nondiscrimination, UD 2 and UD 7. But both the Soviet Union and France wanted to keep Article 6 in the text. Alexei Pavlov of the USSR argued that "apart from attempts against whole groups, such as those against the Jews in Germany, account must be taken of the fact that some civil legislation still contained restrictive provisions regarding juridical personality of individuals. Thus in certain cases a wife had no juridical personality independent from that of her husband" (E/CN.4/SR.58/4). In response to Chairperson Roosevelt's question whether the United States, by prohibiting foreigners from practicing certain professions, was thereby denying their juridical personality, Cassin answered that having a legal personality meant "the most elementary rights which could not be denied to any human being, the *jus gentium* of Roman law. As early as the Middle Ages, canon law had recognized that all men possessed a minimum of rights. That was the minimum envisaged by Article 12 [=6], which could not impair the sovereignty of any State conscious of its responsibilities in respect of foreigners residing in its territory" (ibid.). Roberto Fontaina from Uruguay also wanted the article kept in as long as the right wording could be found (ibid., 5).

The Third Committee received from the commission this text for our Article 6: "Everyone has the right to recognition everywhere as a person before the law" (A/C.3/272). No substantive changes were proposed. Hernan Santa Cruz of Chile recounted the drafting history of the article when he observed that after "the Anglo-Saxon countries in particular had emphasized that the French term *personalité juridique* did not in their opinion have a precise meaning," "the Commission on Human Rights had finally accepted the explanations of the representative of France who had been supported by the representatives of Latin-American countries, the legal systems of which were modeled on French law" (A/C.3/SR.111/224). The Canadian delegate H. H. Carter again gave Nazi Germany "as a recent example" of where "certain persons might be deprived of their juridical personality by an arbitrary act of their government" (ibid., 225). Coming back to use of the word "everywhere," Cassin observed that it was "the Committee's task to prepare the way for a new era in which the fundamental rights of all human beings would be respected. Its duty was to proclaim to the whole world that there was not a single human being who could not possess both rights and obligations. . . .

The basic purpose of Article 5 [=6] became evident if it was considered in conjunction with" Article 4 on slavery, "which was the abasement of the human being from the physical point of view, while Article 5 [=6] was intended to combat and to deny the possibility of his abasement from the legal point of view" (ibid., 226). This article was adopted unanimously (ibid., 229).

Article 6, on the human right to be "a person before the law," is the first of what can be seen as seven articles specifically on legal human rights. By the middle of the twentieth century, this set had become part of the legal systems of all civilized nations, including that of Germany. But with his own personal directives Hitler totally subverted the Weimar Constitution and sidestepped the civilized values enshrined in the German legal system. The Nazification of that system was so thorough that scholars still debate whether we can truly speak of a "legal" system in the Germany of those years. It should not surprise us that the UD drafters had a strong reaction to that subversion, for it made the Holocaust possible. As a corrective, the drafters wanted to lay bare the deeper moral human rights that should have but did not prevent this subversion of radical democracy then as now with authoritarian leaders who would be dictators.

Article 7
Equality Before the Law

Shunning the concept of the inviolability of the person of the King of England and the bounds of the monarch's protective screen, the [US] founders disclaimed any notion that the Constitution generally conferred similarly all-encompassing immunity upon the president [of the United States].

—Judge Victor Marrero of the Federal District Court in Manhattan, October 7, 2019

All are equal before the law and are entitled without any discrimination to equal protection of the law. All are entitled to equal protection against any discrimination in violation of this Declaration and against any incitement to such discrimination.

As the date of the epigraph from Marrero shows, the United States was facing a grave constitutional crisis when one of the later versions of this book was written. In that light, it is striking how John Humphrey, the first director of human rights in the UN Secretariat, began the second sentence of this article: "Public authorities and judges, as well as individuals are subject to the rule of law" (E/CN.4/AC.1/W2/Rev.2). Everyone is so subject, presidents included. The idea of "the rule of law" is precisely that it covers the highest public officials as well as the lowest citizens and aliens of the realm. It is therefore unfortunate that in the Third Session of the commission, René Cassin of France convinced his colleagues that the phrase "public authorities and judges" was not necessary because they were included in the all-inclusive word "all" in "*All* are equal before the law . . ." But as Marrero's judgment against the US president and his family, associates, and companies shows, it needs to be spelled out for all to see. Article 7 does that on a world scale.

This phrase "equality before the law" was and still is a standard refrain in constitutions worldwide. Humphrey collected these late 1940s samples (E/CN4/AC.1/3/Add.1): "All Afghan subjects . . . are free to enjoy all right[s] conferred by Shariat Law" (Art.10); Brazil's Article 141, Egypt's Article 3, and El Salvador's Article 5 stated simply that "all are equal before the law." So does the Fourteenth Amendment of the United States Constitution when it declares that "all persons born or naturalized in the United States . . . are citizens of the United States and of the State wherein they reside." Many constitutions include a brief or long list of domestic nondiscrimination items that are meant to undergird this equality before the law. In the 1940s Cuba's Article 20 mentioned "sex, race, colour or class, and any other kinds of discrimination destructive of human dignity." Czechoslovakia's Article 128 said that "all citizens of the Czechoslovak Republic shall be in all respects equal before the law . . . whatever be their race, their language or their religion," as Iraq's Article 6 also did.

As their social history changes, nations can add an item to this nondiscrimination list or take one away if it has become objectionable. One recent noteworthy addition has to do with "sexual preference," which Portugal added in 2005 (Article 13) and South Africa (Amendment par.9(3)) and Bolivia (Article 14) in 2009.

For a long time this Article 7 was combined with UD Article 2 as one article. When Peng-Chun Chang of China moved that these be split off from each other, the Third Session of the commission went along with that split. Article 2 was allowed to keep the long list of nondiscrimination items, while Article 7 got the protection "against incitement to such discrimination" or against what we would call "hate speech." The difference between them was one of scope: while UD Article 2 and the second sentence of UD 7 are universal or international in scope because they are anchored in the *Universal* Declaration, the rights of which are unalienable, the first sentence of UD 7 can be seen or understood as being just domestic or national in scope. That is how Cassin of France explained the difference. He pointed out that the first sentence of "Article 6 [=7] had a more limited field [than UD 2] and defined the legal status of all human beings within the national limits of sovereign Powers of States. The former [read UD 2] set forth the principle of non-discrimination, whereas in the latter [read first sentence of UD 7] the individual was ensured protection against discrimination within his own country" (E/CN.4/SR.75/2).

So the reader meets with a possibly confusing difference in scope between the first sentence of UD 7, which is domestic in scope, and the second sentence of the same article, which is universal in scope because anchored in the declaration. In the Third Committee, South Africa sought to fix this problem by proposing the deletion of the second sentence of Article 7, the one that has an international scope because it is anchored in the UD (A/C.3/SR.111/226). Speaking for his country, C. T. Te Water argued that the committee was engaged in "an attempt to codify the rights of man. It could not be claimed, however, that the declaration included all [human] rights. For that reason, the concept of equality before the law should not be limited to the principles laid down in the declaration" (A/C.3/SR.111/229). South Africa did not want there to be a text with universal human rights that could be used to stand in judgment over domestic legal systems. Any use of the Universal Declaration had that effect, including this second sentence of UD 7.

Several delegations wanted South Africa to withdraw its proposal to delete that second sentence of Article 7, while others called for a roll-call vote to show where everyone stood on this crucial issue. Such a vote is done not just by a show of hands but by officially recording how each nation voted on an issue. Among the second group was Alexei Pavlov of the USSR. He "observed that the South African representative had proposed the deletion from Article 6 [=7] of the very words which might inconvenience the Government of the Union of South Africa in view of its policy of discrimination against the non-European population of the country. Numerous facts could be cited to prove that such discrimination existed." He then spoke of 250,000 Asians in Natal and Transvaal deprived of their right to vote; of even "broader" discrimination against Asians, women, and murderers in South West Africa; of women who could not own land in South Africa, whose children only received "three years of [noncompulsory] free schooling" in contrast to white children, "who received free compulsory schooling till the age of 15"; and of Indians "whose mortality rate was shocking." He ended his peroration by pointing out that "the colour line was strictly drawn in theaters, parks, restaurants, cafes and railway trains. Millions of people paid in blood and tears for the policy of discrimination pursued by the Government of the Union of South Africa." Pavlov suggested that "if the South African amendment was not withdrawn, the vote should be taken by roll-call, in order to show who agreed with the representative of the Union of South Africa" (A/C.3/SR.112/236).

Te Water responded that "the difficulty which European civilization was facing in its struggle for survival in that country had not been properly appreciated. Only experience on the spot could bring such understanding; he wished it were possible for many representatives to obtain that experience. In view of what had been said in the debate, he withdrew his amendment" (A/C.3/SR.112/240). Te Water's point that the Universal Declaration could then or might someday be improved upon was a fair one to make. But in this particular case—deleting the second sentence of UD 7—that was hypocritical and backfired. Cutting out all universally applicable human rights, which is what the ones in the declaration are, would have left the South African people with just their own domestic and racist apartheid system. Te Water's colleagues probably were stunned when he lauded the 1948 South African system as exhibiting "the most complete equality before the law" (A/C.3/SR.111/230). The disputed sentence was adopted by forty-six to none with one abstention, presumably from South Africa.

The last phrase of UD 7, about protection "against any incitement to such discrimination," which is our equivalent of "hate speech," has its origin in a Soviet proposal to the Sub-commission on the Prevention of Discrimination and the Protection of Minorities. After a long and intense debate in which he at the end gained the support of Australia and China, A. P. Borisov of the USSR got that subcommission to adopt this statement: "The Sub-Commission recommends to the Human Rights Commission the inclusion in the proposed Convention or in the Declaration of Rights, at appropriate places, of clauses condemning incitement to violence against any religious groups, race, nation, or minority" (E/CN.4/Sub.2/SR.8/16–17). One of those appropriate places was, of course, UD Article 7.

In the Second Session of the commission, Alexandre Bogomolov and Pavlov from the USSR carried on the fight for inclusion of this clause. With support of Alexander Easterman from the World Jewish Congress, the representative from Belgium shortened the lengthy Soviet statements to which objections were being raised and came up with the phrase that we have at the end of our Article 7. This Belgian spin-off was adopted by ten votes to none with four abstentions (E/CN.4/SR.35/3). It survived in the Third Session of the commission over opposition from the United Kingdom, Uruguay, and the United States, which did not want to include what to them was a measure of implementation that told states what to do. In the Third Committee there was almost no discussion of this incitement clause because the South African amendment to delete the whole second sentence (including this clause) took all the air out of the room.

Curiously, the UD drafters saw no real conflict between this right to protection against incitement in UD 7 and the rights of freedom and speech (UD 19) and of association (UD 20), which Nazis, fascists, and white supremacists presumably also have. That makes UD 7's clause about protection against hate speech all the more important. In Articles 19 and 20 everyone is said to have the right to practice freedom of speech and association, while here, in Article 7, everyone is said to have the right to be protected against the kind of speech that incites to hatred and violence. Countries differ on how they deal with hate speech and incitement to discrimination. Section 137(c) of the Dutch criminal code criminalizes "deliberately giv[ing] public expression to views insulting to a group of persons on account of their race, religion, or conviction or sexual preference." This has been used to muzzle extreme speech from white supremacists, racists, and hate-mongers. We in the United States recently experienced the lack of this protection, witnessing the full blooming of hate speech.

Leading up to and on January 6, 2021, the then president of the United States invited an insurrection in the oldest democracy of the world. That day his followers stormed and entered the US Capitol, which is the symbol of democracy for millions around the world. Research has started to show that among these followers of his were numerous domestic terrorists, hate groups, and white supremacist groups that have been spreading hatred throughout the land for some decades. They had been encouraged by him to come to Washington on this day to help him block a peaceful transition of power to the man who was to take his place on January 20. The insurrection failed, and he was impeached for a second time on Wednesday, January 13. As Judge Marrero noted in the epigraph to the article, even the president of the United States has no immunity from prosecution or impeachment. The message for history should have been that no one is above the law. Unfortunately, forty-three senators of the opposition party voted "not guilty" and thereby robbed the fifty-seven who voted "guilty" of the sixty-three votes (two-thirds majority) needed to convict this would-be US dictator. Throughout the book, I often refer to Hitler's Germany as an example of what the UD drafters were seeking to avoid. They knew that every democracy needs to be constantly vigilant to protect what it has, so it will not be lost.

Article 8
Having Fundamental Rights

A Bill of Rights is what the people are entitled to against
every government, and what no just government should
refuse, or rest on inference.
    —Thomas Jefferson

In its proper meaning equality before the law means the
right to participate in the making of the laws by which one is
governed, a constitution which guarantees democratic rights
to all sections of the population, the right to approach the
court for protection or relief in the case of violation of rights
guaranteed in the constitution, and the right to take part in
the administration of justice as judges, magistrates,
attorneys-general, law advisers and similar positions. . . .
All the rights and privileges to which I have referred are
monopolized by whites, and we enjoy none of them.
    —Nelson Mandela (while on the run)

---

*Everyone has the right to an effective remedy by the competent
national tribunals for acts violating the fundamental rights granted
him by the constitution or by law.*

This article originated as a brand-new idea very late in the drafting process. We therefore cannot construct it from the bottom up. There is no
survey of constitutional entries that John Humphrey pegged as support
for it and there are no René Cassin rewrites or early drafting stages. If it
is true that the UD drafters operated with the presumption that human
beings are naturally free-roaming creatures, then we should see Article 8
as laying down two parts of the structure needed for this free roaming.
As the opening Jefferson citation implies, people must have basic or fundamental rights so as not to bump into each other, and they must have
an effective remedy with which to pursue violations of these basic rights,
including those perpetrated by authorities.

    This article began as a merger of two similar amendments to already
adopted articles, one by Cuba to UD 6 on being a person before the
law (A/C.3/224) and one by Mexico to UD 7 on equality before the law
(A/C.3/266). The Mexican one set the stage by stating that besides
protection against discrimination, "there should likewise be available to

every person a simple, brief procedure whereby the courts will protect him from acts of authority that, to his prejudice, violate any fundamental constitutional rights." This supposes that every country has a constitution where those basic rights are listed. Many did and do, but F. Percy Corbet of the United Kingdom was "troubled by the words 'fundamental rights.'" She said that "her country had no written constitution," though she did think that "the Mexican amendment contained a new idea which called for careful consideration" (A/C.3/SR.112/237). Responding to Corbet, Hernan Santa Cruz of Chile thought her problem "might be met if the last phrase of the Mexican amendment were altered to read: 'the fundamental rights granted him by the constitution or the law'" (ibid., 239–40). He wanted to see the idea included in the declaration, possibly in UD 10 about legal protections, and liked having "safeguards against authorities who might attempt to infringe the individual's constitutional rights" (ibid., 239). The addition of "or by law" was made by a unanimous vote.

The mention by Mexico of "acts of authority" that violate someone's constitutional rights is interesting, for while the phrase did not survive into the final text, it shows that Mexico was thinking about accountability of public authorities and judges. In legal circles, the lack of this kind of accountability is called "state sovereign immunity," meaning states and certain of their officials cannot be held accountable for their official acts. I already reported that this idea had been removed from Article 7 because France had argued that it was included in the opening term, "All," in "All are equal before the law . . ." with which that article starts.

The Mexican delegate Pablo Campos Ortiz appreciated the support he received from Uruguay and Cuba "concerning the importance of the new element which his delegation wished to include in the Declaration of Human Rights: the right to an effective, simple and brief procedure as protection against the abuses of authority. That new fundamental right warranted a new article," he said (A/C.3/SR.112/234). Ignoring the part about "abuses of authority," Eleanor Roosevelt of the United States sympathized with Mexico's attempt to "give assurance of effective judicial remedy for acts violating fundamental constitutional rights" (ibid.). While also not mentioning Mexico's reference to abuses by authorities, Venezuela thought the amendment would "greatly increase the practical value of the declaration." It suggested that the beginning of the new article be changed to read, "Everyone has the right to an effective remedy by the competent national tribunals" (ibid., 235).

Yugoslavia did not miss Mexico's point about abuses by public authorities. But instead of applauding the approach taken, it found the amendment difficult to accept because Mexico "sought, in effect, to permit the judicial branch of a Government to correct abuses committed by the executive branch; it could therefore be applied only in those States where a definite separation between the two existed. The idea had been borrowed from the Bogota declaration; it was no doubt suited to the system of government prevailing on the American continent, but it was quite incapable of universal application" (A/C.3/SR.112/235). Mexico had indeed borrowed its amendment from Article 18 of the American Declaration of the Rights and Duties of Man adopted in Bogotá, Columbia, in April 1948. The whole of that article read, "Every person may resort to the courts to ensure respect for his legal rights. There should likewise be available to him a simple, brief procedure whereby justice will protect him from acts of authority that, to his prejudice, violate any fundamental constitutional rights" (E/CN.4/122/5).

I need to remind my reader that UD Article 8 started out as a Mexican amendment to what is our UD 7, which deals with protection against discrimination. Speaking after Yugoslavia made its point about the judicial branch not needing to correct abuses by the executive branch, Salomon Grumbach of France mentioned "Nazism with its millions of victims [which] had rested on discriminatory laws" (A/C.3/SR.112/237). He did not link his Nazi observations explicitly to Mexico's brand-new idea of everyone's protection of the fundamental right against abuses by authorities, as he might easily have done. For the Weimar Constitution had been bypassed and members of the SS did not swear allegiance to it or to upholding the fundamental rights of the Weimar Constitution. They instead swore allegiance to their Führer, Hitler. This was their oath: "I swear to you, Adolph Hitler—as the Führer and Chancellor of the Reich—loyalty and bravery. I pledge to you and to my superiors, appointed by you, obedience unto death, so help me God." Lawyers and judges took similar oaths. We must see these oaths in the context of the establishment in 1933 of "special courts" that had jurisdiction over the various decrees by which Hitler ruled. These courts did not attach any importance to how statutes were phrased or to any actual crimes, but instead operated with bogus categories of criminality like "enemies of the state," "economic parasites," "asocial elements," "destructive outsiders," and "parasites in daily life." These Hitlerian categories remind those of us living under authoritarian-type regimes of how the lines between different branches of government are constantly being blurred.

It remains for me to make the point that constitutions in the 1940s did reflect Article 8's call for protection of basic legal and constitutional rights (E/CN.4/AC.1/3/Add.1). The 1940 Cuban Constitution tells us that "every detained person shall be placed at liberty or delivered to a competent judicial authority within twenty-four hours following the act of his detention" (Art.27). And within seventy-two hours that detained person must, "at the disposition of a competent judge," be released or committed to prison. Article 20 of the 1946 Ecuador Constitution stated that "no person may be deprived of his life or his liberty or of his property without previously being heard and convicted in a trial in accordance with the laws." The Fourteenth Amendment of the United States Constitution tells us that "no State shall make or enforce any law which shall abridge the privileges or immunities of citizens of the United States; nor shall any State deprive any person within its jurisdiction the equal protection of the laws." Article 23 of the 1931 Ethiopian Constitution tells us that "no Ethiopian subject may be arrested, sentenced or imprisoned, except as prescribe by law." UD Article 8 universalizes these domestic pronouncements.

In the 113th meeting on October 26, 1948, the Third Committee voted by forty-six to none with three abstentions to adopt this amendment: "Everyone has the right to an effective remedy by the competent national tribunals for acts violating the fundamental rights granted him by the constitution or by law." The decision as to its position, whether as an amendment to an already adopted article or as a separate article, "would be left to the proposed drafting sub-committee," which decided to give it a place of its own. We saw that many of the supporting nations picked up on Mexico's initial reference to "acts of authority" that violate their own citizens' fundamental constitutional rights. This original phrasing reminds us that not just individuals or groups but public authorities can also gravely violate basic human rights. It often happens all over the world, as US members of minority groups are being reminded daily.

Article 9
No Arbitrary Arrest

We know that Maduro's armies are riddled with persecution, torture, threats, and wrongful arrests.
—Juan Guaido

We believe that the way you dress and the shoes you wear are not probable cause for questioning or arrest.
—Luis Gutierrez

No one shall be subjected to arbitrary arrest, detention or exile.

"Habeas corpus" is a Latin phrase that means "you have the body," just as you might say to someone, "You have the keys," indicating—when the two of you are going somewhere—that your friend should proceed and start the car. So "you have the body" is addressed by a judge or other legal official to a warden or other custodian who has someone in custody. The warden who has the body (i.e., the person) is asked to proceed and produce evidence of the charges against the detained person or else release that person. If those charges do not make legal sense, the body must be set free and the person (whose body that is) must be given his or her freedom. The underlying assumption of this legal procedure is that "individual liberty is guaranteed," which is how the 1946 Haitian constitution put it. You can well imagine that in Hitler's Germany and in numerous localities today, corrupt officials can always find a "reason" for your being profiled, interrogated, or arrested. UD Article 9 forbids that by saying that "no one shall be subjected to arbitrary arrest, detention or exile."

The refrain that an arrest had to be legal and not arbitrary ran throughout John Humphrey's constitutional survey (E/CN.4/AC.1/3/Add.1). Many constitutions went on to give details of what the arresting authorities had to do. In Haiti the warrant for the arrest had to be from "a legally authorized official" and "a copy of it left with him [the arrested person] at the time of his detention" (Art.12). Article 32 of the Honduras Constitution recognized the guarantee of habeas corpus, as did the constitutions of Brazil (Art.141, No.23), Costa Rica (Art.41), Cuba (Art.29), Ecuador (Art.187), Paraguay (Art.26), and Uruguay (Art.17). When the Latin phrase "habeas corpus" was not used, another way of saying the same thing was used, as in the revised 1907 Liberia Constitution: "No place shall be searched, nor person seized on a criminal charge, or suspicion, unless upon a warrant lawfully issued, upon probable cause by oath, or solemn affirmation" (Art.1, sec.9).

At the level of the Working Group of the Second Session, what is now the whole of our Article 9 was just the first sentence of what then was a longer article that also included details of the type of trial that was to follow, which became our UD 11. At the time, that first sentence stated that "no one shall be deprived of this personal liberty or kept in custody except in cases prescribed by law and after due process" (E/CN.4/21/AC.2/SR.3/9). Alexander Easterman of the World Jewish Congress "drew the Group's attention to the danger of using the word 'law' in the first sentence of the article. Strictly speaking, the actions of the Nazis were legal" (ibid.). The US and Philippine delegations supported this observation.

In the full Second Session, Easterman's colleague from the congress, F. R. Bielenfeld, repeated the plea when he argued that the text of the first sentence "should specify the nature of the law. Under the Nazi regime thousands of people had been deprived of their liberty under laws which had been perfectly valid" (E/CN.4/SR.36/3). He therefore suggested that the word "law" here be defined as "law conforming to the principles of the United Nations" (ibid.). In my comments on UD Article 8, I showed how arbitrary the categories of Nazi crimes like "enemy of the people" and "social misfit" were. Germans' everyday life was shot through with arbitrary "official" behavior. A known Nazi opponent was refused a driver's license. A man in Leipzig who owned a fleet of taxicabs had a disagreement with the Ministry of Transportation and was told by the Munich Court of Appeals that "the Constitutional provisions mentioned [in the Reichstag Fire] Decree have been stripped of their previous meaning entirely as regards the rights of individuals against the police" (Ingo Müller, *Hitler's Justice: The Courts of the Third Reich* [Cambridge, MA: Harvard University Press, 1991], 49). "The Petty Court of Wilster put into a state home all children whose fathers had not sent them to join the Hitler Youth, since 'anyone keeping his children out of the Hitler Youth . . . is abusing his parental authority'" (ibid., 139). And so on.

A similar arbitrary character permeates official behavior in present-day authoritarian regimes. Freedom House is an organization that grades nations on the political and civil freedoms they allow their citizens to enjoy. Its 2018 report has the title *Democracy in Crisis*. Of the 195 countries assessed, 88 (45 percent) were rated free, 58 (30 percent) partly free, and 49 (25 percent) not free. That means a quarter of the world's nations had dictatorship-type regimes shot through with Nazi-type arbitrariness. Close to another third had only some type of "rule of law," and not even half of the world's nations (88 of the 195 surveyed) experienced the rule of law that lies behind the ban of UD Article 9.

In their discussion of the draft covenant the drafters were also writing, Charles Habib Malik of Lebanon pointed out to his colleagues "that 'arbitrary arrests' did happen and they had to be condemned. Therefore, the word 'arbitrary' was probably the most important word in the entire Article, and must be retained" (E/CN.4/AC.1/SR.23/6). Chile also wondered about this article being "open to the Nazi interpretation of arrest for any offence" (ibid., 5). Still, no changes were made, but the matter became a moot point when the Third Session (by ten votes to four with two abstentions) adopted the single sentence sponsored by the United Kingdom and India that we now have, which does not include the phrase, "except in cases prescribed by law and after due process." Hansa Mehta spoke for the majority when she said that the idea was to "lay down principles and not become involved in [legal] details" (E/CN.4/SR.54/4).

That idea of just stating principles and leaving out extra details also prevailed in the Third Committee. The temptation was great to add details like the right to be quickly informed of the charges, to be brought before a court or to be let go (proposed by Cuba, Ecuador, France, the USSR, and Uruguay), to be compensated for illegal arrest (Cuba, Ecuador, the USSR, Mexico, and Uruguay), to not be jailed for breach of work contract (Cuba, Ecuador, Mexico, and Uruguay), or to not be deprived of one's freedom for mere failure to carry out obligations of a civil character (Cuba, Mexico, Ecuador, the USSR, and Uruguay). Attempts were made by these nations (in the parentheses) to add these or other habeas corpus details, but none of them succeeded. There was, however, a great deal of support for adding "or exile" at the end of the article. The voting got so complicated that it took no fewer than thirteen voting sessions (several by roll call) to do this. A Soviet proposal to put the phrase, "except in the cases and according to the procedure prescribed by prior legislation," back in was rejected by twenty votes to six with five abstentions (A/C.3/SR.114/256). The UD drafters were just as suspicious of communist legal systems as of fascist ones. In fact, they were suspicious of all domestic legal systems that did not allow for some kind of outside moral standard of oversight, which is what they felt their declaration should be.

Article 10
Fair Public Hearing

When I speak of the fear, intimidation, arrests, and public shaming of intellectuals and religious leaders who dare to speak their minds, and then I tell you that I'm from Saudi Arabia, are you surprised?

—Jamal Khashoggi

Everyone is entitled in full equality to a fair and public hearing by an independent and impartial tribunal, in the determination of his rights and obligations and of any criminal charge against him.

The winner of the 2019 European Sakharov Prize on human rights was Ilham Tohti, a Uighur intellectual who got life in prison for agitating for more freedom for the Uighur ethnic Muslim minority in western China. Hu Jia, who won that same prize in 2008 and spent most of the last two decades in prison and house arrest, had supported Tohti for this prize in 2016. He told Gerry Shih of the *Washington Post* (October 25, 2019) that "since then, the condition of the Uighur people has gone off a precipice, something like the Jews of Europe historically."

Indeed, there were in Hitler's Germany no independent and impartial tribunals where people could get a fair hearing, as there also are not for the Uighurs living in China's Xinjiang Province. Hitler ruined the independence of the courts with his appointment of Nazi cronies at all levels of the justice system and by the establishment of special courts that dealt with the crimes listed in his own decrees. He both subverted the old, established system and created alongside it a new one that functioned as revolutionary courts usually do. Throughout the entire system, prosecutors and judges came to use extremely vague categories of interpretation such as the doctrine of criminal types, under which someone could be condemned and shot to death not for committing a crime but for being a "criminal type"; the doctrine of creative interpretation, which allowed judges to "adapt" the Weimar Constitution to life under the Führer; the teleological method, which led judges to look for an ideological meaning and intent behind the laws; the concept of a material crime, which was any activity that ran counter to the National Socialist world view and which was closely linked to effusive, medieval codes of honor and loyalty; and the doctrine of grasping the essences, according to which judges grasped the whole of a situation and did not linger too much on the details of a case (Ingo Müller, *Hitler's Justice: The Courts of the Third Reich* [Cambridge, MA: Harvard University Press,1991], chapter 9).

John Humphrey, the first UN director of human rights, started a small controversy when he submitted this (my italics) Article 27: "There shall be access to *independent* and *impartial* tribunals for the determination of rights and duties under law. Everyone has the right to consult with and be represented by counsel" (E/CN.4/AC.1/3/Add.1/1). Though Article 112 of the USSR Constitution at that time stated that "judges are independent and subject only to law" (ibid., 244), Vladimir M. Koretsky of the USSR nevertheless opined that "these [italicized] terms might be dangerous and unnecessary to use in connection with tribunals of a sovereign state" (E/CN.4/AC.1/SR.3/6). His objection fits with what we today might refer to as "illiberal democracies" where the lines between different branches of government are intentionally blurred, as they are in Poland, Hungary, Turkey, and many others today. Outside criticism is rejected. When Ralph L. Harry of Australia asked Koretsky for an explanation, he responded that "the expression 'independent and impartial tribunals' might be considered as an invitation to evaluate the courts of the judiciary of independent governments. The possibility of such evaluation, he felt, should be eliminated. He said he might be in favour of the phrase 'open tribunals'" (ibid.). This fit Article 111 of the Soviet Constitution, according to which, "In all courts of the Union of Soviet Socialist Republics cases are heard in public, unless otherwise provided by law" (E/CN.4/AC.1/3/45). Harry responded that "in his opinion it is just as important for courts to be independent or impartial as to be open" (E/CN.4/AC.1/SR.3/6).

Eleanor Roosevelt, as chair, tried to clear up the "misunderstanding" with Koretsky. She pointed out that in the United States and the United Kingdom "the terms 'independent and impartial' were always used in connection with courts. She did not feel that either adjective was intended as a criticism" (E/CN.4/AC.1/SR.3/7). To which Koretsky responded that "such a term might be found in many Constitutions but that it should not appear in the language of an International Bill of Rights" (ibid.). Putting Roosevelt on the spot, he "pointed out that in a specific case the courts of certain countries might justify aggression of certain persons against others because of the colour of their skin. He wondered who would be in a position to say such courts were or were not impartial" (ibid.) As it did with other UD articles, the Soviet Union objected to any outside standard by which judicial systems of countries could be judged and found wanting.

The Third Session adopted this sentence for the article: "In the determination of his rights and obligations and of any criminal charge against him, everyone is entitled in full equality to a hearing by an independent and impartial tribunal" (E/CN.4/SR.54/8). The phrase "in full equality" was added upon the insistence of the Soviet Union with a French assist. In response to objections that this idea was covered by UD Article 7 (on equality before the law), Alexei Pavlov rightly argued that "equality before the law and equality before the courts were not synonymous. He could," he said, "quote many examples to show that coloured and white people were in theory equal before the law but that such was certainly not the practice of the courts" (ibid., 9). The words "and public" were added in the Third Committee as the result of a Cuban amendment.

At the start of this essay, I pointed to similarities between Hitler's treatment of the Jews and China's treatment of its Uighur Muslim minority in Xinjiang Province. Authoritarian regimes often look upon dissidents as lawbreakers and "sick" people. They therefore have no interest in giving those "patients" a fair public hearing. For if the behavior at issue is thought of as resulting from an illness or virus, then the problem of guilt or innocence does not arise. That is in effect what the Xinjiang Communist Youth League said in October 2017. The league intended to reassure Uighurs who might have been disturbed by rumors about a million of their people having been put in "reeducation camps" to wean them of their "religious virus." I quote at length from the speech:

If we do not eradicate religious extremism, the violent terrorist incidents will grow and spread all over like an incurable malignant tumor. Although a certain number of people who have been indoctrinated with extremist [Sufi Islam] ideology have not committed any crimes, they are already infected by disease. There is always the risk that the illness will manifest itself at any moment, which would cause serious harm to the public. That is why they must be admitted to the re-education hospital in time to treat and cleanse the virus from their brain and restore their normal mind. We must be clear that going into a re-education hospital for treatment is not a way of forcibly arresting people and locking them up for punishment, it is part of a comprehensive rescue mission to save them. (*New York Review of Books*, February 7, 2019, 39–40)

My hope is that after reading a passage like this just after living through the COVID-19 pandemic, the text of UD Article 10 strikes my reader as an essential component of an international bill of human rights and therefore also of domestic regimes.

Article 11
Innocence and Nuremberg

Nullum crimen, nulla poena sine lege praevia.

───────────

(1) *Everyone charged with a penal offence has the right to be presumed innocent until proved guilty according to law in a public trial at which he has had all the guarantees necessary for his defense.*

(2) *No one shall be held guilty for any penal offence on account of any act or omission which did not constitute a penal offence, under national or international law, at the time when it was committed. Nor shall a heavier penalty be imposed than the one that was applicable at the time the penal offence was committed.*

This article deals with the fundamental concept of being "innocent until proved guilty." To do that requires that there be a previously existing law that defines the crime with which you are charged and under which you are found guilty, after which the punishment can be meted out to you, who at that point are no longer seen as innocent. That is the point of the old Latin phrase "Nullum crimen, nulla poena sine lege praevia" (no crime, no punishment without previous law) that I quoted in the epigraph. Latin adjectives can be added, like *sine lege scripta* (without written law), *sine lege certa* (without well-defined law), or *sine lege stricta* (without exact law). They all say that someone cannot be found guilty of a crime or be punished for an offense unless he or she was judged to be so under a *previously existing* law that must be *exact*, suggesting that it better be *written* so as to be *well defined*.

In other words, Article 11 of the Universal Declaration forbids the making of retroactive laws that are shaped or written *after* the alleged criminal act took place just to find some person or persons guilty and that were not written for the common good of a nation. You have seen Nazi examples of this approach to justice if you have already read some of the other legal UD birth stories in this book. I first discuss paragraph 1 of this article, where the emphasis falls on the national or domestic realm of law making, and then paragraph 2, where it falls on the international precedent set by the Nuremberg trials, which had just finished when the declaration was written and where famous Nazi leaders were judged and found guilty.

The concept of being "innocent until proved guilty" summarizes a set of ideas (not necessarily using these exact words) scattered throughout modern constitutional history that focuses on legal procedures for not losing one's liberty except after being judged in a court of law, in a fair and public trial where one has had all the means necessary for one's defense. The Nazi model of criminals as sick people (see Article 10) dismissed the need for any of the protective measures enumerated in Article 11 and others we have been discussing.

While the concept of innocence until proved guilty is well known in some nations, such as the United States, it was not prominent in John Humphrey's 1940s constitutional survey. I found it in Cuba's 1940 Constitution (Art.26) and in the French Declaration of the Rights of Man and of Citizen of August 1789. René Cassin, the French delegate, took the idea from his own country's eighteenth-century text. Rewriting Humphrey's Articles 6 and 26, he came up with what was then Article 9: "No one shall be held guilty of any offence until legally convicted" (EN/C.4/AC.1/W.2/Rev.2/2), which was soon changed to simply say "until proved guilty."

We owe the opening phrase, "Everyone charged with a penal offense," to the fact that there was a difference between the French and English versions of the text, where the former was limited to criminal law ("Toute personne accusee") and the latter spoke more generally just of "innocence." With support from the United States, the United Kingdom proposed that the text should read, "Everyone charged with a penal offence is presumed innocent." Uruguay pointed out that the Bogotá text (Article 26), which was drawn up by some twenty Latin American nations, "corresponded exactly with the formula proposed by the United Kingdom representative" (E/CN.4/SR.55/14). This helped cement the insertion of this "innocent until proved guilty" language from the Third Session on.

Alexei Pavlov of the USSR "pointed out that the first sentence of paragraph 1 . . . contained the important principle of innocence until proved guilty, which represented great progress for the inquisitionary trial concepts of the Middle Ages to which Nazi Germany had reverted" (E/CN.4/SR.54/14), on which point he was clearly right. China also "favoured the retention of the paragraph 1" (ibid). Twice a subcommittee was set up to work out some of the details for the first sentence of UD 11. The first time, the members (United Kingdom, India, France, China, and Yugoslavia) put parentheses around the part of the sentence on which they could not agree, like this: "Everyone charged with a penal offence is presumed innocent until proved guilty according to law (in a public trial at which he has had all guarantees necessary for his defence)" (E/CN.4/SR.55/13). The United Kingdom spoke against the part in parentheses on the grounds that this matter was dealt with in the preceding article, which speaks of a "fair and public hearing." Egypt was lukewarm because it felt that "if the Commission decided to keep the part in parentheses, the word 'public' should be deleted" (ibid., 15). There was, however, a strong sentiment for the idea of the trial being held in public. France pointed out that the commission struggled with wanting to make the text shorter, while at the same time seeing a need for more details. But its delegation did "not think the words in parentheses superfluous" (ibid., 16). The vote went eight to six, with two abstentions, against the parenthetical phrase.

The chairperson asked a second subcommittee (of France, Lebanon, and the USSR) to come up with a new draft of the same first paragraph. This time there were no parentheses, but there were two sentences instead of one. The first sentence, as we now have it, was adopted by ten votes to three, with three abstentions. The second sentence dealt with trials being "public" except when "in the interest of public morals or security" that could not be done, which was an idea the Soviets wanted to see included. The word "public" was kept in but not the Soviet exceptions.

This brings us to the second paragraph of UD Article 11, which deals with the thorny issue of the nonretroactivity of laws and how that relates to the UD drafters' views on the Nuremberg trials, which were about to finish, and to the Tokyo ones that had just started in 1946. In its UD seventieth anniversary postings in December 2018, the Office of the UN High Commissioner for Human Rights uses UD 11(2) as a springboard for its discussion of international war crimes trials dealing with the 1995 Srebrenica massacre and the 1994 genocide in Rwanda. That posting makes the point that UD Article 11(2) paved the way for the tribunals and special courts set up for Sierra Leone, Cambodia, the former Yugoslavia, Rwanda, and others, eventually leading to the establishment of the International Criminal Court in 2002. My explanation of the construction of 11(2) undergirds the commissioner's springboard.

Humphrey covered the basics in his Article 26: "No one shall be convicted of a crime except by judgment of a court of law for violation of a law in effect at the time the commission of the act charged as an offense, nor be subjected to a penalty greater than that applicable at the time of the commission of the offense." He had found plenty of backing in his survey of constitutions for the idea that, as the 1946 Brazilian one put it, a person should only be prosecuted and sentenced "in the form of a previous law" (Art.141). Article 26 of the Costa Rican one put it bluntly: "The law shall have no retroactive effect." Egypt's Royal Rescript No. 42 of 1923 announced in its Article 6 that "penalties may only be inflicted in respect of offences committed after the law providing for them has been promulgated." The 1911 one of Greece too stated that "no punishment may be inflicted unless previously fixed by law" (Art.7). The 1814 Constitution of Norway stated that "no law may be given retroactive effect" (Art.97).

Clearly, on its face the idea of nonretroactivity was not a thorny issue. If the drafters were to address only the Member States of the United Nations individually and not collectively as a group or as an organization, then the italicized word "national" in 11(2) might have been enough: "No one shall be held guilty for any penal offence on account of any act or omission which did not constitute a penal offence, under national *or international* law, at the time when it was committed. Nor shall a heavier penalty be imposed than the one that was applicable at the time the penal offence was committed." The italicized words "or international" in the middle of this quotation are the stickler.

Because there is an overlap between the preparations for the writing of the Universal Declaration that began in April 1946 and the conclusion of the Nuremberg war crimes trials in October of that same year, one might think that there is a very close connection between these two pivotal events, but there is not. While both came out of the cauldron that was the Holocaust—and in that sense share a deep connection—textually and legally the majority of the UD drafters wanted to keep their distance from these Nuremberg trials. Some delegations thought that at least some of the Nuremberg charges were not firmly grounded in pre-existent international law, which to them conflicted with the idea of the nonretroactivity of laws that they wanted to enshrine in the declaration.

When Article 11 arrived at the Second Session of the commission, it ended with this retroactivity clause: "and which shall be pursuant to law in effect at the time of the commission of the act charged" (E/CN.4/57). Wanting to make sure that the declaration's ban on nonretroactive lawmaking did not conflict with the judgment at Nuremberg, both the Philippines and Belgium proposed that a second paragraph be added, like this: "This [nonretroactivity] provision shall not, however, preclude the trial and conviction of persons who have committed acts which, at the time of their commission, were regarded as criminal by virtue of the general principles of law recognized by civilized nations" (E/CN.4/SR.37/3). The phrase "general principles of law recognized by civilized nations" was taken from Article 38 of the Charter of the International Court of Justice, the legal arm of the United Nations. The Nuremberg trials were clearly on the minds of the drafters. These two nations wanted to make sure that the Universal Declaration supported what had happened at the Nuremberg trials, where twenty-one high-level Nazis stood trial, twelve got the death penalty by hanging (one doing it himself), three were acquitted, and the rest received prison sentences.

Carlos Romulo of the Philippines said their amendment was "especially concerned with the Nuremberg War Crimes Trial and with all major War Crimes Trials, which, according to the original text of Article 10 [=11], would be illegal" (E/CN.4/SR.36/12). The reason here is that, strictly speaking, not all the Nuremberg charges, such as the one of crimes against humanity, were based on the Hague Conventions that bore the legal weight of these trials. The Nuremberg guilty verdicts, it was felt, were as much drawn from the conscience of humanity as from legal precedents. Yet as Fernand Dehousse of Belgium explained, the amendment was meant to prevent "the possibility of German historians, discussing the responsibility for the war, using the original text, to try and prove the illegality of the War Crimes Trials, especially at Nuremberg" (ibid., 13). These two nations wanted the UD text to support what had been decided at Nuremberg. But as I relate, the majority of the drafters did not see it that way, and this Philippine-Belgian paragraph was pared down to just the words "or international" that we have in the middle of UD 11(2).

All along, the Soviets had been opposed to the language used in the Philippine-Belgian amendment. They did not like the phrase "general principles of law recognized by civilized nations" because, as they saw it, that phraseology demeaned colonial peoples for whose liberation the communist block was actively fighting in and outside the United Nations. This block's opposition to the text may have been a key factor in the demise of the proposal. China sought to avoid the clash by proposing to replace "civilized nations" with "grave crimes against humanity" (E/CN.4/SR.37/3), to which substitution Belgium objected because the new phraseology covered "only one of three categories of crimes which had been defined and pronounced punishable according to international law" at Nuremberg (ibid.). The other two crimes that China's phrasing left out were the making and conspiring to make aggressive war and the violation of the laws of conducting war as developed by the 1899 and 1907 Hague Conventions and thereafter. The Chinese substitute phrase, "grave crimes against humanity," was rejected as too narrow. The United States also opposed what was referred to as "the Nuremberg clause." The result was that the Second Session adopted the Philippine-Belgian paragraph by eight votes to one with eight abstentions (ibid., 4). The real trimming took place in the Third Session.

There China (E/CN.4/SR.54/14), India, and the United Kingdom (E/CN.4/99) all proposed the deletion of the entire second paragraph of UD 11. Such deletion was opposed by France and the World Jewish Congress. Speaking for the latter, Franz Bienenfeld defended its retention, saying that "omission of that paragraph would be contrary to the principles of the Hague Convention of 1907 as well as the principles established by the International Military Tribunals at the Nuremberg Trials. Those principles protected the law of humanity against violations by national laws (as had happened in the case of Nazi Germany). Omission of that paragraph would constitute a step back in international law" (E/CN.4/SR.54/13). A subcommittee (of the United Kingdom, India, France, China, and Yugoslavia) was appointed, and it suggested this as the text for Article 11(2): "No one shall be held guilty of any penal offence on account of any act or omission which did not constitute a penal offence, under national or international law, at the time it was committed" (E/CN.4/SR.56/4). To bring the text closer to that of Article 38 of the International Court of Justice, Belgium sought to insert the phrase "the general principles of" before the word "international" in this new second paragraph. But when it ran into difficulty, Belgium withdrew its amendment and the Third Session adopted this second paragraph of Article 11 in a vote of twelve to zero with three abstentions (ibid., 7).

Of course, as you know, 11(2) ends with a sentence that is not part of what the just-cited Third Session adopted: "Nor shall a heavier penalty be imposed than the one that was applicable at the time the penal offence was committed." This Panamanian amendment (A/C.3/220) reached all the way back to Humphrey's first proposal, which then was Article 26 and it had also been suggested in the Third Session. Except for minor changes, it was now added to the UD text by the Third Committee in a vote of sixteen to eight with fourteen abstentions (A/C.3/116/273). The United States suggested that in both sentences of Article 11 the word "penal" be inserted before the word "offence," which was also accepted (ibid., 274). All other amendments pulling in different directions were rejected.

Cuba had not been part of the earlier debates on the article but, as a new voice in the Third Session, it wanted to make sure that the vague wording of 11(2) would *not* be seen as supporting the Nuremberg judgments. It therefore proposed this additional text: "Every accused person has the right to be judged by tribunals established prior to the offence with which he is charged" (A/C.3/224). By way of explanation, Guy Perez Cisneros noted that "in view of legal and moral principles which it could not surrender, the Cuban delegation was equally averse to voting in a way which might be taken as a direct or indirect approval of the Nuremberg judgements. The proposal to include in article 9 [=11] a reference to the Nurnberg Trials would weaken rather than strengthen the article and might be considered as an indirect criticism of the trial as it would stress the contradiction between the precept *Nullum crimen sine praevia lege penale* (no crime without a previous criminal law) and the method adopted at Nurnberg" (A/C.3/116/268). When the Cuban amendment was rejected in a vote of eighteen to eight with seventeen abstentions (ibid., 274), Mexico, Venezuela, and Cuba explained that they would interpret the word "international" in 11(2) as meaning "positive international law" (ibid.). This showed that they disapproved of creating special tribunals and statutes for specific crimes after they were committed, as they felt had been done at Nuremberg. These three nations basically opted for a very strict reading of the Old Latin saying with which I began this birthing story. They seem to have wanted all the Latin adjectives in their version of the saying: "Nullum crimen sine praevia scripta lege penale" (no crime without a previous written penal law). I take it that Cuba thought the *scripta* (written) aspect would automatically include the *stricta* (well-defined) aspect of the previously established law.

While these three nations opposed any UD support for the Nuremberg judgment because that tribunal was established after the crimes were committed, other delegations felt that because of its emphasis on nonretroactivity, the UD text did not give enough support to the Nuremberg outcome. They felt that there was a difference between nonretroactivity on the domestic level and internationally. Adrian Carton de Wiart from Belgium, for instance, "feared that its [11(2)'s] adoption might be used as a basis for the argument that such trials as the Nurnberg Trials had been illegal. He agreed with those who had held that those trials had been based on the laws of human conscience which were higher than national laws" (A/C.3/116/266). Alexandre Contoumas from Greece also argued that "the idea of non-retroactivity in criminal law was included in the general legal principles of his country" but that this principle "in the declaration of human rights might, by implication, cast doubt on the validity of the trials of war criminals in general, and of the trials of Nuremberg and Tokyo in particular" (ibid., 270). He proposed that the secretary should mention these "doubts" about this paragraph in his report to the General Assembly, which would have the last say on the text before its official adoption.

The middle ground between these extremes was taken up by those who had no doubt that the UD text struck the right balance. They felt the Belgian fears were "unwarranted," for (in the words of Benigno Aquino of the Philippines) "it was obvious that considerations of international peace and welfare must supersede national considerations" (A/C.3/SR.115/266). The communists also supported the middle way. Pavlov of the USSR said he saw "no ground for fears expressed by the Belgian representative. The crimes of those brought before the Nurnberg Tribunal had constituted a glaring violation of all the laws of war; they had, in effect, been crimes under international law. There was no cause to fear that the adoption of paragraph 2 of article 9 [=11] in Paris—a city which but a few years ago had itself been under Hitlerite occupation—would be considered by anyone an amnesty for those crimes" (ibid., 267). Ljubomir Radevanovic of Yugoslavia noted that "from the penal point of view international law had not been codified; it was based on custom. . . . At the Nurnberg Trials, the German war criminals had tried to invoke that principle [of nonretroactivity]. The Nurnberg Military had rightly rejected that concept. The *nulla poena sine lege* principle was almost universal in its application in national law. It was inadvisable to propose identical solutions for the same problems in those two fields

of law" (A/C.3/SR.116/272). He would vote for Article 11 on the sup-
position that it "did not cast doubt subsequently on the validity of the
judgments pronounced by the Nurnberg Tribunal" (ibid., 273).

The whole of the second paragraph, with the Panamanian second sentence (but without the word "penal" in it), was adopted by nineteen
votes for with six against and nineteen abstentions (A/C.3/SR.116/273).
Right after that, on the recommendation of the United States, the word
"penal" was inserted twice in the paragraph before the word "offence."
The whole of Article 11, as amended, was adopted by forty-two votes to
none, with two abstentions (ibid., 274).

I realize that I far overshot my usual target in the word count for each
of these birth stories. My excuse is that the dates of the writing of the
declaration and the Nuremberg trials are too close for me not to point
out that the word "international" in the middle of the second paragraph
of UD 11 cannot bear the weight that some scholars and officials, including the Office of the UN High Commissioner for Human Rights, have
put on it.

Article 12
The Right to Privacy

Privacy is dead and social media holds the smoking gun.
—Pete Cashmore, CEO of Mashable

No one shall be subjected to arbitrary interference with his privacy, family, home or correspondence, nor to attacks upon his honor and reputation. Everyone has the right to the protection of the law against such interference or attacks.

On October 16, 2017, James Vacca, a New York City activist on citizens' right to know, told his fellow council members, "When the Department of Education uses an algorithm to assign children to different high schools and a child is assigned to their sixth choice, they and their family have a right to know how that algorithm determined that their child would get their sixth choice. They should not merely be told that they were assigned to a school because an algorithm made the most efficient allocation of school seats. What is considered to be most efficient? Who decided this?" (Ben Green, *The Smart Enough City: Putting Technology in Its Place to Reclaim Our Urban Future* [Cambridge, MA: MIT Press, 2019], 106).

As Vacca argued, we live in a deeply conflicted world between our algorithm-determined lives and the social contract view of the state, where major decisions are made by an informed public for the good of that public. This applies not just to what schools our children are assigned to but also to where bus stops or street lights with sensors are placed and even to how much of a punishment is meted out to a criminal, to say nothing about how COVID-19 has changed our world and made all of us more digital than we ever thought we would be.

No fewer than forty-four of the then fifty-six UN Member States had various protections of this right to privacy built into their constitutions. The variety was enormous. Article 3, section 1, of the Philippines' constitution said that "the right of the people to be secure in their persons, houses, papers and effects against unreasonable searches and seizures shall not be violated." Poland's Article 100 protected "the home and the hearth of the citizen," while Sweden's Article 16 said that the king was "not to disturb or allow to be disturbed the peace of any person in his home." Turkey's Article 71 stated that "the life, property, honour, and residence of each individual are inviolable." The United States' Fourth Amendment said that "the right of the people to be secure in their persons, houses, papers and effects, against unreasonable searches and seizures shall not be violated." These are only partial citations from the forty-four that in the 1940s had privacy provisions in their constitutions (E/CN.4/AC.1/3/Add.1/Article11 [=12]). (Today some forty countries have laws that focus on the technology of privacy invasion and data protection.) It was not easy for the UD drafters to find the common denominator of all the surveyed constitutions, work them up into an initial draft, and then entertain amendments of national delegations that sought to lift up their own way of defining this right.

John Humphrey, the first director of human rights in the UN Secretariat, got these privacy discussions started when he submitted an article on privacy rights that he borrowed from Panama. It read, "No one shall be subjected to arbitrary searches or seizures, or to unreasonable interference with his person, home, family relations, reputation, privacy, activities or personal property. The secrecy of correspondence shall be respected" (E/HR/3; E/CN.4/AC.1/11). In this First Drafting Session, Lebanon and the United Kingdom questioned the vagueness of the words "arbitrary" and "unreasonable" (E/CN.4/AC.1/SR.4/6), but the consensus was that the substance of the article should in some form be included in the bill being drawn up. Based on the discussion, René Cassin, the French delegate, was asked to rewrite Humphrey's list, and he submitted this text: "Private life, the home, correspondence and reputation are inviolable and protected by law" (E/CN.4/21/53).

In the Working Group of the Second Session Alexandre Bogomolov from the Soviet Union asked the French representative how "respect for reputation" fit into this lineup. Cassin responded that "this meant the right of the individual to be protected from slander against his reputation" (E/CN.4/AC.1/SR.5/2). When Panama asked why this article did not mention protection of the individual person whose privacy was the subject of discussion, Cassin noted that "the protection of person had already been covered by the article on slavery," which is our UD 4 (ibid.) When he was asked by Panama why "activities" were not mentioned, Cassin responded that those were covered by "the Declaration as a whole" (ibid., 3). The group forwarded the following text to the Second Session where it was adopted by fourteen votes with twelve abstentions (E/CN.4/SR.37/8): "Everyone shall be entitled to protection under law from unreasonable interference with his reputation, his privacy, and family. His home and correspondence shall be inviolable."

This version was sent to countries for their comments, which were discussed in the Second Drafting Session. Chile, Australia, and the United Kingdom indicated that they liked the version submitted by the United States, except that they felt that "freedom from interference" was too weak and should be made stronger. Taking this in, Chairperson Eleanor

Roosevelt from the United States proposed the US version of the article with the insertion of "under law" to strengthen the protection. It read like this: "Everyone is entitled to protection under law from unreasonable interference with his reputation, family, home, or correspondence." It was unanimously adopted and sent on to the Third Session (E/CN.4/AC.1/SR.36/7). Note that this US version does not contain the concept or terminology of privacy, which is the heartbeat of the article.

This changed when China submitted the following text to the session: "No one shall be subjected to unreasonable interference with his privacy, family, home, correspondence or reputation." It was adopted by nine votes to three, with four abstentions (E/CN.4/SR.55/4) and sent on to the next drafting stage. The word "privacy" up front, followed by a comma, suggests that people have a special zone of privacy around them. It shows that punctuation matters, for without that comma one could think of the human right to privacy as merely a list of protected spheres of our lives, containing only the items mentioned in Article 12—family, home, correspondence, honor, and reputation, which today we might translate into physical, informational, decisional, proprietary, associational, and intellectual privacy items. However, the comma in the article indicates that whatever we put on that list, these items belong under one single umbrella of the basic human right to privacy.

Unfortunately, in the Third Committee the article ran into problems of a parliamentary kind. At the time, the United Nations had two working languages, English and French, which did not always say the exact same thing. The chairperson happened to overlook this fact when he allowed in quick succession two votes to proceed on a Russian amendment (E/800). The first sentence of that Russian text said one thing in English ("No one shall be subjected to arbitrary interference with his privacy, family, home, correspondence, honour, or reputation") and, according to some drafters, something else in French ("ni d'atteintes à son honneur et à sa réputation"). After the chairman had asked for a vote on the Russian text, which passed in a vote of twenty-three to twelve with six abstentions (A/C.3/SR.118/311), disagreement broke out as to whether that was a fair vote because some had voted on the basis of the English translation of it and others on the basis of the French translation. Not realizing what had happened the chairperson (Charles Habib Malik from Lebanon) put the second Russian sentence (quoted shortly) also up to a vote, and it too passed with a similarly large majority. He then, as was the custom when parts of a text were adopted, called for a vote on the whole of the Russian text.

Immediately several minority nations spoke up, saying they had voted for the first Russian sentence on the basis of the French text that spoke of "attacks" (atteintes à son honneur et à sa reputation) and not on the basis of the English text, which allowed for "interference with one's reputation and honor," which, as the French delegate had said, was absurd. Guy Perez Cisneros of Cuba, whose delegation had proposed a text that did make this difference clear (A/C.3/232), argued that "as there were [at that time] two working languages [in the UN], the French was as authentic as the English, he had voted in favour of the French text" (A/C.3/SR118./312). Roosevelt from the United States agreed and said she had voted against the first Russian sentence because she agreed with the French representative that "it was absurd to speak, in the English text, of interference with honor and reputation, as that sentence did" (ibid.). Chile had also voted on the basis of the French text (ibid., 313). Cassin therefore proposed to alter the "imperfect" English text and amend it to fit the French version so it would read "nor to attacks upon his honour and reputation" (ibid.)

The chair once again read the French and English texts of the USSR amendment, the end of the latter being altered to read, "nor to attacks upon his honour and reputation" (ibid., 314). The implication was that the whole of the USSR text in this altered form was now to be voted on. But Peng-Chun Chang of China pointed out that "the Committee could not be asked to vote on the whole of an amendment the wording of which was different from the text on which the vote had [already] been taken, in parts. Rather, it should take a second vote on the first paragraph, and be given an opportunity to reject it. The United Kingdom supported that observation. But the chair said he "could not agree with the Chinese representative. . . . Since there were two working languages, either text could be taken as a basis. The French text before the Committee had not been altered in any way; but the English text had been made to correspond to it" (ibid., 314).

Alexei Pavlov of the USSR said that "the wrangle" in which the committee had been engaged was unworthy of it and asked that his amendment be put to the vote "immediately" (ibid., 315). The chair did just that, and the English version of the whole Russian text (as quoted at the end of the previous paragraph), which was submitted as a substitute for what it had received from the commission, was adopted in a vote of twenty-nine to seven with just four abstentions. As you can see, in order to work out their compromises, the UD drafters at times "wrangled' too much.

I must also report that the Saudi delegation felt that "unreasonable" was too vague and proposed "illegitimate" instead (A/C.3/255). It received support from the Soviet Union because it "was more precise and less open to subjective interpretation" (A/C.3/SR.118/306). Since this adjective sounded too much like "illegal" and would seem to give ultimate authority to national legal systems, a middle way had to be found between it and the word "unreasonable," which, in the words of Karim Azkoul from Lebanon, "was open to various interpretations and therefore dangerous" (ibid., 308). The middle way was found when Ann Newlands of New Zealand proposed the word "arbitrary" (A/C.3/267). This word had already been used with "arbitrary arrest" in Article 9 and in the drafts for Article 15, where the declaration says that no one is to be "arbitrarily deprived" of his nationality. She added that the word "signified everything that was not in accordance with well-established legal principles" (A/C.3/SR118/276). Because it had received a great deal of support, the word "arbitrary" was the term used in the Russian text that was adopted in the abovementioned vote of twenty-three to twelve with six abstentions.

Article 12 presents a pretty good consensus shaped from among an enormous variety. You might say that the Universal Declaration was written from the ground up, from the norms that states already had in their own constitutions to an international generalization of those same norms. From that point of view, the comma after the word "privacy" in the article as we have it is very telling. It could be that Panama's push for the inclusion of "activities" (A/C.3/280) and the French opening phrase of "sa vie privée" were more prescient than they seemed at the time.

Article 13
Freedom of Movement and COVID-19

> The rights of men, as citizens of the world, shall be limited to
> the conditions of universal hospitality. We are speaking
> here . . . not of philanthropy, but of right; and in this sphere
> hospitality signifies the claim of a stranger entering foreign
> territory to be treated by its owner without hostility. The latter
> may send him away again if this can be done without causing
> his death; but, so long as he conducts himself peaceably, he
> must not be treated as an enemy. . . . This right to present
> themselves to [world] society belongs to all mankind in virtue
> of our common right of possession of the surface of the earth
> on which, as it is a globe, we cannot be infinitely scattered,
> and must in the end reconcile ourselves to existence side by
> side: at the same time, originally no one individual had more
> right than another to live in any one particular spot.
>
> —Immanuel Kant

---

(1) *Everyone has the right to freedom of movement and residence within the borders of each state.*

(2) *Everyone has the right to leave any country, including his own, and to return to his country.*

Reading Article 13, on the human right to movement, one is struck by its abstract, bare-bones approach. We are told that we have a human right both to freedom of movement within our own country and to leave it and return to it if we want to. No limits are mentioned in the text. Is that kind of freedom a human right in the age of COVID-19? That seems totally out of place. Read that quotation from Kant again. He apparently thought that all of us human beings own planet Earth together. The climate crisis (see UD 28) does point in that direction, but can we really, as "citizens of the world," roam around on it, visit family and friends in other parts if we want to, and return to where we started out? Not in March 2020, when I am writing this. But the ability to come and go as you please, even across borders, seems to be what Kant has in mind.

If we substitute the word "ideally" for Kant's word "originally," we come closer to what Article 13 means today in a world stricken by COVID-19 and other disasters. It then reads like this: "Ideally no one individual ha[s] more right than another to live in any one particular spot" on this planet. Kant must think that where you find yourself is largely a matter of accident. Right he is. The drafters' struggle with this article was to make the ideal fit into their own real Holocaust world, which for us would be a post–COVID-19 one, whatever that will look like. As fellow humans we therefore ideally owe each other hospitality for commerce, travel, respite, and safety, medical or otherwise. That could mean shelter in place. I do not know how you feel about this total freedom even on an ideal level, but you will see that a good many of the UD drafters did accept Kant's ideal. The bare-bones text shows as much.

A good half of the constitutions that John Humphrey, the first UN director of human rights, looked at (E/CN.4/AC.1/3/Add.1/67) included a right to freedom of movement. Many of them qualified it with limitations based on "police regulations" (Chile), "cases of criminal responsibility" (Cuba), "limits prescribed by law" (Ethiopia, Honduras, the Philippines), "an executed sentence" (Panama), "legislative restrictions of a hygienic nature necessitated by epidemics" (Turkey).

It is therefore no surprise that the *Drafting Committee* set up by the Human Rights Commission submitted a version that had a general limitation built into its text. Charles Habib Malik of Lebanon told his colleagues that "the intent of the Article was to guarantee freedom of movement within a country subjected to conditions . . . and also the liberty of emigrating from a country and changing nationality. He wondered, however, if 'emigration' covered the case of mere travel, which ought also to be included" (E/CN.4/AC.1/SR.13/8). This right of transit can also be found in the second paragraph of a US submission stating that "every person shall, subject to equitable immigration and deportation laws, be free to enter, travel through or over, and remain temporarily in the territory of another state, provided always that he observes local laws and police regulations" (E/CN.4/AC.1/11/13). Ralph L. Harry of Australia also agreed that the article needed to deal with "the facilitation of movement throughout the world" (E/CN.4/AC.1/SR.4/4).

The First Drafting Session came up with this three-sentence article: "There shall be liberty of movement and free choice of residence within the borders of each State. This freedom may be regulated by any general law adopted in the interest of national welfare and security. Individuals may freely emigrate or renounce their nationality" (E/CN.4/36/Add.2/5). Note that it stipulates "welfare and security" oversight for each nation but not one for cross-border settlements. So the Working Group of the Second Session adopted a note asking "Members of the United Nations to co-operate in providing such facilities" for rescue and cross-border resettlement (E/CN.4/AC.2/SR.9/12). "Dr. Weiss from the International Refugee Organization supported the proposed comment, which would facilitate the resettlement of individuals under supervision of IRO" (ibid., 13). Founded in 1946 to help with the mass of refugees caused by World War II, the International Refugee Organization is active around the globe. The changes added in the whole of the Second Session created this long two-paragraph article: "1. Subject to any general law not contrary to the purposes and principles of the United Nations Charter and adopted for specific reasons of security or in general interest, there shall be liberty of movement and free choice of residence within the border of each State. 2. Individuals shall have the right to leave their own country and, if they so desire, to acquire the nationality of any country willing to grant it" (E/600). You can see that the drafters were searching for a way to uphold the Kantian ideal but make it realistic by injecting outside controls. The "national welfare" of the first version was changed to controls coming from the United Nations or its affiliated agencies like today's World Rescue Organisation or even the World Health Organization, which designated COVID-19 a global pandemic.

In the Second Drafting Session the drafters rethought their UD text because they now were comparing that text with the one they were drawing up for a legally binding international convention or covenant. Since no limitations had yet been put into that covenant text, many felt, as Chile put it, that "no limitations" should be put in the UD text (E/CN.4/AC.2/SR.36/7). The main issue was whether the general limitations on possession of human rights spelled out in what was then UD Article 2 (now UD 29)—which included a reference to "the purposes and principles of the United Nations"—were sufficient and would make a limitation in Article 13 unnecessary. Lebanon's distinction between a "declaration, which laid down the absolute, positive principles on which the rights of man were based, and the convention, which indicated the limitations of those rights" (ibid.), expressed the prevailing mood. Chairperson Eleanor Roosevelt proposed the deletion of the limitations from the UD text, which was done in a vote of five to one with one abstention, with this result: "(1) Everyone has the right to freedom of movement and residence within the borders of each State. (2) Everyone has the right to leave any country, including his own."

The Third Session upheld this idealism. When urged on by Chile, India, Belgium, and Australia, it approved by eleven votes to one, with four abstentions, this text. A. J. D. Hood from Australia "fully concurred in the remarks of the Chilean representative," who had called the right to movement a "fundamental human right" and had not wanted to see "any limitations to that right" (E/CN.4/SR.55/9). Hood went on to argue that "freedom of movement was unquestionably one of the fundamental rights of man, and it should form the subject of a statement of principle. To subject it to reservations would be to deprive the Declaration of all its force" (ibid., 11). But the battle for limitations was not yet over.

In the Third Committee the Soviet Union resubmitted its amendment to have the rights in Article 13 limited by the "laws of each state" (E/800). It was supported in this effort by Poland and Saudi Arabia. The latter rightly observed that "in times of national crisis due to various political or economic causes, every Government made use of its right to regulate freedom of movement within its territory" (A/C.3/SR.120/320). A. Appadorai from India pleaded that "the provisions of article 11 [=13] were essential for the indigenous inhabitants and the Asians living in Africa" (ibid., 317). This was in 1948, and South Africa had just begun to pass the first of many apartheid laws. Appadorai did not want to see the USSR limitation spread from "the Asian population in Africa [to] the inhabitants of many other countries" (ibid.). This Soviet attempt failed by large majorities (ibid., 325). Cuba and Egypt proposed to limit the right to freedom of movement and residence to just a right within one's own country, which one was also free to leave "by his own will" (Cuba/A/C.3/232) or "only of his own accord" (Egypt/A/C.3/264). They did not address the right to move about the world in a Kantian fashion. These two amendments were roundly rejected. Panama proposed that the rights of Article 13 be circumscribed by "temporary" restrictions (A/C.3/280). This too was rejected, though it did receive some US support.

The only successful amendment was the Lebanese one that proposed to add the phrase, "and to return to his country," to the end of Article 13(2) so that it would end up reading like this: "Everyone has the right to leave any country, including his own, and to return to his country (A/C.3/260). It is hard not to think again of the opening quote from Kant when one reads Lebanon's explanation of this proposal. Karim Azkoul "recalled that article 11 [=13] was intended to cover all movements inside and outside a given State. According to that article any person had the right to leave any country, including his own. The ideal would be that any person should be able to enter any country he might choose, but account had to be taken of actual facts. The minimum requirement was that any person should be able to return to his own country" (A/C.3/SR.120/316). This was in the fall of 1948 after the Israeli war of independence had begun the previous June, which caused huge numbers of Arabs to flee and be pushed into neighboring Arab lands. Seeing this, Lebanon sought and got "assurance of the right to return" as a minimum concession to the Kantian ideal. The amendment passed unanimously in a vote of thirty-three for, zero against, and eight abstentions (ibid., 325).

Ernest Chauvet of Haiti noted,

The principle of the individual's right to move freely about the world had been recognized before national States had reached their present state of development. The various barriers erected by those states failed to take account of the importance of the human element, the ties of family and friendship, which were often stronger than the ties which attached the individual to the sometimes unstable Government of his country. The World belonged to all mankind. Government restrictions ran counter to the aspirations of the universal conscience; they might be tolerated as a temporary necessity, but there could be no question of including them in the declaration which was intended primarily to educate the masses. Its principles should not be political, but educational, social, and humane, and should remain faithful to the great Declaration of Human Rights of 1789. (A/C.3/SR.120/318)

The Belgian representative was "impressed" by the Haitian statement and "agreed that freedom of movement and freedom of residence should be guaranteed throughout the world," which is why he objected to any limitations. "The main purpose of the declaration of human rights," he said, "was to make a public declaration of what the conscience of the world was thinking" (A/C.3/SR.120/322). Benigno Aquino of the Philippines responded to Haiti's statement with the observation that even temporary restrictions conflicted with "the exercise of free movement, not only within a country but also from one country to another. His delegation considered that article to be one of the most effective means by which to break down the walls of silence which cut off whole countries from the rest of the world" (ibid., 318). Roosevelt of the United States "expressed sympathy with the ideal upheld by the representative of Haiti, especially when he explained that every man should have the right to settle in the country of his choice. Economic consideration had, however, forced certain countries to take legal measures to restrict immigration. . . . A declaration of human rights should not contain principles the application of which was rendered impossible by existing circumstances" (ibid., 319). But if we think the ideal is really ideal, why not state it in the face of the real? And is that not true of the entire declaration?

Article 14
The Right to Asylum

> Every refugee in this world is forced out, like a tree pulled
> out of the ground by a storm.
> —Ai Weiwei

---

(1) *Everyone has the right to seek and to enjoy in other countries asylum
from persecution.*

(2) *This right may not be invoked in the case of prosecutions genuinely
arising from non-political crimes or from acts contrary to the purposes
and principles of the United Nations.*

There is a difference between the "*per*secutions" in paragraph 1 and the
"non-political" "*pros*ecutions" in paragraph 2. Paragraph 1 is about being
unjustly pushed out of your own country because of war, poverty, persecution, or lack of protection by the authorities. Paragraph 2 says that this
protection does not count if you have engaged in nonpolitical criminality. Do not commit a heinous crime and then ask for protective asylum in
the country next door.

The 1951 Refugee Convention defines a refugee as a person who, "owing to well-founded fear of being persecuted for reasons of race, religion, nationality, membership of a particular social group or political
opinion, is outside the country of his nationality and is unable or, owing
to such fear, is unwilling to avail himself of the protection of that country." In today's world of more and more failing states (like Syria, South
Sudan, Yemen, Afghanistan, Democratic Republic of Congo, and others),
the number of internally displaced persons is also very large and creates
many refugees inside their own country.

I strongly encourage you to go to the website of the United Nations
High Commissioner for Refugees and study its most recent global refugee report. The one for 2019 tells us that by the end of 2019, 79.5 million people (that is, roughly 1 percent of the world population) had
been forced to leave their homes. That included people displaced within
their own nations and nearly 26 million refugees, around half of whom
were under eighteen. As the top sourcing nations that yielded this flood
of people in trouble, the site lists Syria, Venezuela, Afghanistan, South
Sudan, and Myanmar, all of which you probably have read about. The
site lists Turkey, Colombia, Pakistan, Uganda, and Germany as the top
hosting countries that took in many millions of refugees. Obviously this

altruism among nations needs to be increased, which even this defective article can help do.

Chinese artist Ai Weiwei, from whom I took the opening quote about refugees being like uprooted trees, was himself such a tree. He told a Canadian interviewer, "My father was exiled and I grew up in the camps. We faced all kinds of discrimination and unfair treatment, so I have a natural understanding of people being seen as different" (Ai Weiwei, *Humanity* [Princeton, NJ: Princeton University Press, 2018], 66). His astonishing film *The Human Flow* is a three-hour tour through today's refugee camps and their horrific conditions. It shows you how deeply broken the world's refugee system is.

The first big crack in that system can be seen right here in Article 14 of the Universal Declaration. The article does not say that everyone has the human right to find and be given asylum from persecution in other countries. It only says that everyone has the right *to seek and to enjoy* such a right once it is given by another country. The drafting of this article is an uneven story of the right to be *granted* asylum being first left out, then put in, and finally being left out. And there was lots of disagreement about the role the United Nations was to play in all this.

While it was left out of both John Humphrey's early text and René Cassin's rewrites, the right to be granted asylum was first put in by the Working Group of the Second Session. That group had received this imperfect text from the First Drafting Session: "Everyone has *the right to escape* persecution on grounds of political or other beliefs or on grounds of racial prejudice by taking refuge on the territory of any State willing to grant him asylum" (E/CN.4/21; (italics added). Paul Weiss, the representative of the International Refugee Organization, immediately spoke up against this "very imperfect" version of what was needed. He hoped the Drafting Committee "would reconsider the [imperfect] wording with a view to sponsoring more positive action" (E/CN.4/AC.2/SR.5/4). Alexander Easterman of the World Jewish Congress also contended that "Article 14 afforded a right of escape with no corollary of a right to access to the country of reception. Many refugees from Germany had been denied this right which had resulted in the death of thousands. Moreover, Article 14 failed to implement Article 7 [=3], since persons who were denied the right to asylum frequently died and thus were denied the right to life" (ibid.) These comments were "strongly supported" by the representative of the International Union of Women's Catholic Organizations (ibid.).

Chairperson Eleanor Roosevelt of the United States "thought it would be dangerous to raise any false hopes in the Declaration and doubted whether it was within the province of the United Nations to tell Member States that they must grant asylum" (E/CN.4/AC.2/SR.5/4). General

Carlos Romulo (Philippines) countered by saying, "It was not so much a question of raising false hopes as of establishing a principle to be followed by all" (ibid., 6). After some more skirmishing, the general reiterated his view that the "onus of finding asylum" should not be put on the individual and proposed this wording: "Everyone shall have the right to seek and be granted asylum from persecution. This right shall not be accorded to criminals nor to those whose acts are contrary to the principles and purposes of the United Nations." This was adopted by the working group and also by the Second Session itself, in the latter by eleven votes to one with five abstentions (E/CN.4/SR.37/10). The sole negative vote came from the United Kingdom, which had wanted to go back to the weaker version of the text but was rebuffed in a vote of eleven to four with two abstentions (ibid.)

Given that the implementation of this right of asylum involves more than one country, it is not surprising that Humphrey's survey of national constitutions (E/CN.4/AC.1/3/Add.1) showed only a few that contained this right. Cuba and France were among the clearest. Article 31 of the Cuban Constitution stated that Cuba "offers and recognizes the right to asylum to those persecuted for political reasons provided that persons thus sheltered respect the national sovereignty and the laws." France's was even more direct: "Anyone persecuted because of his acts in favour of liberty has the right of asylum on the territories of the Republic." Given that in those days the term "democracy" raised all the hackles of the Cold War, Yugoslavia's Article 31 is intriguing: "Foreign citizens persecuted on account of their struggle for the principles of democracy, for national liberation, the rights of the working people, or the freedom of scientific and cultural work, enjoy the rights of asylum in the Federal People's Republic of Yugoslavia."

Discussions of a possible role for the United Nations to play dominated the next two drafting phases. The Drafting Committee's Second Session had set up a small subcommittee that proposed this two-sentence text as the first paragraph: "Everyone shall have the right to seek and may be granted asylum from persecution. The United Nations is bound to secure this asylum in agreement with Member States" (E/CN.4/AC.1/49). The United States, Lebanon, Australia, and the USSR objected because it put the onus of granting asylum on the shoulders of the UN, which they felt should not be given an explicit role in a declaration that was not supposed to include measures of implementation and only deal with principles. A Soviet proposal to "bar Fascists and Nazis from the right to find asylum" was rejected in a vote of four to one with two abstentions because it was felt such activities were covered by the second paragraph, which was like ours and was adopted in a five-to-two vote. The second sentence of paragraph 1, calling on the UN, was rejected "by three votes for and three against" (E/CN.4/AC.1/SR.37/13). The slightly changed first sentence ("Everyone has the right to seek and may be granted asylum in other countries from persecution") was adopted by six votes for, none against, and one abstention (ibid., 14). The words "may be" did not go unnoticed.

At the start of the Third Session, Toni Sender of the American Federation of Labor thought the new wording was "highly unsatisfactory" and that "the permissive character of the phrasing 'may be granted asylum' deprived the article of any real value" (E/CN.4/SR.56/7). Franz Bienenfeld of the World Jewish Congress "stated that the right to asylum was implicit in the concept of the right to life" that was already in the declaration. "In demanding the right to asylum, refugees were not asking for permanent homes but for temporary safety from persecution" (ibid.). After stating the right of everyone to seek asylum, the French proposal included this second sentence: "The United Nations is bound to secure them such asylum," after which came the usual 14(2) statement (E/CN.4/182/Add.8/3). This led Roosevelt from the United States to observe that the French proposal could probably not be accommodated "as the [Economic and Social] Council had asked the Commission to make a study on the right to asylum" (E/CN.4/SR.56/9). Both Belgium and Lebanon backed the French call for a UN role, but that proposal was rejected in a close vote of six for, five against, and five abstentions (ibid., 12).

At this point a totally new idea was interjected because a subcommittee proposed that the first paragraph be made to read, "Everyone has the right to seek and be granted asylum *as humanity requires*" (E/CN.4/SR.57/2, italics added). This qualifying clause, as it came to be called, did not help clarify matters at all. According to Charles Habib Malik from Lebanon, this "broad and vague" new phrase should be voted on separately, and he "would rather see [it] deleted and be replaced by the previously rejected French proposal to entrust the United Nations with the problem of asylum" (ibid., 3). Belgium, Chile, and China supported that idea. The chairperson pointed out that the subcommittee had done what it did "partly because the Chinese representative had indicated the danger of an unqualified right of persons to seek and be granted asylum" (ibid., 5). At this point Lebanon also pressed hard for a revote on the French text. Hansa Mehta from India pointed out that "the United Nations could be instrumental in providing permanent asylum only. It was a human right, however, to seek and be granted temporary asylum from persecution. That right was not covered in the French proposal" (ibid., 6).

Roberto Fontaina from Uruguay sought to clear up some "misconceptions," he said. "The task of the Commission consisted in drafting principles. The question of implementation would be considered by the Commission during the discussion of the Covenant. The Commission's sole concern at the present time was to lay down the principle that a person persecuted for political reasons had a right to asylum. The determination of how asylum should be granted belonged to the Covenant." He added that the necessary mechanism for granting asylum "should be provided by the United Nations" and ended up supporting a reconsideration of the French proposal. He was followed in this by the Philippines and Panama, whereupon Lebanon "formally moved that the French proposal about the UN acting on the matter in concert with its Members be resubmitted for consideration" (E/CN.4/SR.57/9). After the qualifying clause "as humanity requires" was deleted in a vote of fourteen for and one against with two abstentions, the resubmission of the French proposal calling for a UN role was again rejected in a close vote of seven for and eight against, with one abstention. That once again allowed for a vote on "Everyone has the right to seek and be granted in other countries asylum from persecution." It passed in a remarkable twelve-to-one vote with four abstentions (ibid., 11). The meeting closed at 1:20 p.m., and it would seem that the crack I noted at the start of our story was removed.

At the time this article was being debated by the Human Rights Commission, the United Nations generally was seized by the question of what to do about the waves of refugees caused by the 1948 Arab-Israeli War. One of those waves overlapped with the debates in the Third Committee. So the Saudi delegation proposed that "and be granted" be deleted from the article (A/C.3/241) and the United Kingdom delegation proposed that the relevant paragraph read, "Everyone has the right *to seek, and to enjoy* in other countries, asylum from persecution" (A/C.3/253, italics added). Both of these proposals were accepted, which means that the lessons learned from the Holocaust were lost when the time came to deal with waves of Arab refugees. The neighboring Arab nations were greatly burdened by the roughly 750,000 Palestinians who were pushed out of their Palestinian territories when the State of Israel was formed. Below the surface lay the right of these refugees to repatriate to their places of birth once the war was over. The general feeling was that since it was the United Nations that had partitioned Palestine, that organization was to some extent responsible for the refugee problem.

Karim Azkoul of Lebanon sought to save the integrity of this article with the argument that "a statement of a [human] right should not . . . depend on the possibility of states to comply with that right. If it were part of the birthright of man, it should be established, even if, for accidental reasons, it did not seem possible to ensure immediate implementation" (A/C.3/SR.121/335). This to me is the heart of what I call the transcendence or superiority of human rights over national or domestic legal systems. The idea received support from several delegations. Justino

Jimenez de Arechaga of Uruguay thought that the United Kingdom delegation had confused "immigration and the right to asylum" (which people today also often confuse), which to him were "two different things" (ibid., 334). Pablo Campos Ortiz of Mexico seconded these thoughts, while Agha Shahi of Pakistan argued that the right to asylum was implicit in the right to freedom of thought and expression because people often want to flee their home country when these rights are violated. "After condemning the Nazi and fascist ideologies and the conception of the absolute state, Mr. Shahi emphasized the necessity of guaranteeing to everyone not only the right to seek asylum but also the possibility of enjoying that asylum" in a nontrivial way. His delegation did not think that by voting for a human right to be granted asylum, "a country would seriously endanger its immigration policy" (ibid., 337).

The attempt to keep a real asylum right in the text failed when (in addition to most Arab states) the United Kingdom, Australia, New Zealand, India, the United States, Norway, China, Greece, Sweden, and Venezuela also voted for the UK-Saudi proposals that cut the right to be granted asylum from the UD text (A/C.3/SR.122/344). If only three of these had voted differently, the moral foundation stone for today's fight against the world refugee crisis would not have had this crack in it. The hypocrisy of the deletion votes is shown up when we compare those with Uruguayan Enrique Rodriguez Fabregat's comment that "the same conviction as had moved [his delegation] to support the Jews in their persecution now inspired it to defend the cause of the Arab refugees" (A/C.3/SR.118/292).

Article 15
The Right to a Nationality and Statelessness

The very phrase "human rights" became for all concerned—
victims, persecutors and onlookers alike—the evidence of
hopeless idealism or fumbling feeble minded hypocrisy.

—Hannah Arendt

(1) *Everyone has the right to a nationality.*
(2) *No one shall be arbitrarily deprived of his nationality nor denied the
    right to change his nationality.*

Imagine you are one of the seven hundred thousand Rohingya citizens
who (after the 1962 coup by General Ne Win) were pushed out of Burma
into Bangladesh because your government says you do not really belong
there. It says you are not "really" a citizen because you cannot trace your
lineage back to 1824 when the British colonized Burma, though they did
not use the term "Rohingya" when they categorized the different ethnic
and religious groups living in Burma at that time. Your government says
it is not violating paragraph 2 of this article because you are all Muslim
interlopers in "their" Buddhist country.

Offhand, having a nationality may not seem to be a human right, but
as the Rohingya example shows, having one can turn out to be crucial to
survival. The 1954 Convention relating to the Status of Stateless Persons
defines a "stateless person" as "a person who is not considered as a national by any State under the operation of its law." So there is a conflict
here between Burma rejecting you and Article 15 saying that you have a
human right to a nationality. Who is going to give you that nationality?
Must Bangladesh give you its citizenship? Will it be the United Nations?
This question of UN involvement dominated the debates on this article.
The drafters had to find phraseology that could not be undone by appeals to the idea of national sovereignty, which was the standard Soviet
objection to universal rights of this kind. I tell this drafting story from
the perspective of René Cassin, who fought the hardest to have the UN
play a role in addressing the problem of stateless people.

When the first UN director of human rights, John Humphrey, did his
survey of extant constitutions (E/CN.4/AC.1/3/Add.1), he ran into the
same basic models we have today. Some countries give nationality or

citizenship based on bloodline and others based on where you are born. He found a bloodline (plus naturalization) example in Article 88 of the Polish Constitution stating that citizenship could be acquired "if the parents are Polish citizens or by naturalization granted by a competent State authority." The US Fourteenth Amendment indicates that "all persons born or naturalized in the United States, and subject to the jurisdiction thereof, are citizens of the United States and of the State wherein they reside." That is a-born-on-the-soil example to which naturalization is added, which is how I got my own US citizenship. Humphrey's Article 32 (E/CN.4/AC.1/11/36) begins with an interesting blend of both these acquisition strands: "Everyone is entitled to the nationality of the State where he is born unless and until on attaining majority he declares for the nationality open to him by virtue of descent," to which he added two more paragraphs banning arbitrary deprivation and identifying the right to be able to change one's nationality, both of which you find in UD 15(2).

French delegate Cassin, who was asked to rewrite the Humphrey list, changed that first sentence to this simple one: "Everyone has the right to a nationality," to which he added this paragraph: "It is the duty of the United Nations and Member States to prevent the absence of nationality, which is contrary to human rights and against the interest of the community of mankind" (E/CN.4/AC.1/W.2). By enlisting the United Nations to combat the problem of statelessness, Cassin put his pen on what seventy-five years later is still a deep wound in the system. It is estimated that today there are over ten million stateless people in the world. Every year the United Nations High Commissioner for Refugees bestows the Nansen Refugee Award, which is given to people or organizations that seek to reduce statelessness. In 2019 that award was given to Azizbek Ashurov, a lawyer in Kyrgyzstan whose organization helped more than ten thousand people gain citizenship in the Kyrgyz Republic. Among them were two thousand children who now have the right to education whereas before they did not.

At the start of the Second Session's Working Group on the declaration, Alexandre Bogomolov of the USSR asked France "what was meant precisely by the sentence 'everyone has the right to a nationality'" (E/CN.4/AC.2/SR.5/11). He wanted to know "on whom the obligation [to give nationality] was to be imposed, since the principle seemed an infringement of the sovereign rights of States" (ibid., 12). Cassin replied that "as a result of the war there were thousands of stateless persons all over the world constituting a grave social issue. . . . Whilst the United Nations had no power to grant nationality, a duty remained to call attention of Member nations to a situation which would become increasingly serious" (ibid., 11).

As Cassin noted, the drafters were aware that thousands of stateless persons roamed around Europe after the war searching for a new political community to join. That would include Hannah Arendt, from whom the opening quote of this essay was taken. The hypocrisy she talks about is that of nations that refused to take in and give shelter to the flood of refugees that broke upon Europe right after World War II. She herself was such a stateless refugee from 1937 (when Germany took away her German citizenship) till 1951 when she became a US citizen. This experience of national homelessness led her to believe that there are no human rights outside of having citizenship in a state that honors human rights.

In the Second Session itself, Belgium also drew attention to the problem of statelessness. Over objections from the United Kingdom not to place "a heavy and impossible burden" on the United Nations, the session adopted this Belgian text in a vote of twelve to two with one abstention: "Everyone has the right to a nationality. All persons who do not enjoy the protection of any Government shall be placed under the protection of the United Nations. This protection shall not be accorded to criminals, nor to those whose acts are contrary to the principles and aims of the United Nations" (E/CN.4/SR.3/13).

Right at the start of the Second Session of the Drafting Committee "the Chairman, speaking as representative of the United States, suggested deletion of article 15" (E/CN.4/AC.1/SR.39/7). Cassin responded that "the purpose of article 15 was to express one of the general principles of mankind and to affirm that every human being should be a member of a national group. The United Nations should contribute to putting an end to statelessness by urging the necessary measures upon sovereign states" (ibid). He mentioned the Nansen passports introduced by the League of Nations as a precedent. Alexei Pavlov of the USSR again raised objections based on national sovereignty that would block any UN enforcement action of this kind. In a vote of three to three with zero abstentions, the Drafting Committee decided *not* to delete this article, and to keep the simple first sentence in the text (in a vote of three to three with one abstention), but it also decided to delete the second sentence that called for a role played by the United Nations.

So what arrived at the Third Session of the commission was just this one sentence: "Everyone has the right to a nationality," and nothing else. The Soviet Union proposed to add a paragraph saying "the procedure of depriving a person of his nationality must be determined by national laws" (E/CN.4/95), which sidestepped the problem of statelessness. The United Kingdom and India jointly proposed this substitution for 15(1): "No one shall be arbitrarily deprived of his nationality," which also mostly ignored that problem. France resubmitted its own article calling on the UN and its Member States "to prevent statelessness" and to place people who are stateless "under protection of the United Nations" (E/CN.4/82/Add.8/4.). The upshot was that the UN protection for stateless persons was rejected by a vote of nine to six with one abstention. The UK-Indian proposal containing just our 15(2) was adopted in a vote of ten to three with three abstentions. The simple first sentence ("Everyone has the right to a nationality") was removed in a vote of six to five with four abstentions.

Cassin observed that "a human being had a number of [human] rights; one of them being the right to be attached to a national group; and the Declaration should contain a provision covering that right" (E/CN.4/59/8). If you think, as Cassin did, that human rights must express deep human needs and capabilities, he had a point. For nationality connects to a person's right to the full development of his personality (see UD Articles 22, 26, and 29). Nationality brings with it not just essential protection but also connections to history and culture. It gives people a sense of belonging to their own group (if they are lucky) or to the wider multicultural national community that has come to shape today's nations. When seen in light of UD 21, it fleshes out a person's right to self-determination and control over his or her environment. (See Johannes Morsink, *Inherent Human Rights* [Philadelphia: University of Pennsylvania Press, 2009], chapter 4).

That left in the text only our 15(2), which had in it the word "arbitrary." In the Third Committee Uruguay proposed that that word be changed to "unjustly" (A/C.3/268) on the grounds that "an arbitrary act was usually an act committed against law, but it could be a just act if it contravened an unjust law," which meant that "unjust" was a "higher standard of justice to which the laws on deprivation of nationality should conform" (A/C.3/SR.123/349). In seeking to reduce statelessness, "justice should be the standard not mere legality, and justice was a concept that could be defined on an international level" (ibid., 353). Going in the opposite direction, the Soviet Union proposed that the word "arbitrary" be understood to mean "[not] in any other manner or in any other case than as provided for in the laws of the country concerned" (E/800). Pavlov argued that "the United Nations was not a world Government set above the Governments of various States; it could not dictate to those States in matters in respect of which no obligations were imposed by the Charter" (ibid., 356). Guatemala wanted to see the word "arbitrary" deleted without a replacement (ibid.). All these amendments dealing with the word "arbitrary" in 15(2) were rejected and 15(2) itself, as received from the Third Session, was adopted "unanimously" (ibid., 361). Innocuous words, it seems, can carry big messages.

We see the same moral transcendence in the Third Committee debate over the reintroduction of the simple first sentence of 15(1), "Everyone has the right to a nationality." Its reintroduction came from Uruguay (A/C.3/268), Lebanon (A/C.3/260), and France (A/C.3/244). The

French proposal also included a new third paragraph asking "the United Nations . . . to concern itself with the fate of stateless persons." Eduardo Anze Matienzo of Bolivia went so far as to say that "nationality was an inalienable human right. It was independent of the legal status of the place of birth. In law, a nationality might be regarded as transitory; but as a right it was inherent" (A/C.3/SR.123/351). After pointing out that "individuals should not be subjected to action such as was taken during the Nazi regime in Germany when thousands had been stripped of their nationality by arbitrary government action," Eleanor Roosevelt of the United States asked "how it would be possible to realize that right. [She] would like to be able to feel, as the Bolivian representative did, that such a right was inalienable, but that attitude hardly seemed realistic" (ibid.). Arguing that "the declaration . . . should not include mention of the duties of Governments or of the United Nations," she also indicated that if the majority wanted 15(1) included, her country would not object (ibid., 352).

Numerous delegates made strong statements pleading for the reintroduction of "Everyone has the right to a nationality" into the text of Article 15. Some (Norway and Lebanon) wanted that sentence plus a UN role, while others (Guatemala, Australia, and Chile) wanted it back in, but without a UN role. Chile charged that the Soviet Union "had apparently misunderstood the purpose of the declaration; that purpose was not to impose laws on any sovereign State, but to enable the people of a State to judge for themselves whether the laws under which they lived were in conformity with the principles of the declaration. If the Hitler regime were still in existence the result of not adopting 15(1) would be to justify the acts of that regime rather than protect individuals against them" (A/C.3/SR.123/357).

Cassin of France argued that "although the members of the Committee remained government representatives, in the drafting of a declaration of universal import they met as an Assembly seeking the universal good. They could not close their eyes to the fact that, in an international order based on the principle of national sovereignty, the existence of persons rejected by their countries was a source of friction. The declaration should proclaim that every human being had the right to a nationality, just as if it proclaimed that everyone had the right to marry; it was not called upon to implement either right" (A/C.3/SR.123/358). The first paragraph 15(1) was added back in in a vote of twenty-one to nine with six abstentions (A/C.3/SR.124/359).

Article 16
Marriage and the Family

The family, consisting of a more or less durable union,
socially approved, of a man, a woman and their children is a
universal phenomenon present in each and every society.
—Claude Levi-Strauss

(1) *Men and women of full age, without any limitation due to race,
nationality or religion, have the right to marry and to found a family.
They are entitled to equal rights as to marriage, during marriage and
at its dissolution.*
(2) *Marriage shall be entered into only with the free and full consent of the
intending spouses.*
(3) *The family is the natural and fundamental group unit of society and
is entitled to protection by society and the State.*

Though I do not know the details, it would seem that something like
Levi-Strauss's conception of marriage (based on historical research) was
the one most of the UD drafters had in mind when they adopted the first
paragraph of this article: "Men and women of full age . . . have the right
to marry and found a family." Some kind of male-female coupling is
probably necessary if societies are to continue to exist, though it is of no
help to the millions of members of the LGBTQ community whose sexual
identities do not fit into this traditional definition.

That is why today some thirty nations allow for gay marriage and often
for the adoption of children by such couples, as can be seen in this this
comment by John McDargh: "The best part of being married is that now
when we walk down the street, people won't just see two guys and a kid,
they'll have to see a FAMILY" (Patricia Gozemba and Karen Kahn, *Court-
ing Equality: A Documentary History of America's First Legal Same-Sex Marriages* [Boston: Beacon Press, 2007], 209).

To accommodate different approaches to marriage, many countries
have civil and religiously sanctioned ones. Already in 1948, Article 16 of
Belgium's constitution stated that "civil marriage shall always precede
the religious ceremony, except in cases to be established by law if found
necessary" (E/CN.4/AC.1/3/Add.1/98).

John Humphrey avoided controversy by submitting this initial text to
the First Drafting Session: "Everyone has the right to contract marriage
in accordance with the laws of the State" (E/CN.4/AC.1/3/Add.1/98).

But in the Working Group of the Second Session (E/CN.4/AC.2/SR.6), the International Union of the Catholic Women's League and the International Federation of Christian Trade Unions objected to giving the same "remedies for breach of marriage" for men and women (E/CN.4/ AC.2/SR.6/3). They were supported by Charles Habib Malik from Lebanon, who started the Second Session itself with this two-sentence proposal for the article: "The family deriving from marriage is the natural and fundamental group unit of society. It is endowed by the Creator with inalienable rights antecedent to all positive law and as such shall be protected by the State and Society" (E/CN.4/SR.37/11).

Malik gave a lengthy rationale, the gist of which was that "society was not composed of individuals, but of groups, of which the family was the first and most important unit; in the family circle the fundamental freedoms and rights were originally nurtured. It therefore deserved greater prominence, he thought, than that given it in the original text. . . . He had used the word 'Creator' because he believed that the family did not create itself. That word might give rise to objections, but he would very much like to have it retained. He also contended that the family was endowed with inalienable rights, rights which had not been conferred upon it by the caprice of man" (E/CN.4/SR.37/11–12). Alexandre Bogomolov, who represented the Soviet Union, disagreed. He "pointed out that varied forms of marriage and family life existed in the world, each form corresponding to the special economic conditions of the people concerned. Different religions had different ideas regarding the position of women in the family; some religions allowed polygamous families and some did not accord an equal status to men and women. He also reminded the Representatives that many people did not believe in God, and that the Declaration was meant for mankind as a whole, whether believers or unbelievers" (ibid.).

The first Lebanese sentence ("The family deriving from marriage is the natural and fundamental group unit of society") carried by nine votes to five, with four abstentions. The second sentence, about God and the family having inalienable rights, was rejected both in the Second Session and in the Second Drafting Session. The second time was because representatives did not go along with Malik's suggestion that they read "Nature" instead of "God" into his amendment's reference to the "Creator" (E/CN.4/AC.1/SR.38/8). UD 16's second sentence, "Marriage and the family shall be protected by the State and Society," harking back to an earlier Byelorussian proposal, was also adopted.

An exchange took place between Chile (which "thought it should be established that men and women had the same fundamental right to dissolve marriage, although this was not recognized in all countries") and August Vanistendael, the representative of the International Federation of Christian Trade Unions. The latter repeated his earlier warning that "the dissolution of marriage was unacceptable to millions of Christians" (E/CN.4/AC.1/SR.38/13). This did not affect the outcome since the session kept the received text: "Men and women shall have the same freedom to contract marriage in accordance with the law." But it did help adoption of a UK-inspired proposal that gave us the first version of the article's middle sentence: "Marriage shall not be contracted without the full consent of both intending spouses and before the age of puberty" (ibid.)

In July 1948 the Third Session began with a long query from Amalia C. de Castillo Ledon, the vice-chairperson of the Commission on the Status of Women. She pointed out that back in January of that year, her commission had submitted this text to the Human Rights Commission: "Men and women shall have equal rights to contract marriage or dissolve marriage in accordance with the law" (E/CN.4/SR.58/9). She said her commission

was aware that a certain section of public opinion had protested against that text on religious grounds, which the Commission understood and respected. But since the Commission had been appointed to safeguard the rights and protect the interests of women throughout the world, it had been obliged to take account not only of groups that did not recognize divorce, but also of the existing situation in countries where, divorce being legally recognized, the relevant legislation usually placed women at a disadvantage. The Commission on the Status of Women had not thought that the text it advocated would be against the religious principles of certain groups, since even religious doctrine provided for the dissolution of marriage in certain cases, although extensive restrictions were applied. The Commission had been guided above all by concern at existing conditions, under which inequalities were too often sanctioned to the detriment of women and the family. In many countries grounds for divorce for men differed from those for women. In many cases the law denied a woman the most elementary right to express her opinion, to take her own decisions or sometimes even to receive alimony for herself and her children. It was the duty of the Commission on Human Rights to examine every aspect of the problem and to find a just and humane solution. The Declaration must plainly state the principle of equality of men and women in marriage. (Ibid., 10)

The Third Session heard this advice but took no action. Instead, it approved the much weaker phraseology of "equal rights as to marriage" that was used in a US proposal. Leaving out the middle sentence, that proposal (with French changes that I put in italics) read as follows: "Men and women *of full age have the right to marry and to found a family and* are entitled to equal rights as to marriage. The family *(deriving from marriage)* is the natural and fundamental group unit of society and is entitled to protection." The first italicized phrase was an addition and the second a deletion. Each summarized a long discussion that was marred by procedural obstacles. This US text, as amended by France, was adopted to be the whole of what was then Article 13, our 16 (E/CN.4/SR.62/11). Immediately the Soviet Union pointed out that "inadvertently" the middle sentence about full consent of the parties had been left out. It proposed this remedy: "Marriage may be entered into only with the full consent of both spouses; men and women shall have equal rights both during the marriage and in its dissolution" (ibid.) The idea of equal rights in the dissolution of marriage, Alexei Pavlov said, was "to protect the woman from the loss of property which she frequently incurred as a result of divorce" (ibid.). By eleven to zero with four abstentions, the first Russian sentence, "Marriage may be entered into only with the full consent of both spouses," was adopted, while the second Russian sentence was rejected in a vote of seven to six with six abstentions.

The Third Committee had representatives on it of all fifty-six Members of the United Nations, while the Human Rights Commission, from which it received the UD text for review, had only eighteen members. That is the reason I try to always give the reader a good look at what this Third Committee did. I report on three major changes the Third Committee made. Each time I put the change made in italics.

First, you can see that the italicized addition in the first sentence ("Men and women of full age, *without any limitation due to race, nationality or religion,* have the right to marry and found a family") harks back to the nondiscrimination demands of UD Article 2. This insertion was proposed by Mexico (A/C.3/266). It is an exception in the UD lineup because all along delegations had agreed not to repeat the strong denunciation of discrimination in Article 2. But by a vote of twenty-two to fifteen with six abstentions, an exception was made (A/C.3/SR.125/375). Pablo Campos Ortiz of Mexico said that he "was convinced that a certain idea should be repeated again and again if the need arose. . . . There had been notorious cases of discrimination in marriage, particularly by the Nazis" in the 1935 Nuremberg marriage laws (A/C.3/SR.124/364). The roll call shows that support for the nondiscrimination clause came mostly from communist and Latin American delegations. The United Kingdom, the United States, Australia, New Zealand, and Canada did not want to see the nondiscrimination provisions of Article 2 repeated. Most Muslim-majority nations also voted against this repetition. Begum Shaista Ikramullah, the Pakistani delegate, said "her delegation was opposed to the Mexican amendment because it completely disregarded the religious factor as a hindrance to marriage" (A/C.3/SR.125/374). Jamil Baroody spoke for Saudi Arabia and defended that country's own amendment proposing that the phrase "legal matrimonial age" be inserted in the first paragraph. He noted that "the word 'full' in paragraph 1 of the basic text was ambiguous, because it did not necessarily mean 'of full age according to law.' In any case, the law was not the same in all countries or even within all parts of the same country, as for example in the United States of America. 'Full age' might also cover aged and decrepit couples whose marriage might not be desirable" (A/C.3/SR.124/363). Saudi Arabia's call for a change from "full age" to "legal matrimonial age" (A/C.3/240) was rejected in a vote of twenty-four to four with seven abstentions (A/C.3/SR.125/376). Ecuador voted against it because of worries that this proposal "could result in the State making the right to marry and found a family conditional upon unacceptable restrictions" (ibid., 368).

This legal specificity did not fit well with the Mexican call for nondiscrimination. Indeed, according to Saudi Arabia, "the authors of the draft declaration had for the most part taken into consideration only the standard recognized by western civilization and had ignored more ancient civilizations which were past the experimental stage, and the institutions of which, for example marriage, had proved their wisdom down through the centuries. It was not for the Committee to proclaim the superiority of one civilization over all others or to establish uniform standards for all the countries in the world" (A/C.3/SR.125/370).

Second, we owe the addition of the italicized phrase in the second sentence ("They are entitled to equal rights as to marriage, *during marriage and when divorced*" [later changed to "and at its dissolution"]) to the USSR amendment (E/800). René Cassin of France pointed out that the commission "had not specifically mentioned divorce, contenting itself with a broad general formula 'as to marriage' because divorce did not exist in some countries and because it wished to respect the varying legislation on marriage in all countries" (A/C.3/SR.124/363). Belgium said it would support the USSR amendment (ibid., 365). Bodil Begtrup of Denmark "thought article 14 [=16] one of the most important in the declaration, particularly for women." She asked Chairperson Eleanor Roosevelt of the Commission on Human Rights "to define the exact meaning of 'equal rights as to marriage.' For if the term 'marriage' covered the case of dissolution of the contract, article 14 [=16] should not contain the word 'divorce.' If, however, that idea were not contained in the text, her delegation would" support the USSR amendment (A/C.3/ SR.125/367). Karim Azkoul of Lebanon answered her when he said the commission had "discussed at length the term 'as to marriage' and had decided it covered all phases of marriage." He explained that "if an average person read the declaration, he would have the impression that the General Assembly of the United Nations had put marriage and divorce on the same footing. But marriage was an institution, whereas divorce was merely an exceptional and regrettable aspect of that institution" (ibid., 372). Roosevelt backed him up, saying that "the Commission on

Human Rights had interpreted the term 'marriage' in its widest sense. Article 14 [=16], in its original draft, dealt with all stages of marriage in the contract to divorce" (ibid., 373). These answers did not satisfy the majority of drafters, for the Soviet proposal to add "during marriage and when divorced" at the end of the first paragraph was adopted in a close vote of seventeen to sixteen with nine abstentions (ibid., 376).

The third change the Third Committee made was to insert the two italicized words into the third sentence of the article, as follows: "Marriage shall be contracted only with the *free and* full consent of the intending spouses." We owe this change to Lebanese amendment (A/C.3/260). (The word "both" was deleted when the French amendment A/C.3/244 was adopted.) Cassin of France noted that "the reason for specifying that marriage might be contracted only with the full consent of the intending spouses was that the custom still existed whereby parents, guardians or others arranged marriages without consent of the spouses. Marriage was a basic right; it should not be negotiated like a treaty or a business deal" (A/C.3/SR.124/363). Azkoul of Lebanon followed that up by explaining that "he had a practical end in view in proposing the addition of the words 'free and' before the words 'full consent' (A/C.3/260). Parents could force a girl to give her full consent to a marriage she did not wish, but, logically, they could not force her to give her free consent" (ibid., 364). The Dominican Republic and Poland spoke up in favor of this addition (A/C.3/SR.125/369, 371). The amendment was adopted by a lopsided vote of thirty-six for, none against, and five abstentions.

The fourth and last change in the Third Committee was also the result of the USSR amendment (E/800). It proposed the italicized addition to the end of the third paragraph of the article, as follows: "The family is the natural and fundamental unit of society and is entitled to protection *by society and the State.*" This amendment was simply an attempt to reinstitute protection that you might recall had been part of earlier versions of the article and was adopted by a handsome majority (A/C.3/SR.125/377). While the United States (ibid., 373) felt that simply calling for protection was enough, the United Kingdom worried that this "might be interpreted as giving the State overriding authority over the family" (A/C.3/SR.124/365). France thought the text "adequate" but did also note that this protection "should not be provided solely by the State; it must be provided at all stages from the social group to the world community not only by public bodies but also by private or religious institutions, wherever they existed" (A/C.3/SR.125/374).

Pavlov rejected the idea that the USSR amendment was unnecessary. "On the contrary," he said, "unless it was explicitly stated that it was for the State and society to protect the family, which was the natural unit of society and the fate of which might determine the fate of the nation, a family in need of protection would not know where to turn" (A/C.3/ SR.124/366). Since I am writing this at the apex of the coronavirus pandemic in the United States, I must also share this prescient Polish observation that "there were countless cases in which the family needed the protection of society and the State: it has to be assisted through special provisions related to expectant mothers, nurseries for infants, food priorities in emergencies or in under-developed countries, and the like" (A/C.3/SR.125/371). I leave it to my reader to fill in the last clause.

Article 17
Property and Essential Needs

The right of every family to a decent home . . .
 —Franklin Roosevelt's Second Bill of Rights

We have built an economy without shock absorbers.
 —Joseph Stieglitz

———————

(1) *Everyone has the right to own property alone as well as in association with others.*

(2) *No one shall be arbitrarily deprived of his property.*

What Stieglitz meant in the opening quote from the *New York Times* of April 17, 2020, was made abundantly clear a few days later when that paper announced its new project of telling the world the kind of America we need in this age of tremendous and still soaring inequality in all sectors of life. Thousands died due to a lack of health care and adequate protective gear at work. Unless very big changes are made, the road ahead for those who survived the coronavirus pandemic will be very bumpy indeed. There were no shock absorbers because in the United States—unlike in other developed countries—there is no workable safety net for 80 percent of the workforce. The virus has laid bare the cruel underbelly of unfettered American capitalism that also exacted enormous death tolls from many other countries. All these nations, to use the words of Article 17 drafters, failed to make the human right to "the essential needs of decent living" a reality for most of their citizens.

Millions of us, even in well-off strata of Western nations—certainly including those pushed to the edge in the American gig economy—suddenly saw what our "essential needs of decent living" were when faced with the sudden arrival of a health pandemic. Additionally, thousands more forgot about the word "decent" because they were also suddenly made homeless due to a lack of money for their rent or mortgage payments. Who, we should ask, really is the guardian of our *human* rights, those rights to "the essential needs of decent living" that include a minimum of personal property that US president Franklin Roosevelt also said every human being should have to supply those essentials for him- or herself and his or her family? Things like owning a profit-making business, owning an estate, and acquiring stocks or works of art are all part of a flourishing economy, but they cannot be counted as a minimum requirement for human dignity.

The unfortunate aspect of this drafting story is that the UD drafters buried this crucial phrase "essential needs" inside the much broader economic perspective covered by this article. We do find this phrase "essential needs of decent living" in the Bogotá Declaration that twenty-one nations of Latin America adopted in April 1948 in Bogotá, Columbia. Article 23 of this regional text says that "every person has a right to own such property as meets the essential needs of decent living and helps to maintain the dignity of the individual and of the home" (E/CN.4/122/6). At one point the UD drafters copied this entire text—except for the word "private"—for their own declaration (E/CN.4/AC.1/SR.38/6). That happened after they failed to find a common denominator among national statements.

From the start it was obvious that the drafters had to thread their way through a multiplicity of different national views on property rights. John Humphrey looked at more than fifty constitutions, and in forty-two of them he found entries he could roughly match with our Article 17. His own submission to the First Drafting Session had four paragraphs, but only the first ("Everyone has a right to own personal property") and the last ("No one shall be deprived of his property without just compensation") survived in some way. The two middle sentences dealt with the right to share in "profit-making" enterprises and with the state's right to "determine those things that are susceptible of private appropriation" (E/CN.4/AC.1/11). The early drafting stages of this article focused on finding, as the Soviet Union put it, "some abstract formula which made allowance for different social systems" (E/CN.4/AC.2/SR.8/2). This resulted in the Second Session of the commission adopting this text: "Everyone has the right to own property in conformity with the laws of the state in which such property is located. No one shall be arbitrarily deprived of his property" (E/CN.4/SR.27/12). Since the state is in control here, this text lacks the moral transcendence the UD drafters were trying to achieve. But that soon changed.

At the start of the Second Session of the Drafting Committee, Hernan Santa Cruz of Chile "recalled the text of the draft adopted by the Inter-American Juridical Committee at the Bogota Conference; 'Everyone has a right to own private property as meets the essential needs of decent living, and helps to maintain the dignity of the individual and of the home.'" He made the following pitch. "He thought that article 14 [=17] was wrong, because a [human] right was not affirmed if it was stated at the same time that it could be suspended by law. The question to be decided was whether ownership of property was an essential and fundamental right. The idea of ownership was regarded from angles in different countries; it was necessary to find a minimum common denominator or, if that proved impossible, to abandon the question altogether" (E/CN.4/AC.1/SR.38/3).

When the United States asked "who would define 'essential needs,'" Santa Cruz answered that "Bogota did not limit the right to property; it merely established to what extent it was to become an essential [human] right, and each country would be free to determine reasonable limits in that connexion" (E/CN.4/AC.2/SR.8/3). Geoffrey Wilson of the United Kingdom liked the Chilean suggestion. René Cassin of France noted that any text arrived at would have to be a result of compromise since the Chilean proposal "was likely to displease some countries" (E/CN.4/AC.1/SR.38/4). Santa Cruz "could not agree" with the French representative. "The purpose of the declaration, which was to establish essential [human] rights, should not be forgotten. If states were allowed to legislate on the matter, all that remained would be an abstract right" (ibid). Alluding to Cassin's call for compromise language, he said that "the easiest way would be to adopt a definition of the [human] right to ownership of property, and that provided by the text adopted at Bogota seemed the most suitable" (ibid.)

Alexei Pavlov of the USSR "agreed with the French representative that property should be subject to the laws of the land. . . . In soviet countries common ownership was the basis of the regime, and such countries would be opposed to the adoption of any other system. He concluded that it was necessary to retain the idea that ownership applied alike to private [profit-making] ownership and common ownership, in conformity with the laws of the different states" (E/CN.4/AC.1/SR.38/4). Santa Cruz responded that "the conception held by the USSR fitted perfectly into the framework of the text which he had proposed . . . [and] that at least part of the property held [in the Soviet system] should be held as an essential right" (ibid., 5).

The reader now has met the two leading opponents in these property debates. First Chile would get the upper hand and then the Soviet Union. Chile's moment came when the Second Session of the Drafting Committee adopted this Bogotá text in a vote of three to two with three abstentions. Pavlov asked for the deletion of the word "private" because "in the USSR private [profit-making] property was not the essential basis of 'decent living' for individuals" (E/CN.4/AC.1/SR.38/5). The United Kingdom agreed with that and proposed the deletion of the word "private" from the just-adopted text, which was done. After that E. J. R. Heywood of Australia proposed that the phrase "and not be arbitrarily deprived" be added to the adopted Bogotá text, which was also done (ibid., 7).

Now it was the turn of the Soviet Union to get the upper hand. This happened in the next drafting stage, which was the Third Session of the commission. The adopted Bogotá text came under fire when the Soviet Union argued that any UD text "should be acceptable to Members of the United Nations with differing economic systems." He gave his own country's constitution as an example of one that "recognized the right to private property resulting from individual labour and not from the exploitation of others. But besides private property there was another system of property, and that was socialist and collective property" (E/CN.4/SR.49/8). The context makes it clear that "private" property was the kind that made a profit by exploiting others, for Pavlov went on to say that "it was possible to prove that private property had acted as a brake on progress and ensured the continuance of extreme poverty and wealth. It would be possible also to prove the superiority of a property regime where the land belonged to the peasants and the factories to the workers. If, therefore, any statement about private property was to be put in an international document, mention must also be made of the other form of property." That is why he wanted to have property regimes "determined by the laws of individual countries. That was an expression of the equality of the two systems." He concluded that "the USSR could never agree that only private property could be guaranteed" (ibid.). As you can see from these quotations, for the communist countries there was a big difference between private profit-making property and collective or commonly held property.

Instead of the Bogotá text that was on the table, the USSR wanted go back to what had been decided in the Second Session of the commission. Into that text it wanted to insert the phrase I italicized: "Everyone has the right to own property, *either alone (individually) or in community (association) with others* in conformity with the laws of the state in which such property is located. No one shall be arbitrarily deprived of his property" (E/CN.4/SR.59/3). Pavlov explained that "the amended article would also cover what was known in the USSR as personal ownership of property, which differed from private property, as understood in Western countries, because it was based on income earned from collective work" (ibid.). This fit the USSR constitution of 1936, which permitted "the small private economy of individual peasants and handicraftsmen based on their personal labour and precluding the exploitation of the labour of others" (Article 9).

A drafting subcommittee (of the United Kingdom, France, the USSR, and the United States) was set up. It suggested this two-sentence text: "1. Everyone has the right, alone as well as in association with others, to own property (*in accordance with the laws of the country where the property is located*). 2. No one shall be arbitrarily deprived of his property." The discussion focused on the phrase I italicized. Afanasi Stepanenko of the Byelorussian Soviet Socialist Republic supported the phrase so that "the principle of national sovereignty, laid down in the [UN] Charter," would be respected (E/CN.4/SR.61/5). The Soviet Union argued that this italicized clause "would prevent the view of others from being imposed on it" (ibid.). The United Kingdom thought the parenthetical clause unnecessary (ibid., 3). "In reply to Mr. [Karim] Azkoul (Lebanon) the Chairman explained that according to the Drafting Sub-Committee's text, everyone had a dual [pre-political?] right to own property, either by himself, or in association with others, and these two forms of ownership were not mutually exclusive" (ibid., 4).

The vote against inclusion of the parenthetical phrase ("in accordance with the laws of the country where the property is located") was eight against, four to retain, and two abstentions. A USSR amendment that "arbitrarily" in the second sentence of UD 17 be replaced by "illegally" was also rejected. But the Soviet victory lay in the unanimous adoption by the Third Session of its proposal of the phrasing, "Everyone has the right, alone as well as in association with others, to own property." That is what was passed on, together with the right of not being "arbitrarily deprived" of one's property.

I tell what happened in the Third Committee mostly with voices not heard in the commission. Chile offered an amendment (A/C.3/249) that literally copied the just-discussed Bogotá text. Cuba also wanted to see the Bogotá text restored but incorporated into its amendment (A/C.3/232) changes that accommodated the demands of the Soviet Union. In the first Bogotá sentence, it inserted the by now familiar Soviet (italicized) line, "Every person has the right to own such property, *alone as well as in association with others*, as meets the essential needs of decent living and helps maintain the dignity of the individual and the home." Belgium also inserted in the second sentence "Everyone has the right to legal protection" before "against arbitrary confiscation of his property." These insertions did not help the Latin American cause to see the Bogotá text restored. Drafters like the United States lumped the Chilean and Cuban amendments together, saying they were both "undesirable" since "it would be difficult to define the exact meaning of 'decent living' referred to in these amendments" (A/C.3/SR.126/382). After both Cuban sentences were rejected in solid votes (ibid., 387), Santa Cruz of Chile "withdrew his amendment" as well (ibid., 388).

As was to be expected, the Soviet Union repeated its standard proposal (E/800) that "1. Everyone has the right to own property alone as well as in association with others in accordance with the laws of the country where such property is situated," and "2. No one shall be arbitrarily, i.e. illegally, deprived of his property." It did not receive much attention except that Sweden spoke up on its behalf. Ulla Lindstrom "said she had taken little part in the debate on the draft declaration as she had found the basic text generally acceptable; it included, in fact, principles which were already being applied in Sweden" (A/C.3/SR.126/382). She had considered proposing her own amendment to add "in his own country" to the text of the article, but decided not to in the hope that "draft article UD27 [=29] as well as the laws of various countries would cover her point." She then said she would "support paragraph 1 of the Soviet amendment." She would also vote for paragraph 2 because "the word 'illegally' was clearer and more restrictive than 'arbitrarily'; the latter might, for example, be interpreted to conflict with Swedish law which allowed the expropriation of private property for public use" (ibid.). China supported the Swedish hope that the limitations spelled out in UD Article 29 would suffice. Peng-Chun Chang realized that "the right to private property was abused, but expressed the view that article 27 [=29] was the appropriate place for strengthening the limitations to the various rights" (ibid., 388).

The Soviet amendment (E/800) was never voted on because it got caught up in votes that were taken on Haitian and Belgian amendments that introduced a new element into these debates. First, Emile Saint-Lot of Haiti pointed out that the USSR proposal "would be a concession to nationalism that was contrary to the purpose of the universal document under discussion" (A/C.3/SR.126/383). "In order to correct the unduly individualistic nature of the basic draft of Article 15 [=17], yet not to go to the other extreme of setting up national laws as a criterion for determining the limits of the right to own property, he proposed the addition to paragraph 1 of the sentence: 'This right shall be exercised in conformity with the public interest'" (ibid., 383). Referring to the same USSR proposal, Belgium also noted that "there was no reason for the declaration . . . to contain a reference to national laws." Its representative also "opposed the Cuban and Chilean amendments because the concepts of 'essential needs' and 'decent living' were vague." He therefore proposed this substitute for the basic text: "Within the limits of public interest, everyone is entitled to own property alone as well as in association with others" (ibid.). While Uruguay saw a slight difference between these two amendments in that the Haitian one "would constitute a concrete criterion to be used in implementation of rights set forth in the declaration" (ibid., 384), other nations did not see things this way. They all figured that both these texts simply reproduced the public-interest demands spelled out in UD 27, which is our UD 29. Interestingly, these two public-interest amendments introduced a theme that Humphrey had also found in his constitutional survey.

Just before the Belgian text, "Within the limits of public interest, everyone is entitled to own property alone as well as in association with others" (A/C.3/325), was to be voted on, the Soviet Union asked whether it could insert its own phrase, "in accordance with the laws of the country where the property is located," into that Belgian text. Fernand Dehousse, Belgium's representative, said he could not do that because "the concept of public interest, to his mind, was more flexible and progressive than the concept of national laws" (A/C.3/SR.126/389). "Mr. Pavlov (USSR) then moved, as an amendment to the Belgian amendment, the addition of the words" that I italicized earlier. When the chairperson put that Soviet subamendment up to a vote, it was rejected by twenty-five votes to eleven with six abstentions (ibid.). Right after that, both the Belgian and Haitian amendments were rejected by solid majorities. The chairperson rejected a Soviet request to have its own amendment as of yet put up for a separate vote. Pavlov appealed that ruling but was rebuffed by the committee.

Two final observations. Article 17 is unique in that it is not carried forward and codified in later legal international human rights instruments. Also, the first paragraph of Article 21 of the 2007 UN Declaration on the Rights of Indigenous Peoples (A/RES/61/295) tells us, "Indigenous peoples have the right to the lands, territories and resources which they have traditionally owned, occupied or otherwise used or acquired." Article 2 of this UN Declaration refers to the same properties as "ones they possess by reason of traditional ownership." The UD drafters, however, were focused on the human rights of individuals as flesh-and-blood creatures and not on any kind of group rights, human or other. So they did not consider whether the phrase "in association with others" might cover the rights of indigenous peoples to their ancestral lands..

Article 18
Freedom of Thought, Conscience, and Religion

When we blindly adopt a religion, a political system, a literary dogma, we become automatons.
> —Anais Nin

People wo are captured by religious extremism—male or female, old or young—have their consciences destroyed, lose their humanity and murder without blinking an eye.
> —President Xi Jinping

Everyone has the right to freedom of thought, conscience and religion; this right includes freedom to change his religion or belief, and freedom, either alone or in community with others and in public or private, to manifest his religion or belief in teaching, practice, worship and observance.

The major world religions are much older than the nations where they have their habitats. It would therefore have made sense if the drafters had let those ancient religious traditions have a major voice in deciding the scope of religious liberties in various regions of the world. But they did not take that kind of historical institutional approach. They very much came to their list of religious liberties from the bottom up, beginning with John Humphrey's survey of extant constitutions (E/CN.4/AC.1/3/Add.1). There they found no fewer than forty-five constitutional statements ranging from announced state religions (Hanafi Islam in Afghanistan, the Roman Catholic Apostolic Church in Argentina, and evangelical Lutheranism in Scandinavia) to strident anticlericalism in Mexico. They were looking for the common denominator among this great variety.

Humphrey's survey showed that the great majority of nations gave quite a wide scope of religious freedom to their citizens. The range included the freedom of religious practice in the Soviet Constitution, where "the church is separated from the State, and the school from the church," and where citizens "had freedom of religious worship and freedom of anti-religious propaganda" (Art.124), as well as the United States' famous First Amendment, according to which "Congress shall make no law respecting an establishment of religion, or prohibiting the free exercise thereof." Article 14 of the Belgian Constitution stated that "religious liberty and the freedom of public worship are guaranteed, unless crimes are committed in the use of these liberties." It then added that "no one shall be compelled to join in any manner whatever in the forms and ceremonies of any religion, nor to observe its days of rest" (Art.15). Similarly, Article 53 of the Colombian Constitution stated that "no person shall be molested by reason of his religious opinion, or be compelled to profess beliefs or observe practices contrary to his conscience."

Many of these constitutions did put limits on the practice of religion, which, as the Icelandic one put it, "must not [go] against morality and public order" (Art.63). That limitation occurred regularly in the survey. Even Article 13 of the 1940s precommunist Chinese Constitution noted that "the people shall have the freedom of religious beliefs." Not so today, when, as the quotation at the start of this essay shows, President Xi Jinping equates being a Uighur Muslim with being an extremist whose conscience is destroyed and who no longer knows right from wrong and therefore endangers public order and the security of the state.

Humphrey summarized this enormous variety for the First Session of the Drafting Committee with this simple Article 14: "There shall be freedom of conscience and belief and of private and public religious worship" (E/CN.4/AC.1/11/18). As you can see, Humphrey did not use the word "religion," which omission did not get fixed until the Third Session. The enormous variety of religious practices led Charles Habib Malik of Lebanon to underscore "that the Committee recognize the fundamental human right for differing fundamental convictions, as in religion, to exist in the same national entity" (E/CN.4/AC.1/SR.8/13). That same kind of range led René Cassin of France to stipulate that the practice of religion "can be subject only to such limitations as are necessary to protect public order, morals and the rights and freedoms of others" (E/CN.4/Add.2/7).

The Working Group of the Second Session cut out the "limitations" that Cassin had put in because it was thought that those were dealt with in what became our UD 29. The group discussed the five aspects of religious freedom mentioned by Frederick Nolde, who spoke for the Commission of the Churches on International Affairs. These were freedom of worship, of observance, of teaching, of association, and of practice (E/CN.4/AC.2/SR.6/9). Four of them found their way into the text that the Second Session adopted: "Individual freedom of thought and conscience, to hold and change beliefs, is an absolute and sacred right. Every person has the right, either alone or in community with other persons of like mind and in public or private, to manifest his beliefs in teaching, practice, worship and observance" (E/CN.4/95).

At the start of the Third Session of the commission, the representative of the Agudas Israeli World Organization, which was devoted to strengthening Orthodox Jewish institutions, noted the omission of "religion" in the opening lineup, even though this Article 18 was "the foundation for religious freedom" (E/CN.4/SR.60/5). He said that freedom of religion could be found in the 1789 French Bill of Rights as well as in the American Bill of Rights of 1791. Borrowing from the US submission, he proposed that the article start with, "Everyone has the right to freedom of religion, conscience and belief" (E/CN.4/SR.60/6), which was done. But note that "thought," which is part of our final text, was not mentioned here either. That too was fixed in what Geoffrey Wilson of the United Kingdom thought had been a discussion that carried "metaphysical considerations . . . too far" (ibid., 14). But first the session returned to the question of limitations.

The Soviet Union wanted to see this right practiced "in conformity with national laws and public morals" (E/CN.4/SR.60/7). Egypt also proposed that the practice of this Article 18 as well as several other articles be subject "only to such limitations as are prescribed by law and necessary to protect public order and health, morals and the fundamental rights and freedoms of others" (ibid.). Malik of Lebanon responded that "a limitative clause of that nature might distort the exact meaning intended in article 16 [=18]. The article dealt with the rights and freedoms that were above the law and, as it were, outside it. A provision based on religion or morals could not be amended by the law. He would be opposed to such a formula" (ibid.). He referred the Egyptian representative to what became UD Article 29, which spells out limitations on the practice of any and all human rights. The minutes tell us that "the Chairman [Eleanor Roosevelt] and Mr. Lopez (Philippines) concurred in the views of the Lebanese representative" (ibid., 8). The Soviet-Egyptian view was rejected in a vote of ten to five with one abstention (ibid., 9).

At this point Malik proposed a text that looks much like our end product: "Everyone has the right (is entitled) to freedom of religion, conscience and belief; this right includes freedom to change his religion or belief, and freedom, either alone or in community with other persons of like mind and in public or private, to manifest his religion or belief in teaching, practice, worship or observance" (E/CN.4/SR.60/9). When the Soviet Union observed that Malik's proposal "made no allusion to 'freedom of thought'" (ibid., 10), that term was quickly added and made first on the list.

Cassin of France argued that "freedom of thought had a metaphysical significance," a statement not unlike what Anais Nin says in my opening quotation in this essay. "It was an unconditional right which could not be subjected to any restrictions of a public nature. The other rights, however important they might be, were subject to certain limitations. There was a great difference in degree between freedom of thought and of opinion" (E/CN.4/SR.60/13). Is that because exactly what we are thinking is always private, while opinions get expressed and are open to inspection and curtailment? And which comes first, religion or thought? Salvador Lopez of the Philippines felt that since this article was "intended essentially to protect religious freedom," the right to freedom of religion should be mentioned before thought (ibid.). Peng-Chun Chang of China agreed with Cassin "that according to European ideas, freedom of thought was the basis of freedom of belief. Although belief implied thought, freedom of thought had in the course of history actually preceded freedom of belief. But the right to those freedoms implied the right to change them. He therefore suggested simply saying: 'the right to freedom of thought, religion and belief,'" also placing thought first (ibid.).

As I indicated, Wilson of the United Kingdom felt that all this was pushing "metaphysical considerations . . . too far" (E/CN.4/SR.60/14). A subcommittee of France, Lebanon, the United Kingdom, and Uruguay was appointed to find a solution. It proposed the following text: "Everyone has the right to freedom of thought, conscience and religion; *this freedom includes the freedom to change his religion or belief,* and freedom, either alone or in community with others, in public or private, to manifest his religion or belief in teaching, practice, worship and observance" (E/CN.4/SR.62/12; italics added). The Third Session adopted it in a vote of eleven to zero with four abstentions (ibid.).

In the Third Committee Muslim-majority nations disputed the italicized clause because it conflicts with the Sharia prohibition on leaving one's Islamic faith. Defending Saudi Arabia's proposal (A/C.3/247) to delete it, Jamil Baroody "pointed out that throughout history missionaries had often abused their rights by becoming the forerunners of a political intervention and there were many cases where peoples had been drawn into murderous conflict by missionaries' efforts to convert them" (A/C.3/SR.127/391). His main examples were the "bloody and unjustifiable crusades . . . [that] had as their real economic and political purpose the acquisition of a place in the sun for the surplus populations of Europe" (ibid., 392). He continued, "Those who believed in God should admit that all human beings, regardless of their religion, were equal before Him. As to those who did not believe in God, they should understand that in playing upon the religious beliefs of others they might draw the world into a new murderous crusade" (ibid.). He therefore "wished the [Third] Committee to make the declaration as clear as possible and omit any pretext for exciting hatred and encouraging dangerous differences of opinion" (ibid.). He was supported by Begum Shaista Ikramullah of Pakistan, who "stressed the necessity of not adopting any article which might shock the religious sentiments of the different peoples" (ibid., 399).

Fernand Dehousse of Belgium had agreed with Saudi Arabia's "criticism of intolerance and showing to what extremes of fanaticism and sectarianism in the religious and other fields could lead." But Belgium could not agree "to delete an entire section of text dealing with external manifestations of freedom of conscience. It would be unnecessary to proclaim that freedom if it were never to be given outward expression; if it were intended, so to speak, only for the use of the inner man. It was necessary, however, to stress the external manifestations of creeds by which expression was given to beliefs. In that sense the Saudi Arabian amendment was also restrictive" (A/C.3/SR.127/395). A few minutes later, "the Chairman announced that the delegation of Saudi Arabia had withdrawn its first amendment (A/C.3/247) and that it formally proposed" to just cut the words "to change his religion or belief, and freedom" (A/C.3/SR.127/396). Abdul Abadi of Iraq "supported the amendment submitted by Saudi Arabia in its new form" (ibid., 402).

Those other "restrictive" amendments mentioned by Belgium were the ones by the USSR that were designed to circumscribe these rights by the "laws of the country concerned and the requirements of public morality" (E/800); the Peruvian one that focused on just "the right to freely profess a religious faith and to express it in thought and practice, both in public and private," but did not mention either freedom of "thought" or of "conscience" (A/C.3/225); and a longer one submitted by Sweden (A/C.3/247) that was meant to protect "individuals who have religious beliefs different from the officially acknowledged religion, or who have no religious belief whatever, against manifestations of religious fanaticism." To achieve that goal, Sweden proposed to add at the very end of the text this further clause: "provided that this does not interfere unduly with the personal liberty of anybody else." None of these amendments were accepted, and the text the Third Committee adopted in a vote of thirty-eight to three with three abstentions was the same one it received from the Third Session (A/C.3/SR.128/406). The countries that proposed restrictive amendments were told that Article 29 took care of limitations to the practice of all human rights, including the ones in Article 18.

To help explain the rejection of the Saudi proposal to delete explicit mention of the right "to change his religion or belief" from the text of Article 18, I cite some more observations. Benigno Aquino of the Philippines "stressed that while men agreed in general as to what they considered as their essential freedoms, they frequently differed in the profession of their opinions and faiths. Nothing could show that more clearly than the statement by the representative of Saudi Arabia. For him, religion was the manifestation of an emotion; for others [e.g., Aquino himself] it was the expression of faith. It was therefore inevitable that the definition of freedom of religion should give rise to differences of opinion" (A/C.3/SR.127/395). He could therefore not vote for the Saudi amendment, nor for the one by Peru, for that one "retained only one form of freedom of thought: freedom of religious thought" (ibid.). Cassin of France also argued that "one of the most important corollaries of freedom of thought was the freedom of the individual to change his opinion" (ibid., 397). Chang of China told his colleagues that "it was pluralistic tolerance, manifesting itself in every sphere of thought, conscience or religion, which should inspire men if they wished to base their relations on benevolence and justice. . . . [He] said he had heard with sympathy and respect the objections raised by the representative of Saudi Arabia. For the countries of the Far East the nineteenth century, with its expansion of Western industrialism, had not always been very kind and he admitted that missionaries had not always limited themselves to their religious mission" (ibid., 398).

Jamil Baroody "asked the French representative whether his Government had consulted the Moslem peoples of North Africa and other French territories before accepting that text, or whether it intended to impose it on them arbitrarily. He also asked other colonial powers, notably the UK, Belgium and the Netherlands, whether they were not afraid of offending the religious beliefs of their Moslem subjects by imposing that article on them. He reminded the representative of Lebanon that 40 percent of the Lebanese population was Moslem, and asked him whether the whole of that population had authorized him to approve article 16 [=18] *in toto*." Baroody closed by saying that "to mention the individual's right to change religion was superfluous, as that particular freedom was implied in the principle of freedom of belief." He said that Chang had been "over-optimistic in believing that missionaries should be given a chance not to repeat past mistakes. [He] did not question the high personal integrity of most missionaries, but he feared that many would still be used for the end of certain alien political forces" (A/C.3/SR.127/404). The Saudi amendment to drop the disputed text was rejected by twenty-two votes to twelve with eight abstentions (A/C.3/SR.128/405).

When Saudi Arabia asked for a roll-call vote, the tally was twenty-seven to five with twelve abstentions. The five votes that wanted the clause removed came from Afghanistan, Iraq, Pakistan, Saudi Arabia, and Syria, all Muslim-majority nations (A/C.3/SR.128/406). After the proposed deletion was rejected, the rest of the article spelling out the right to various manifestations was adopted in a vote of thirty-four to one with ten abstentions, the only negative one presumably coming from Saudi Arabia.

Other Muslim-majority nations, such as Syria, Iran, Turkey, and Pakistan, in the end voted for Article 18 as we have it.

We need to remember that the declaration includes Article 2, which includes "religion" on its list of nondiscrimination items. That makes religious persuasion or practice one of the bases on which no one is supposed to be discriminated against. For example, one cannot be barred from participation in government (Art.21) on the basis of religious belief or practice, assuming that the limitations of UD 29 are also adhered to.

Article 19
Information, Opinion, and Expression

Freedom of information is a fundamental human right and is the touchstone of all the freedoms to which the United Nations is consecrated.

—UN General Assembly resolution, December 14, 1946

Free expression is the base of human rights, the root of human nature and the mother of truth. To kill free speech is to insult human rights, to stifle human nature and to suppress truth.

—Liu Xiaobo

Everyone has the right to freedom of opinion and expression; this right includes the freedom to hold opinions without interference and to seek, receive and impart information and ideas through any media and regardless of frontiers.

In the flow of the text of this article, the reader can see that the rights to freedom of opinion and expression come *before* the right to freedom of information. While this third-listed right "to receive and impart information and ideas" is not an afterthought, it does seem to have a bit of a lesser status. But I put "information" up front in the essay title before the others because I discovered that the text of Article 19 (as seen here) was recommended to the Human Rights Commission by its own Sub-commission on the Freedom of Information and of the Press (E/CN.4/84). From there this text found its way to the finish line without substantive changes. I therefore share with my readers what the subcommission members who actually wrote this text thought, instead of tracing the article's path through its UD drafting stages, which is my normal procedure.

I think you will see that in a time when we are trying to sort facts from fiction, it makes sense to emphasize the right to freedom of information. Since 2004, two thousand American newspapers have stopped operations, meaning many people are now living in what are called "information deserts." The result is that without good information, it is hard to shape our opinions responsibly and exercise our human right to freedom of expression. Can we get good local news from the internet? From our favorite news channels or feeds?

The UN Economic and Social Council (ECOSOC)—the parent body of the Human Rights Commission—had mandated that this Sub-commission on Freedom of Information and of the Press be created "to examine what rights, obligations and practices should be included in the concept of freedom of information" (E/325/4). ECOSOC had also been asked by the General Assembly to organize a huge after-the-war conference on the subject of freedom of information and the press (E/325), stipulating that "all Delegations to the Conference shall include in each instance persons actually engaged or experienced in press, radio, motion pictures and other media for the dissemination of information" (E/CN.4/Sub.1/2/3), to which mix we would, of course, add all kinds of social media platform owners and managers. The General Assembly Resolution (59/I) that called for this conference (which I quoted at the beginning of this essay) stated that "freedom of information is a fundamental human right and is the touchstone of all the freedoms to which the United Nations is consecrated. Freedom of information implies the right to gather, transmit and publish news anywhere and everywhere without fetters. As such it is an essential factor in any serious effort to promote the peace and progress of the world" (A/229).

The subcommission was given the job of preparing for this conference. It recommended to ECOSOC that the site for the conference be in Europe because "of the special importance of the Conference to peoples of States which had been occupied by the enemy, had suffered under Fascist restrictions on information and continued to lack adequate material information facilities as a result of the devastation brought about by the war" (E/441/3). It was held in Geneva, Switzerland. Living within our own silos of information, in our own era of "fake facts" and with numerous governments seeing "the press as the enemy of the people," we can readily see why the question of freedom of information dominated international discourse in the late 1940s when liberal democracies had to fight for their lives against very strong currents of authoritarianism. In his reply to a United Nations Educational, Scientific and Cultural Organization questionnaire, Arthur Compton, an American Nobel Prize–winning physicist, pointed out that "the individual has the right to expect society to protect him against known untruths sponsored by the state under the guise of truth, against intentional obstruction to the growth and availability of useful knowledge and against indecency and the spread of hatred that will mar his mental attitude and make co-operation difficult" (E/CN.4/Sub.1/49). Then as now, this was not an easy protection to provide.

The Second Session of this subcommission discussed and wrote our Article 19. Eleven nations were represented in that session: the Netherlands (chair), the United States, Norway, Canada, France, Panama, Philippines, the USSR, the United Kingdom, Uruguay, and Czechoslovakia. The Commission on Human Rights asked them to review and give advice on these versions of UD Articles 17 ("1. Everyone is free to express and impart opinions, or to receive and seek information and the opinion of others from sources wherever situated. 2. No person may be interfered with on account of his opinions.") and 18 ("There shall be freedom of expression either by word, in writing, in the press, in books or by visual, auditory or other means. There shall be equal access to all channels of communication.") (E/CN.4/Sub.1/36). After some initial back and forth, a committee of three was appointed, consisting of Andre Geraud of France, G. R. Ferguson of Canada, and A. R. K. Mackenzie of the United Kingdom. That group of three submitted two texts to their colleagues from which to choose (E/CN.4/Sub.1/SR.27/2).

Mackenzie, the chair of the group, explained that text A was a redraft by Ferguson of an earlier proposal and read as follows: "Everyone shall have the right to freedom of opinion and expression; freedom to seek and receive information and the opinion of others by any medium, within and beyond the borders of his land; and having regard to the rights of others, to transmit all information and opinion without limitation." Text B was "largely written" by Geraud and was based on the famous French Declaration of Rights of 1789. It read as follows: "The free communication of thoughts, opinions, and facts, regardless of frontiers, is one of the rights of man. Everyone has, therefore, the right to speak, to write, to print, to employ freely all modes of expression, being liable only for the abuses of this freedom in cases determined by the law of nations." The main question about these two texts turned out to be whether to place limitations on any of the rights at issue.

D. L. Sychrava of Czechoslovakia was dissatisfied with text B because "no liberty of information or of the press could be conceived of, if such liberty were prejudicial to the common welfare. The problem at issue was to define the word 'liberty' and the limitations thereto. The greatest crimes in history had been committed in the name of liberty. He felt that the expression 'law of nations' was inadequate and required clarification" (E/CN.4/Sub.1/SR.27/3). Both the United States and the Dutch chair responded that any limitations could be removed because they were dealt with in other articles of the draft declaration, like our UD 29. The United States and France also sparred on the need for limitations, with the United States wanting none and France thinking that "deletion of all mention of limitations would be an unrealistic approach to the problem" (ibid. 5). Zechariah Chafee of the United States, supported by Mackenzie of the United Kingdom, presciently "observed that merely to state that a person would be held responsible only in cases determined by law was no protection against tyranny" (ibid.). By eight votes out of eleven, it was decided to delete the limitation "by the law of nations" from text B and, by seven votes, to delete the phrase "having regards to the rights of others" from text A.

At the beginning of the next meeting, the chair invited David A. Halperin, representative of the Co-ordinating Board of Jewish Organizations, to address the group. Taking his place at the subcommission table, he agreed that "there was justifiable reluctance to incorporate restrictions on freedom in the Bill of Human Rights; but experience had shown that certain limitations were indispensable for the common good. The prevention of dissemination of prejudice and hatred was at least as necessary as the prevention of obscenity. The freedom to disseminate hatred was one of the most important reasons for its survival through the centuries." He concluded that "a positive step by the United Nations to discourage and prevent the dissemination of racial and religious hatred would lift the hearts of millions of men and women throughout the world" (E/CN.4/Sub1/SR.28/2-3).

After that speech, Mackenzie of the United Kingdom proposed the following text for adoption: "Everyone shall have the right to freedom of *thought* and *communication*; this shall include freedom to hold opinions without interference; and to seek, receive and impart information and ideas by any means and regardless of frontiers" (E/CN.4/Sub.1/SR.28/3). Except for a difference in tense and the two terms I put in italics, this is what became UD 19. You may remember that our UD 18, on the freedom of religion, also speaks of the rights to "freedom of thought, conscience and religion." When Ferguson of Canada pointed out this recurrence of "thought" in the proposed Article 17 (=19), the subcommission decided to recommend to the Commission on Human Rights that if "thought" could not be removed from UD 16 (=18), then this word in UD 17 (=19) should be replaced by "opinion." Speaking for the International Organization of Journalists, Martin made the case "that freedom of thought or opinion was meaningless without freedom of expression" (ibid., 4). The members agreed with that view and by seven votes decided to replace the word "communication" in the italicized text with the word "expression" (ibid.). We then read in the minutes that "the proposed Article 17 [=19] of the Draft Declaration on Human Rights was adopted by eight votes with one abstention" (ibid.) This text was received by the Third Session of the Human Rights Commission in April 1948.

In the subcommission, the Soviet Union had been on the side of those who wanted to see limitations put on these rights in Article 19. It continued this push when the UN text wound its way through the last UD drafting stages. In the Third Session of the commission, the USSR proposed this amendment to Article 19: "Freedom of speech and the press should

not be used for purposes of propagating fascism, aggression and for provoking hatred as between nations" (E/800). In a long speech, Alexei
Pavlov opposed what he called the "syndicates and monopolies through
which, in many countries, small groups of people had complete control
over standardized news published in their papers," for which he gave
examples from the United Kingdom and the United States. These syndicates, he said, "were frequently connected with other big business con-
cerns and thus reflected a different point of view from that of the people"
in small towns. He "stressed that it was extremely unfair that financial
reasons should prevent the people from having newspapers reflecting
their own views" (E/CN.4/SR.63/3). For us in 2020, the coronavirus has
added to the "monopolization" of the media, which is why we see the
disappearance of small-town papers that give people the local news.

A small drafting subcommittee of the Third Session recommended
two changes in the UN text that brought it to what we now have. Taking
the advice of the Sub-commission on Freedom of Information and of
the Press, it changed the word "thought" (which also occurs in UD 18)
in the second line to "opinion" and changed "by any means" to "through
any media" (E/CN.4/SR.64/2–3). As to the Soviet amendment denying
free speech to fascists, Panama, France, China, Lebanon, Belgium, India, the United Kingdom, Australia, Egypt, Uruguay, and the Philippines
all spoke up against it and in favor of the text recommended by the Sub-
commission on Freedom of Information and the Press. The Soviet amendment was defeated in a vote of thirteen to four with zero abstentions, the
votes in favor coming from the USSR, Yugoslavia, the Ukrainian Soviet
Socialist Republic, and the Byelorussian Soviet Socialist Republic (ibid.,
10–11).

While numerous amendments were proposed, no changes were made
by the Third Committee. The USSR proposed two long amendments
(E/800), the first of which included this sentence: "Freedom of speech
and the Press shall not be used for purposes of propagating fascism, aggression and for provoking hatred as between the nations." The Belgian
representative Fernand Dehousse voted against this amendment because,
he said, even though he "hated fascism as intensely as did the USSR representative, [the word] could not be used in a legal document in which
it was not clearly defined" (A/C.3/SR.128/414). To which Fryderyka Kalinowska from Poland responded that "during the war waged against fascism the Allies knew very well what that word meant."(A/C.3/SR.129/419).
The Yugoslavian delegate Ljubomir Radevanovic also argued that "the
Declaration should not pass over in silence the danger to international
peace and civilization which propagating fascism and aggression and
provoking hatred as between the constituted, nor should it fail to condemn such propaganda and provocation" (ibid., 420).

The Soviet proposal was rejected by twenty-five to ten with thirteen abstentions, mostly because there was not enough agreement then as now on what the term "fascism" meant. We too have not solved the special problem of how tolerant a liberal democratic society should be of those—like Nazi and fascist groups—who themselves are intolerant in word and deed. Guided by this Article 19, in the full knowledge that it is only one of thirty human rights norms, each nation must craft its own solution. Andre Geraud, the French member on the abovementioned subcommission, argued that "the freedom of thought and expression entails certain duties," among which he listed not to publish state secrets, not to promote crime and disorder, not to question fundamental freedoms, and not to establish "actual [information] monopolies on the national or international level" (E/CN.4/Sub.1/SR.5/1). But the wish for limits was easier than getting a consensus on how to phrase these limits.

At one point Chafee of the United States, "replying to a previous remark by Mr. Lomakin from the USSR that governments should label as poison and exclude from the market all false ideas, pointed out that the difficulty lay in determining what poison was. For example, in the United States the doctrine of Communism was frequently labeled poison; yet he felt that it would be contrary to the principle of freedom of information to prohibit discussion of Communism. There must be faith in the capacity of human beings to choose the good from the bad, once they were provided with full information" (E/CN.4/Sub.1/SR.36/5). "Emphasizing the tremendous responsibility of newspapermen, Mr. Sychrava from Czechoslovakia advocated that measures should be taken to prevent dissemination of untruths. From the very beginning the Sub-Commission had felt that certain limitations and restrictions on the freedom of information was necessary, but it had not defined them; the peoples of the world, be it remembered, were not always able to discriminate between truth and untruth. Nevertheless, those restrictions would have to be clearly and effectively defined so as to prevent any abuse" (ibid., 2). It seems that during the writing of this book the human capacity to separate good from evil has not improved and that, given the different universes of information people in the United States tap into, the need for restrictions is much greater than it was when the subcommission on Freedom of Information and of the Press hammered out the text for UD 19. P. H. Chang, the Chinese member, gave an analysis that spoke to this very situation. "What will be the situation," he asked,

when a word is multiplied a million-fold and a voice is magnified for all the world to hear, as it is done through the modern printing presses, telecommunication lines, radio and films? The one on the receiving end does not have a chance to talk back. If he thinks he has in his possession a more accurate version of the truth, a larger collection of facts, or a sounder opinion than which has just

been disseminated, he has no way of getting it across to the same audience. . . .
In other words, there have grown up two distinct groups within the concept of
information: the majority of the people, on the one hand, are passive, listening,
inarticulate and influenced; and, on the other, owners of the media [platforms]
of mass information together with their functionaries—reporting, interpreting,
broadcasting and influencing. (E/CN.4/Sub.1/42/2)

Unlike his fellow members, Chang did not want to restrict or abridge
the freedom of mass information. Instead he called for an enlargement
of the concept "to ensure at all times the right of all persons and people
to receive accurate, objective, comprehensive and representative information" (ibid.). He worried that "in proportion as the speed and quantity of information are multiplied, its quality must also be raised. Freedom
to inform on a mass scale, must not be allowed *to become the freedom to
misinform*—even if there exists very effective modern scientific means to
do so" (ibid.; original emphasis).

Toni Sender, who represented the American Federation of Labor on
the subcommission, "remarked that to ensure individual freedom to hold
and to impart opinion was not enough. It was necessary to also ensure
the right freely to receive information" (E/CN.4/Sub.1/SR.25/5). To
which Mackenzie from the United Kingdom responded that the just-
adopted Article 17 [=19] for the declaration "provided for precisely this
freedom to 'seek information and the opinion of others from sources
wherever situated'" (ibid.). This became our "through any media and
regardless of frontiers" (E/CN.4/Sub.1/48). Roberto Fontaina from Uruguay also argued "that in its fullest sense freedom of information should
be world wide" (E/CN.4/Sub.1/41).

Article 20
Freedom of Assembly and Association

> The reason we form networks is because the benefits of a connected life outweigh the costs. It's to our advantage as individuals and a species to assemble ourselves in this fashion.
> —Nicholas Christakis

> Congress shall make no law . . . abridging . . . the right of the people to peaceably assemble.
> —William Penn

---

(1) *Everyone has the right to freedom of peaceful assembly and association.*

(2) *No one may be compelled to belong to an association.*

This article went from being quite simple to having a lot of details, to once again returning to simplicity. Director John Humphrey's choice of wording for it fits with the opening quotation from Christakis about our human need to create networks and live a connected life: "There shall be freedom to form associations for purposes not inconsistent with this Bill of Rights" (E/CN.4/AC.1/3/Add.1). It was inspired by extant constitutional statements that were also short and to the point. Brazil's Article 141 noted that "freedom of association for legitimate purposes is guaranteed." El Salvador's Article 14 stated that "the inhabitants of El Salvador may associate and assemble peacefully, for any lawful purpose." In Iraq, Article 12 stated that "freedom of . . . forming and joining associations is guaranteed to all Iraqis within such limits as may be prescribed by law." And so on.

Each generation will read UD Article 20 through its own lens of preoccupation. For those of us living in countries whose governments have asked us to "social distance" during a health pandemic, it raises the question as to what the limits are on our human right to "assemble peaceably," as the United States' First Amendment puts it. For example, in April 2020 protesters in different states of the country congregated in front of their state houses without keeping social distance, breaking both federal and state "stay-at-home" orders implemented to prevent them from endangering their own and, more importantly, other people's health. This provision for the protection of "other people's health" places a limit on our right to assemble peaceably. In the next paragraph, I have put in italics the phrases of the text that show that the UD drafters understood this built-in limit on our freedom of assembly.

In line with the wide scope of the Christakis quotation, the American Law Institute had prepared a more detailed text that was submitted by the Panama delegation for inclusion in the declaration: "Freedom to form with others associations of a political, economic, religious, social, cultural, or any other character *for purposes not inconsistent with these articles* is the right of everyone" (Article 5). René Cassin, the French delegate, who was asked to streamline what Humphrey had done, took over this Panamanian list of human associative activities. In his Article 23, Cassin added still more associative fields: "There shall be freedom of peaceful assembly and of association for political, religious, cultural, scientific, sporting, economic, and social purposes *compatible with this Declaration.* No other restriction shall be placed on the exercise of this right except for *the protection of public order.*" The "public order" limitation at the end is standard in constitutions then and now. This list of fields gives quite a range to the exercise of the human freedom to assemble and associate with others, like-minded or not. Article 6 of the constitution of the Dominican Republic included this freedom as one "inherent to the human personality," which fits the notion in the declaration's preamble of "inalienable rights of all members of the human family." But this list was not to last, because in the fall of 1947—that is, before the just-cited versions of UD Article 20 were adopted—the Third Committee of the United Nations was "seized" (meaning occupied) by a dispute over the mention of labor unions in the UD text. A fight broke out between the communist-dominated World Federation of Trade Unions (WFTU) and the International Labour Organization (ILO).

The WFTU had sent a memorandum to the UN Economic and Social Council (ECOSOC), which was the parent body of the Human Rights Commission. The WFTU asked ECOSOC for "guarantees for the exercise and development of Trade Union Rights" (A/374/Annex I). Since ECOSOC oversaw the work of the Human Rights Commission, that in effect meant that the WFTU wanted to see trade-union rights mentioned in the Universal Declaration. The WFTU made the point that World War II had been fought and won in large part because of "the active help of the working class and as a result of its sacrifices" (AC.1/3). These union workers had "borne the brunt of the war" (ibid., 5). When these men and women were decommissioned, they wanted their unions listened to and their rights to organize acknowledged. The story I tell when we get to UD 23(4), which speaks of "the right to form and join trade unions," shows you how strong unions were in the days right after the war and still are in many European countries. Compare that with US president Donald Trump's wanting meat-packing plants in the United States, which were COVID-19 hot spots, to stay open over strong objections of the United Food and Commercial Workers Union.

The WFTU felt that the council had snubbed its seventy million members because it sent their request on to the ILO without first hearing them out. The ILO had been founded after World War I and had lots of experience in this field. Its tripartite structure of workers, owners, and government representatives fit well under the umbrella of a general "right of association," which up to that point had been the theme of Article 20. The communist-dominated WFTU objected to this general way of talking and instead wanted the article to specifically mention the rights of trade unions. ECOSOC also "further resolve[d] to transmit the [same] documents to the Commission on Human Rights in order that it may consider those aspects of the subjects which might appropriately form part of the bill or declaration on human rights" (Resolution 52 (IV)).

This ECOSOC mandate to the Human Rights Commission had its desired effect, for in December 1947 the Second Session of the Human Rights Commission added the phrase "[of] trade union or any other character" to the already adopted list of associative fields that I mentioned earlier. However, five months later, in May 1948, Eleanor Roosevelt proposed on behalf of her country that this list of association fields, to which the right to unionize had been added, "be replaced by these words: 'for the promotion, defence and protection of purposes'" (E/CN.4/AC.1/SR.41/2). Hernan Santa Cruz of Chile objected and warned that both ECOSOC and the UN General Assembly had supported "the recent campaigns of the trade unions for the recognition of union association" in the declaration. He wanted to retain "the catalogue of the political, economic, religious, social and cultural rights long recognized by the Constitutions of almost all the nations of the world, and, more recently, the right of trade union association" (ibid.3). He was right to think of the declaration as far more than a political document. These constitutions thought of the right to assemble more in terms of our need to create all kinds of "networks" and to live "a connected life," as the opening quote by Christakis suggests.

Cassin of France appreciated Chile's reminder and pointed out that "the old declarations on human rights in dealing with freedom of assembly had not had trade union organizations in view" and "wondered whether it would not be possible to leave out the catalogue, but to [just] mention the right of trade union association" (E/CN.4/AC.1/SR.41/3). That was done when the Drafting Committee adopted this text for Article 20: "Everyone has the right to freedom of peaceful assembly and to participate in associations or organization of local, national, or international trade unions for the promotion, defence and protection of interests and aims not incompatible with this Declaration" (ibid., 5).

In the Third Session, which was intent on shortening the document, these union rights (as well as the other fields that had been mentioned) were cut out again. The Chinese representative, Peng-Chun Chang, argued "that any enumeration was dangerous. It might be argued that religious associations, for example, had the same right to be included in article 19 [=20] as trade union organization. He did not see that the latter should be mentioned any more than the former. The purpose of article 19 [=20] should be to grant to everyone freedom to organize or join any association provided only that that was done within the framework of democratic interests. The simplified draft advocated by the Chinese delegation best fulfilled that purpose" (E/CN.4/SR.61/8–9). That proposal (E/CN.4/102) had this simple sentence: "Everyone has the right to freedom of assembly and association." It was adopted in a vote of seven to four with three abstentions and became the first paragraph of our Article 20 (E/CN.4/SR.61/11). One reason for this success was that a draft of the article on work already contained union rights in 23(4). Thus the Third Session was free to cut Article 20 to the bone and pass this lean Chinese text on to the Third Committee.

The Third Committee inserted the word "peaceful" into the text of the article and added this second paragraph: "No one may be compelled to belong to an association." Cuba (A/C.3/232), France (A/C.3/330), and Panama (A/C.3/280) wanted to see the deleted list of association fields restored. The case for a return to such a list was made by Argentina. It bemoaned the fact that "nothing was said of the purpose for which persons might assemble or form associations; yet a specific statement of that nature was necessary. It was important to specify, for example, that every person had the right to associate with others to promote or protect such legitimate interests as trade union interests especially since that right was at that time denied by certain governments" (A/C.3/SR.130/432). These amendments were rejected with large majority votes (A/C.3/SR.131/445).

The Haitian delegate, Emile Saint-Lot, made the interesting prediction that "the declaration when finally adopted would be regarded as a kind of super-constitutional document" (A/C.3/SR.131/431), which is indeed how the document has come to be viewed by countries that have drawn up their own postwar constitutions with an eye to this iconic text. Of course, each country must supply its own details, for, as Saint-Lot also noted, "he did not see how this sparse text could cover the different penal codes of Member States. In every country, there were associations of evil-doers and what would happen when they justified their activities under the terms of article 18 [=20]?" Giving the Ku Klux Klan as an example, he wanted to know "what would be the use of national laws if there was a higher authority to which such organizations could appeal?" (ibid., 432). The Soviet Union also thought "it was essential to prevent the spread and organization [of groups] such as the Ku Klux Klan" (ibid., 439). Its own amendment read like this: "All societies, unions, and other organizations of a fascist or anti-democratic nature, as well as their activity in any form, are forbidden by law under pain of punishment" (E/800). To which Bolivia responded that it "had felt the effects of nazism [*sic*] and fascism, but it believed the surest way to cure those evils was to ensure basic freedoms" (A/C.3/SR.130/435). The countries that wanted these limits put into the text of Article 20 were referred to UD Article 29, which puts limits on the practice of this and all other human rights.

The only amendments accepted by the Third Committee were both proposed by Uruguay. It proposed (A/C.3/268) that the word "peaceful" be added to 20(1) and that a second paragraph be added as follows: "No one may be compelled to belong to an association." There was not a great deal of opposition to adding "peaceful" to 20(1), which was done in a vote of twenty-one to sixteen with six abstentions (A/C.3/SR.131/445).

In the summer of 1948, before this debate in the fall took place, the ILO had adopted the Convention on Freedom of Association and Protection of the Right to Organize and called on governments to take prompt action to ratify it. This might be the reason why Uruguay's second paragraph for Article 20 ("No one may be compelled to belong to an association") was not much discussed in the Third Committee. As my reader may know, a union or closed-shop policy is one where a person's right to continued employment in a certain enterprise is made conditional on his or her joining the trade union that has won the collective bargaining rights for the workers in that enterprise. For instance, New Zealand (a closed-shop country at the time) cautioned the delegates "because it was sometimes necessary to demand that all members of the group concerned should belong to the association," as was often the case in the medical and legal professions (A/C.3/SR.131/438). In 1947 the United States had passed the Taft-Hartley Act, which banned these closed shops, so it is no surprise that the country favored this Uruguayan amendment on not being forced to join an association. So did Saudi Arabia, New Zealand, Australia, and most communist countries. The biggest surprise came when, after 20(2) had been adopted in a vote of twenty to fourteen with nine abstentions (ibid., 445), the Soviet Union said it had voted in favor of adding the paragraph because of the importance it "attached to the voluntary nature which associations and assemblies should present" (ibid., 447).

Article 21
The Right to Participation in Government

> Many forms of government have been tried and will be tried in this world of sin and woe. No one pretends that democracy is perfect or all-wise. Indeed, it has been said that democracy is the worst of Government except all those other forms that have been tried from time to time.
>
> —Winston Churchill

> Beware of one-party states.
>
> —Timothy Snyder, *On Tyranny*, Lesson 3

(1) *Everyone has the right to take part in the government of his country, directly or through freely chosen representatives.*

(2) *Everyone has the right of equal access to public service in his country.*

(3) *The will of the people shall be the basis of the authority of government; this will shall be expressed in periodic and genuine elections which shall be by universal and equal suffrage and shall be held by secret vote or by equivalent free voting procedures.*

While both Hitler and the UD drafters believed that "the will of the people shall be the basis of the authority of government," they looked very differently upon how that will is to be expressed. We recognize that same struggle between democratic regimes and authoritarian strong men in our own day as well. It is true that in the last half of the twentieth century, the end of colonialism and the collapse of communism greatly increased the number of governments installed and operating on the basis of majority rule, but that trend did not hold.

The Democracy Index of 2020 (put out by the Intelligence Unit of the UK magazine the *Economist*) lists only twenty-two countries as being "fully democratic." Among "flawed democracies" it counts India, Brazil, Poland, Hungary, and Mexico (and I would add the United States), while among "hybrid" regimes it lists Ukraine, Armenia, Kenya, and Turkey. Fully "authoritarian regimes" are Kuwait, Myanmar, Russia, Iran, and Saudi Arabia. In her celebratory comments on the seventieth anniversary of the Universal Declaration in 1998, the UN High Commissioner for Human Rights worried that because "the younger generations of adults have little knowledge or memory of their parents' experiences under fascism and communism . . . [they] may be losing faith in the democratic project" (on UD Article 21).

Already in his 1925/26 book *Mein Kampf,* Hitler had defended what he called "the personality principle" of leadership and government and expressed his desire to see that applied "from the smallest community cell to the highest leadership of the entire Reich" ([Boston: Houghton Mifflin, 1971], 448). This principle dictated that the best, strongest, and brightest must rule those who are weaker and less pure. He wrote that "a philosophy of life which endeavors to reject the democratic mass idea and give this earth to the best people . . . [must] make sure that leadership and the highest influence in the [Aryan] people fall to the best minds. Thus it builds *not* upon the idea of majority, but upon the idea of personality" (ibid., 443; italics added). Clearly, we need to heed what UD 21 says about the authority of government and how that is established and maintained.

Unlike authoritarian top-down approaches to government, John Humphrey's survey of extant constitutions led him to propose two articles, one that combined our 21(1) and 21(3) into just one Article 30 that he submitted to the First Drafting Session: "Everyone has the right to take an effective part in the government of the State of which he is a citizen. The State has a duty to conform to the wishes of the people as manifested in democratic elections. Elections shall be periodic, free and fair" (E/CN.4/AC.1/11). Charles Habib Malik from Lebanon sponsored its inclusion. Humphrey also submitted a different Article 31, which became our 21(2): "Everyone shall have equal opportunity of access to all public functions in the State of which he is a citizen" (ibid.). This one was sponsored for inclusion by Peng-Chun Chang, the Chinese representative. Since its story is clear and brief, I relate it first, before I share the details of paragraphs 21(1) and 21(3).

At the start China had submitted this text: "Appointments to Civil Service shall be by competitive examination," which René Cassin of France acknowledged when, on behalf of the First Session of the Drafting Committee, he added, "Such functions cannot be considered as privileges or favours but appointment shall be by competitive examination or by reason of the titles of the ablest" (E/CN.4/AC.1/W.2/5). The Chinese delegate stressed that "all men should have the right to participate in public life by holding public office. He reviewed the experience of China in this matter and pointed out that competitive examination for public jobs had existed in his country for centuries" (E/CN.4/AC.1/SR.9/4). Hernan Santa Cruz of Chile objected: "In his opinion, it was sufficient to establish the principle of non-discrimination in the filling of public offices" (ibid.). As a result, the word "equal" was inserted into the text of

21(2). Malik from Lebanon "did not think that this paragraph even dealt with a human right," to which Chang responded that, like elections, "competitive examinations were also a method of achieving human rights" (ibid., 6). Upon the recommendation of France and the United States, the Working Group of the Second Session unanimously added this second sentence to our 21(2): "Access to public employment shall not be a matter of privilege or favour," but that addition was dropped in the Third Session and the remaining single sentence of 21(2) was accepted by the Third Committee in a unanimous vote of forty-three to zero with three abstentions (A/C.3/SR.134/468).

As I said, originally Humphrey had combined our 21(1) and 21(3) into just one article that Cassin of France, in his official rewrites, had cut into two separate articles, adding details that caught the attention of the Working Group of the Second Session, to which they were sent. In his Article 26, Cassin said that "*Everyone* had the right to take an *effective* part in his government," while in his Article 27 he spoke of "*democratic* elections, which shall be periodic, free, *and by secret ballot*" (E/CN.4/21/79; italics added). That working group zeroed in on issues of nondiscrimination also dealt with in UD Article 2. Afanasi Stepanenko of the Byelorussian Soviet Socialist Republic asked to have "regardless of race, sex, language, religion, fortune, education, national or social origin" inserted into Cassin's Article 26 text (E/CN.4/AC.2/SR.7/9). Speaking for the Commission on the Status of Women, Bodil Begtrup of Denmark said she "would like to see the word 'equal' before 'election'" in Cassin's Article 27 text (ibid.).

When Cassin proposed to change his Article 26's term "everyone" to "citizen," Chairperson Eleanor Roosevelt, alluding to millions of colonial peoples, said she "preferred the retention of the word 'everyone' as including the inhabitants of non-self-governing territories who are not citizens but to whom the Declaration would afford some rights of participation in Government" (E/CN.4/AC.2/SR.7/8). Heppel of the United Kingdom also "disliked the word 'citizen' if it excluded persons in non-self-governing territories. His delegation felt that the Secret Ballot was a form of democratic procedure which was neither understood nor accepted by some of the British African dependencies. Their forms of Native Government were based on old-established customs with which it was the policy of his Government to interfere as little as possible. The principle of developing democratic institutions was fully recognized," he said. He went on to quote "from a report to the [UN] Trusteeship Council from the Commission on Samoa [a British Protectorate], stressing the dangers of arbitrary imposition of western democratic procedure. His delegation was reluctant to accept the words 'secret ballot' in this Article" (ibid.).

At that point "there was a discussion on the wording of the article between the representatives of France, the Philippines and Panama, with (Roosevelt) the Chairman" (E/CN.4/AC.2/SR.7/10). That consultation led to a text that added two new items I italicized: "Everyone *without discrimination* has the right to take an effective part in the Government of his country. The State shall conform to the will of the people as manifested in elections which shall be periodic, free, *fair* and by secret ballot" (ibid., 11). It kept the secret ballot but did not say elections had to be democratic. These issues of citizenship and the longer list of nondiscrimination items were also raised in the Second Session of the Drafting Committee but again without success (E/CN.4/AC.1/SR.41).

In its quest for brevity, the Third Session of the commission cut out almost all of the details the Second Session had put in. After revisiting a range of discrimination issues related to the participation of women and colonial peoples in government and elections, it adopted a three-paragraph text. The first two are what we now have, but 21(3) was shorn to a minimum without any election details: "Everyone has the right to a government which conforms to the will of the people." The Third Session adopted this stripped-down version of UD 21 "by eleven votes with four abstentions" (E/CN.4/SR.62/8). Different readers will focus on different deleted details. What struck me as an American was the deletion from 21(1) that one's participation in government had to be "effective." That detail happened to remind me of the concept of gerrymandered districts in some of our states, where, as a result of political shenanigans, a certain party gets far fewer assembly seats than it really should have. While most of the other deletions were later restored, the word "effective" in 21(1) never was.

The Third Committee received many amendments (A/C.3/296/Rev.1) on how to restore the democratic details that had been lost in the Third Session. The Soviet Union wanted to restore all the election details, but not the word "free" before "elections" in 21(3). With slight variations, Cuba, France, Sweden, and the United Kingdom proposed the reinstitution of election details. Iraq and China wanted to go back to using "citizen" instead of "everyone" in 21(1). Before I discuss the reintroduction of these details, I relate an interesting amendment proposed by Colombia and Costa Rica.

These two nations wanted to add this fourth paragraph to the article: "Every man has the right to make opposition to the Government of his country and to promote its replacement by legal means with equality of electoral opportunities and of access to the means of propaganda" (A/C.3/248). Alberto T. Canas of Costa Rica defended the additional paragraph, saying that if this right to opposition "were lost, all human rights were lost. The Nazi and fascist governments—like all tyrannical regimes—had been able to deprive the people of all fundamental rights precisely because they had first deprived them of the basic right to oppose the Government" (A/C.3/SR.132/449). While not included in UD 21, this right to rebellion and opposition to government found its way into the declaration as the second recital of the preamble.

Even the restored UD Article 21 (about that in a moment) does not explicitly mention the idea of multiparty election systems, which are the hallmark of liberal democratic governments. Early on, Santa Cruz of Chile had "suggested that a provision concerning the right to form political parties be added to Article 26 [=21]" (E/CN.4/AC.1/SR.9/2). He was told by Cassin of France that "the liberty to form political parties already had been mentioned in Article 23 [=20], on freedom of peaceful assembly and of association for political and other purposes" (ibid). At that time our UD 20 still had in it a list of associative purposes. But as I reported in my commentary on that article, this list was later deleted, which left Santa Cruz's suggestion hanging by a thin thread. The Belgian delegation picked it up in the Third Committee, where Fernand Dehousse argued that candidates for office needed to be chosen from "several lists of candidates because the very essence of the democratic system was the electoral competition between different political parties. In the absence of a guarantee based on several lists of candidates, the whole democratic character of free, equal, periodical and secret elections might be distorted" (A/CR.3/SR.132/464). Later, during voting, he proposed to "add the words 'according to the party system' after the words 'which shall be conducted periodically'" to article 21(3) (A/C.3/SR.134/471). But nothing came of that.

Just before the vote on this Belgian proposal was to be taken, Alexei Pavlov of the Soviet Union asked Belgium to withdraw its amendment (ibid., 469). He pointed out that "in his country the bourgeoisie class had ceased to exist. There thus remained only workers and peasants, and the Communist Party by itself was capable of looking after their interests. Did they want the USSR to import a foreign bourgeois class in order to reestablish the party system? . . . Under the prevailing system, there was no justification for the creation of other parties. The Belgian amendment was absolutely irreconcilable with the social structure of certain Member States" (ibid., 471). Belgium withdrew its amendment "as a conciliatory gesture" but did point out that "there existed in the USSR not only the Communist Party, but also the non-party block" (ibid.). Venezuela rightly "regretted this [Belgian] withdrawal" (ibid., 473).

This communist victory does not mean that the Universal Declaration supports one-party election systems. Earlier on, the Commission on Human Rights had asked its Sub-commission on the Prevention of Discrimination and the Protection of Minorities to advise it on the text of its

Article 6, our 2, on nondiscrimination. M. R. Masani, the Indian member of that subcommission, proposed the item of "political opinion" be added to the nondiscrimination list being considered (E/CN.4/Sub.2/SR.4/2). The French member, Samuel Spanien, thought that just the word "opinion" would do (ibid., 6), whereupon W. M. J. McNamara from Australia suggested the addition of "political or other opinion," with which Masani agreed (ibid., 9) and which was then added to the recommended list for the Human Rights Commission (ibid., 12). As a member of the subcommission, Alexandre P. Borisov of the USSR had wondered whether adding this phrase would cover the "opinions of Nazis or Fascists concerning, for instance, the superiority of white race over the black" (ibid., 8). But after the new list arrived at the Second Session of the commission, the Soviet Union sought to have the item of "political or other opinion" deleted from the list of our UD 2. In that session, Lord Dukeston of the United Kingdom said he would vote against the Soviet list that lacked this item "because it did not protect the individual against discrimination on the grounds of political opinion . . . and a one-party Government would not be obliged to take measures to safeguard the freedom of those professing a different political opinion from its own" (E/CN.4/SR.35/3). In a vote of ten to four with three abstentions, the Second Session rejected the Soviet shorter list and "political or other opinion" remained on the list of UD Article 2 (ibid., 5).

Combined with UD 2, UD 21 would seem to demand a multiparty system of government. The declaration does not condone the authoritarian structures of government or single-party systems that, at the time of this writing, are in ascendency around the world and against which Timothy Snyder has warned us in Lesson 3 of his little booklet (see Preface) that tells us how to avoid dictatorship and tyranny. He based his lessons on what he learned from the rise of fascism, Nazism, and communism in the 1930s, 1940s, and 1950s.

The details of 21(3) that were deleted in the Third Session were added back in in the Third Committee. China's proposal to do that had two versions, an earlier one (A/C.3/333) and a slightly altered later one that read as follows: "The will of the people is the basis of the authority of government; this will shall be expressed in periodic and genuine elections, which shall be universal and equal, and shall be held by secret vote, or by equivalent free voting procedures" (A/C.3/SR.133/462). With one important change (discussed below), all these details were added back in by a large majority of thirty-nine votes to three with three abstentions (A/C.3/SR.134/472).

Pavlov of the USSR asked the Chinese representative "if he would accept the following wording for the beginning of paragraph 3: The will of the people *shall be* the basis of the authority of the government" (A/C.3/

SR.134/469; original italics). Belgium agreed with this request (ibid., 470). But France was opposed. Cassin argued that "the expression 'the will of the people *is* the source of the authority . . .' was much stronger than 'the will of the people *shall be* the basis of the authority,' since it stated a principle. That was, in his opinion, a point of fundamental importance" (ibid.). Mr. Chang was agreeable to the change being discussed, for he felt that "'The will of the people *is* the source of the authority . . .' was a positive statement of fact; '*shall be* the basis' on the contrary, would indicate that such was not always the case in certain countries. It was for that reason that he preferred '*shall be* the basis,' it being generally understood that the will of the people should in all cases be the basis of the authority of government. That wording should also satisfy the Argentine representative, since it was no longer a simple statement, but the proclamation of a right" (ibid.; last italics added). As I noted, this new Chinese text passed in a vote of thirty-nine to three with three abstentions (ibid., 472). I reported on this discussion because if the UD is to float above national legal systems as a norm to be adhered to—as its drafters thought it should—then the "shall be" reading is to be preferred.

At this point the minutes record that "*Article 19 [=21], as amended, was adopted by 39 votes to 1, with 1 abstention.*" The sole negative vote came come from Haiti, because its representative felt the term "secret" "might be used as a pretext for any restrictions the non-democratic countries might wish to impose" (ibid.). Pavlov of the Soviet Union, who incorrectly thought he had prevailed in his single-party position, was delighted by this outcome. He said "he had been in favour of the compromise which had finally been adopted, and which had been arrived at as a result of sincere collaboration between many delegations. It was one as one of the all too rare cases when the Committee had adopted progressive ideas. The conciliatory spirit manifested on that occasion was very encouraging, and gave grounds for unbounded hope in the future of the United Nations" (ibid., 473).

Article 22
Social (Security) Justice

Oh sons of earth! Attempt ye still to rise,
By mountains pil'd on mountains, to the skies?
Heav'n still with laughter the vain toil surveys,
And buries madmen in the heaps they raise.

    —Alexander Pope

You need some inequality to grow . . . but extreme inequality
is not only useless but can be harmful to growth because it
reduces mobility and can lead to political capture of our
democratic institutions.

    —Thomas Piketty

---

*Everyone, as a member of society, has the right to social security
and is entitled to realization, through national effort and international cooperation and in accordance with the organization and
resources of each state, of the economic, social and cultural rights
indispensable for his dignity and the free development of his
personality.*

This article opens a wound in the history of human rights. The debates
surrounding it raise the question whether the newer economic, social,
and cultural rights that hail mostly from the nineteenth century and are
found in the second half of the declaration have the same status as the
older civil and political rights that hail mostly from the eighteenth
century and are found in the first half of the UD text. This article's sudden appearance makes the declaration look like the famous Exxon Val-
dez oil tanker that broke into two parts off the shore of Alaska in 1989.
This rift about rights never healed, and in 1976 two legal international
covenants came into force, one for each half of the declaration. What
ties this huge legal but bifurcated human rights system together morally
and aspirationally is that the Universal Declaration is the mother text of
it all, both halves equally aimed at the protection of all members of the
human family.

    The split in this system has been made worse by the health pandemic
that is racing through the world in 2020 as I write the last draft of this
story. Even before this COVID-19 crisis hit us, Thomas Piketty, an internationally renowned economist, predicted that in the twenty-first century

inequality within nations would rise to unacceptable levels, even to the point, as the epigraph says, of "captur[ing] . . . our democratic institutions." That would, of course, undercut all the human rights enunciated in the declaration, including those of UD Article 21 on participation in government.

In the Third Session during the discussion of Article 23 (on work), Charles Habib Malik from Lebanon noted that "until now the Commission had discussed and examined the rights of the individuals as such; the right to life, to freedom of thought, freedom to come and go, to marriage, and so on. Now it was engaged in discussing the rights of the individual as a member of society. It was desirable, therefore, to insert somewhere in the Declaration a statement calling attention to the need to establishing the kind of economic and social conditions that would guarantee those rights" (E/CN.4/SR.64/17). A subcommittee was appointed that came up with a majority proposal, which is our Article 28 (discussed later), and a minority French one: "Everyone, as a member of society, has the economic, social and cultural rights enumerated below, whose fulfillment should be made possible in every State separately or by international collaboration" (E/CN.4/120). With changes suggested by the United States ("through national effort and international cooperation"), Cuba ("indispensable for his dignity and the free development of his personality"), and the USSR ("has the right to social security"), this article was adopted by twelve votes with five abstentions.

The label "social security" caused a great deal of trouble. You can look at it in two ways, either as it occurs in this Article 22 and thus as a general right to social justice that comes with "the realization . . . of the economic, social and cultural rights" spelled out in the rest of the declaration, or as if attached to the second list in Article 25(1), which is what some drafters wanted to do. There it would have fit with the list of things like unemployment, sickness, and disability that is usually connected with the right to social security. In the drafting process this "social security" label and the list of Article 25(1) got separated from each other and were never reconnected. Finding this phrase here in Article 22, we should interpret it in a broad "social justice" sense and as shorthand for what the article calls "the economic, social and cultural rights indispensable for his dignity and the free development of his personality."

When, in the Third Committee the separation of the "social security" label and the list in UD 25 became clear to the drafters, the Syrian delegate Abdul Kayaly "proposed that the phrase social security should be replaced by the phrase social justice, which would express a broader concept" (A/C.3/SR.137/504). This broader Syrian phrase of "social justice" captures, I think, what Piketty had in mind with the quotation I presented earlier. What he says links up with Article 22's claim that "everyone, as a member of society," has the human rights that "are indispensable for his dignity and the free development of his personality." My report shows that a minority of the drafters also would have liked to see the "social justice" label in this bridge article, for it would have fit with what they sought to do with the group of articles that follows this one. Unfortunately, they were blocked by the majority.

Jamil Baroody, the Saudi delegate, explained that the Syrian concept of social justice "conformed to Islamic law" and that there were in Muslim-majority nations several institutions, such as the *zaka* tax and the *waqf* system, that fulfilled that goal. The first is a tax (sometimes voluntary, sometimes not) levied for the purpose of assisting the poor and unemployed. The second takes the income from property placed in trust and uses it for relief of the poor or the unemployed (A/C.3/SR.139/515). These Muslim institutions point to the idea that a nation or society is an organic unit and not just a collection of individuals. Some Western delegates supported the Syrian amendment. France also thought the phrase "social justice" was "the most general term that could be used," and it interpreted UD 22's phrase "social security" "in a broadly humanitarian rather than in a technical sense," which it would have had if attached to the list in UD 25 (A/C.3/SR.137/499). Eleanor Roosevelt also felt that "it would perhaps have been preferable to use a term other than social security and a suggestion to that effect had been made" by Syria (A/C.3/SR.138/501). Belgium suggested that both phrases ("social justice" and "social security") be used in the first sentence of UD 22 so as "to widen the meaning" of the latter term (ibid., 512). But all attempts to change the label of our UD 22 failed and the opening clause "Everyone, as a member of society, has the right to social security" was adopted unanimously by thirty-eight votes to none (ibid., 514). The rest of the article was adopted by thirty-one votes with seven abstentions (ibid.)

The right to the "free development of his personality" goes back to the American Federation of Labor, which had advised the commission that "the supreme test of the state is . . . the way it provides for the full and free development of each individual" (E/CN.4/W.8/2). With support from other Latin Americans, Cuba turned this clause into Article 22's "indispensability" phrase. It wanted that phrasing because it sought to highlight the importance of these newer economic and social rights. Also, the phrase fits with UD 22's opening line of everyone "as a member of society" and emphasizes the idea that the human rights in the declaration belong to people *not* as atomistic individuals but as the social creatures they are.

In spite of its troubled history, the majority of drafters wanted to see Article 22 included because they wanted to draw the world's attention to these newer social and economic rights. As René Cassin from France put it to members of the Third Session, these rights required more "material assistance to be furnished by the State" (E/CN.4/SR.72/4). It probably costs far more to give all the citizens of a state a good education and good health care than to give police protection to all. The realization of the newer rights also requires more international cooperation than that of the older ones. The huge and still rising economic inequality within states makes it impossible for many of the poorer nations to bring the enjoyment of economic, social, and cultural rights to their people without international cooperation. That is the point of Piketty's international blockbuster best sellers, in the latest of which he argues for an "international socialism" where borders have been transcended by a global equality regime *not* dreamed of by even the most radical of the UD drafters. Drawing inspiration from the triumph of nations that I tell in these drafting stories, we ourselves can and should combat the excessive character of the inequality that we see all around us and that keeps millions of people (to use the words of the UD preamble) from enjoying their "inherent dignity and . . . *equal* and inalienable human rights" (my italics). As the eighteenth-century poet Alexander Pope put it, "Heav'n still with laughter the vain toil surveys, / And buries madmen in the heaps they raise."

Article 23
The Right to Work Today

Workers of the world, unite!

   —Karl Marx, *The Communitst Manifesto*

[The US] Congress must embrace an Essential Workers Bill
of Rights: providing truly universal paid family and medical
leave, ensuring all front-line workers have protective equipment to do their jobs safely, directing the Occupational
Safety and Health Administration to establish emergency
safety standards, funding hazard pay and protecting workers' right to collective bargaining and to speak out about
dangerous job conditions.

   —Elizabeth Warren, *New York Times*, April 9, 2020, A27

---

(1) *Everyone has the right to work, to free choice of employment, to just
    and favourable conditions of work and to protection against
    unemployment.*
(2) *Everyone, without any discrimination, has the right to equal pay for
    equal work.*
(3) *Everyone who works has the right to just and favourable remuneration
    ensuring for himself and his family an existence worthy of human
    dignity, and supplemented, if necessary, by other means of social
    protection.*
(4) *Everyone has the right to form and to join trade unions for the
    protection of his interests.*

John Humphrey, the first director of the UN Human Rights Division,
was a socialist law professor at McGill University in Montreal. He had
plenty of socialist friends, especially in Latin America. Passing through
the age of neoliberalism, it is interesting for us to see what serious 1940s
socialist thinkers like Humphrey, René Cassin from France, Hernan Santa
Cruz from Chile, and others thought should be included as workers'
rights in an international bill of rights. To bring us up to date, I quoted
Elizabeth Warren's suggested Essential Workers Bill of Rights at the peak
of the 2020 pandemic in the United States. Warren had dropped out of
the race for US president, and this was the day after Bernie Sanders, the
US democratic socialist candidate for president, also dropped out of the
race. As my US readers know, this lack of good workers' rights cost thou-

sands of US lives. I begin our story with two examples that did not make it into the UD but that reveal the socialist ardor behind Article 23 on the right to work.

Humphrey's H39 (H standing for Humphrey) stated, "Everyone has the right to such equitable share of the national income as the need for his work and the increment it makes to the common welfare may justify" (E/CN.4/AC.1/11/44). While Humphrey meant this article to boost the dignity of all workers whose jobs were important for society, opponents could use it to argue that CEOs and surgeons should earn many, many multiples of what factory-floor workers and nurses earn because what they do is so much more "valuable" than what floor workers and nurses do. Who is to tell?

Cassin did not include H39 in his rewrites. He earned his own socialist stripes when in his rewrite of Article 38 he made the case that a worker should have the right "either by himself or through his chosen representatives or his trade organization, to the collective bargaining of labour conditions, the determination of general plans of production or distribution of goods, and, should the case arise, the supervision and administration of the enterprise in which he works" (E/CN.4/AC.1/W.2/Rev.1/7). (A Wikipedia article on what we today would call "workers' control" gives examples of this in some twenty-seven countries around the world.) Much later in the Third Committee debates, when it was clear that these kinds of provisions would not be included in the declaration, the French delegation indicated that it "would have been glad if, over and above wages and trade unions, the worker could have been brought to realize the dignity of his labour by indicating the possibility of his taking part in the management of the undertaking to which he belonged. However, the French delegation would not insist on those cherished opinions and would vote for article 21 [=23] in its entirety, desiring thereby to give an example of good discipline" (A/C.3/SR.156/678).

Just before Article 23 was adopted by the Third Committee, Enrique V. Corominas from Argentina told his colleagues that "his country had just overhauled its economy and moved away from the idea that central state power only exist[ed] to preserve law and order." "The policy of liberalism had resulted in capitalistic monopolies and the conversion of labour into merchandise without value. . . . Given the choice between the individualism and collectivism, Argentina preferred the concept of the individual in his proper relation to society. The decision as to whether the workers would be a democratic force in the development of civilization would be decided by the result of the vote on article 21 [=23]" (A/C.3/SR.157/686). Remarks like this explain why so many of the rights we find in Articles 23, 24, and 25 of the declaration exhibit a remarkable blend of the socialist welfare state with a market economy.

While Humphrey's H39 was ignored, his H37 also raised eyebrows: "Everyone has the right and the duty to perform socially useful work [and to the full development of his personality]"; the bracketed part added by Cassin was soon deleted. Both the "duty" to work and the requirement that this work be "socially useful" stayed in the text a long time. They reflect UD Article 22's idea that everyone has these human rights "as a member of society." (I used to think about this phrase when, during the coronavirus pandemic, I would hear over the news the phrase, "We are in this together." This can only be a duty, if it is one at all, under normal circumstances when it is not the case that a quarter of the workforce has needed to file for unemployment.) Quite a few Latin American constitutions contained this duty to do socially useful work. Article 14 of the submission by the Inter-American Juridical Committee summarizes this trend succinctly: "Every person has the duty to work as a contribution to the general welfare of the state" (E/CN.4/AC.1/3/Add.1/309). France's 1946 constitutional Paragraph 5 stated that "everyone has the duty to work and the right to obtain employment" (ibid., 311). Article 12 of the Soviet Constitution stated that "in the USSR work is a duty and a matter of honour for every able-bodied citizen, in accordance with the principle of socialism: 'From each according to his ability, to each according to his work'" (ibid., 312).

Charles Habib Malik from Lebanon immediately pointed out that some of the newer social or economic rights "would be true in a socialistic form of society, others would not" and might have to be omitted or rephrased. For instance, the "duty to work" might "in certain countries be considered as leading to forced labour," with which point Eleanor Roosevelt of the United States agreed (E/CN.4/AC.1/SR.9/10). Third Committee submissions for fixing this problem included Cuba's rights "to work . . . and to follow his vocation freely" (A/C.3/232) and Lebanon's rights "to work, to choice of work and to his mode of life" (A/C.3/260). The United States successfully submitted the text closest to what we now have: "Everyone has the right to work, to free choice of employment, to just and favourable conditions of work [and pay] and to protection against unemployment" (A/C.3/363), the bracketed part being rejected because it was covered in the next paragraph. Not everyone liked this shift away from the socialist duty to work to a liberal right to work. Austregesilo de Athayde from Brazil said he "had hoped that the article would mention work not only as a right, but also as a social duty; but in view of the fact that the document being drafted was a declaration of rights, he would not press that point" (A/C.3/SR.139/520).

The communists also did not like the switch from the duty to the right to work. Alexandre Bogomolov told his colleagues in the Second Session that in the Soviet Union "it was normal for the [state] to undertake to provide its citizens with work," implying that the duty to work was not cumbersome there. He added that "in countries where private undertakings existed side by side with the State, and where the State could not accept all the responsibilities connected with the work of its citizens," there the state would need "to take effective action by means of economic measures to prevent unemployment" (E/CN.4/SR.40/6). In the Third Session, Geoffrey Wilson of the United Kingdom said he saw that the right to work was real in "the socialist system, by control of production, and by elimination of economic crises." But he did not think that the United States could easily eliminate unemployment. "In capitalistic states, not counting the Far East, there were some twenty to thirty millions in a state of want who formed a regular army of unemployment. He could however ask that something concrete should be done. Instead of merely making a general statement about the right to work, the relevant article should list measures to be taken to ensure that right" (E/CN.4/SR.49/8–9). The extent of these measures was the subject of much debate.

Instead of the absolute right to work, Roosevelt, speaking for the United States, proposed the "right to a fair and equal opportunity to perform socially useful work." The response by Santa Cruz from Chile reminds us of the opening quotation by Warren about an Essential Workers Bill of Rights. He countered that "President Roosevelt in 1943" had spoken of "a need for a new United States Bill of Rights which would establish the right to useful and remunerative work" (E/CN.4/AC.1/SR.14/6). Cassin from France pointed out that "in two wars, the State had demanded the maximum from millions of men and in these crises had taken over control of the entire economy of the country. Unfortunately, it was a fact that after the crises it had not been possible to find employment for all these men. He admitted that unemployment cannot be overcome immediately, but felt that the Declaration should establish fundamental rights, such as the right to work, for the future. . . . If the Declaration were to be adjusted only to existing conditions it would not achieve a very useful purpose." Countries, he said, "should try to find means to adjust their legislation accordingly" (ibid., 7). That is right on the mark now that in 2020 almost half of American families have lost employment income due to the health pandemic.

This exchange between socialist and market-driven views informs Article 23(1)'s provision that everyone has a human right to "protection against unemployment." Also, the drafters were told that in Article 55 the United Nations Charter holds out the goal of "full employment" for its Member States to aim at. What held them back from stipulating the socialist duty to work was their knowledge that, in the modern world, factors other than a person's ability and desire will play a crucial role in whether employment is available to all those who seek and want it.

Article 23(2)'s stipulation that "everyone, without discrimination, has the right to equal pay for equal work" is an exception to the rule drafters had to not repeat the discrimination ban of UD Article 2. The Second Session of the commission had accepted this text: "Women shall work with the same advantages as men and receive equal pay for equal work" (E/CN.4/57/14). In the Third Session this stipulation led to a disagreement between two groups of women's representatives. Janet Rob, "speaking on behalf of 14 feminine organizations, requested the deletion" of the paragraph. She thought that it "could lead to misunderstanding and was an unnecessary limitation on the word 'everyone' that was used in the first paragraph of the article" (E/CN.4/SR.64/5). But that was not the view of the Commission on the Status of Women, which said it wanted to see the paragraph retained. The UK and Indian delegations, as well as the Belgian and US ones, favored deletion, while, as was their custom, communist delegations took the side of the Women's Commission. Alexei Pavlov of the USSR said that the question of equal pay for equal work "could not be left up to the discretion of the employer who was only too ready to hire cheap labour when he could. It was necessary, therefore, to guarantee that right explicitly" (ibid., 15). He repeated that plea a few meetings later, supported by Afanasi Stepanenko from Byelorussia, who "expressed his astonishment that the representative of India, herself a woman [which goes for Roosevelt as well], was opposed to [the paragraph]. The importance of such a provision was paramount, in view of the fact that women had been discriminated against in the matter of pay almost more than in any other" (E/CN.4/SR.66/9, 6).

The Third Committee created a subcommittee to resolve this and other pivotal issues. The meetings were very productive with a lot of give and take. Our 23(1) was adopted by forty-four votes to none with one abstention (A/C.3/SR.140/686), that being the United States. Article 23(2)'s nondiscrimination ban and clause on equal pay for equal work were adopted by forty-one to three, with five abstentions (ibid., 687). Then a curious thing happened.

After all four paragraphs of Article 23 were adopted separately, the article as a whole was rejected. Besides the nondiscrimination clause, then called 23(2a), the call for enough remuneration to "assure a decent standard of living for himself and his family" (called 23(2b)) also required more discussion. The main bone of contention was not whether Article 23 should say, as it now does, that a worker's pay ensures for the worker and his family "an existence worthy of human dignity." Rather, it was whether the worker's pay should "be supplemented, if necessary, by other means of social protection," which it now also says. When the subcommittee brought 23(2b), which is our 23(3), up for a vote, it was adopted by twenty-seven votes to six (Canada, China, New Zealand,

Syria, the United Kingdom, and the United States), with ten abstentions. The article on work as a whole was adopted by thirty-nine votes to one (the United States), with two abstentions.

As was the custom, delegations quickly rose to explain their votes. On behalf of the United States, Roosevelt said that

> although it was in agreement with paragraphs 1 and 3, it could not accept the second sentence of paragraph 2 [our paragraph 3]. In the first place it would be a matter of long and difficult discussion to decide exactly what was meant by "a decent existence." Secondly, the principle of the supplementation of wages would prove extremely difficult of implementation. Different countries had different methods of social protection to the worker who needed more than he was able to earn. To assess a worker's wages by his needs rather than by the work he performed was, in her opinion, a false principle. She had therefore voted against article 21 [=23], although she fully understood the feelings of the Committee and regretted that she had been unable to support the majority. (A/C.3/SR.158/690)

The United Kingdom and Norway had also not wanted to see the supplements included in a worker's pay but nonetheless accepted the paragraph on the understanding that these supplements could be administered in other ways as well—for instance, under the provisions of UD Article 25. Australia also felt 23(3) "would not bind any State to supplement a person's needs in a form of wages, since part could be in the form of social protection" (A/C.3/SR.158/691). L. I. Kaminsky from the Byelorussian Soviet Socialist Republic, which had sponsored an even stronger family allowance clause, again said the pay should be "sufficiently high to allow workers a decent standard of living and he failed to see what members could find to object to in that" (ibid., 692).

For a good understanding of 23(4), I suggest the reader go back and read the story on Article 20 of the declaration. That one paints the background for this union rights paragraph of Article 23. The list of purposes—including that of unionization—having been deleted from Article 20's right to associate meant that there was a chance to, as of yet, follow the UN Economic and Social Council's mandate that union rights be given a place in the declaration. This was done with the adoption of this Ecuadoran amendment to 23(4): "Everyone has the right to form and to join trade unions for the protection of his interests," which the Third Committee adopted by a vote of forty-one to zero, without abstentions (A/C.3/SR.157/689). Given the enormous strength of the union movement both inside and outside the United Nations, this lopsided vote should not surprise us. It should inspire us to restore those rights in our own neoliberal economies.

Article 24
Rights to Rest and Leisure

Human labour is not merchandise.

—International Labour Organization (1921)

Each person deserves a day away in which no problems are confronted, no solutions searched for: Each of us needs to withdraw from the cares which will not withdraw from us.

—Maya Angelou

Everyone has the right to rest and leisure, including reasonable limitation of working hours and periodic holidays with pay.

At the end of my commentary on Article 23, I recorded the lopsided vote with which "the right to form and join trade unions for the protection of his interests" was put into the declaration. The rights named in Article 24 are often the reason why workers form or join a labor union. In the United States today, only about 10 percent of the labor force is unionized. That is the reason the rights of this UD article are not more widely enjoyed in the richest country on earth.

John Humphrey could only have gotten his simple H43 ("Everyone has the right to a fair share of rest and leisure") from the socialist and communist constitutions in his survey (E/CN.4/AC.1/3/Add.1/352), for only they contained this right. No others did. We find various versions of UD 24 in the constitutions of Brazil ("weekly rest with pay, preferably on Sundays" [Art.157]), Costa Rica ("All manual or intellectual workers shall have the right to paid annual vacations" [Art.54]), Ecuador ("every worker shall enjoy a weekly rest of forty-two continuous hours" [Art.185f]), and the USSR ("Citizens of the USSR have the right to rest and leisure. The right to rest and leisure is ensured by the reduction of the working day to seven hours for the overwhelming majority of the workers, the institution of annual vacations with full pay for workers and employees and the provision of a wide network of sanatoriums, rest homes and clubs for accommodation of the working people" [Art.119]). Hernan Santa Cruz from Chile sponsored it for UD inclusion (E/CN.4/AC.1/SR.11/48).

General Carlos Romulo from the Philippines suggested the deletion of the clause "a fair share of" from the Humphrey text because that kind of language was not part of any of the other rights listed in the declaration. He also suggested this addition to the article: "Rest and leisure should be ensured to everyone by laws or contracts, providing for reasonable limitations on working hours and for periodic vacations with pay" (E/CN.4/AC.2/SR.8/8). Because the drafters saw this additional clause as a measure of implementation, which were not normally included in an article itself, they at first (in the Working Group of the Second Session) voted to add this Philippine text only as a comment and not in the article itself (ibid.) However, in a unanimous vote of eleven with two abstentions, the Second Session itself voted to add these Philippines details that had been put in a commentary back into the article, which is where we have them in UD 24. This was done upon the suggestion of Uruguay and Belgium.

In his rewrites for the First Drafting Session, René Cassin added to Humphrey's H43 (quoted above) the phrase "and to the knowledge of the outside world," thereby linking that article to the right to an education (E/CN.4/AC.1/W.2/Rev.2/7). His colleagues severed the link by removing this phrase. In the Third Committee, the Philippines and Argentina sought to recoup that earlier linkage by proposing this text: "Everyone is entitled to due rest and leisure for his spiritual, cultural, and physical well-being" (A/C.3/358). Similar proposals were made by Cuba and Egypt. Panama wanted to insert after the word "leisure" "in such a measure as may be required for the maintenance of the physical and mental health and well-being of the working man or woman" (A/C.3/280). The United States objected that the phrase "working man or woman" was too "specific" since it would "exclude certain categories of people who worked from [having] the right to rest and leisure" (A/C.3/SR.149/609). Our exact wording comes from a proposal made by New Zealand (A/C.3/359).

The point of these rights to rest, leisure, limitation of working hours, and holidays with pay is that human beings themselves are not commodities. They themselves are not machines or things that can be bought and sold. The labor union movement then and now seeks to unite workers of the world around their needs and therefore also around their rights to rest, leisure, safe working conditions, and days off with pay. In the words of the 1921 International Labour Organization, "Human labour is not merchandise." Cassin used this slogan as the first sentence of his own Article 37 on work: "Human labour is not a merchandise. It shall be performed in good conditions. It shall be justly compensated according to its quality, its duration and its purpose, and shall give a decent standard of living to the worker and his family" (E/CN.4/AC.1/W.2/Rev.1). That would include limited working hours and holidays with pay, which always have been among the objectives of the trade union movement.

Critics of the declaration use these Article 24 rights to make fun of or criticize the very idea of human rights, saying the stipulations of UD 24 clearly are not inherent in human nature. Unionists beg to differ. The grossest violations of these particular human rights are just as repulsive as those of other human rights in the declaration. They point to the factories attached to the concentration camps where "workers" had none of these rights, to the lack of a "living wage" in sectors of some advanced industrial economies, or to the death by fire of hundreds of workers in the Bangladeshi garment district where owners violated all the human rights listed in UD Articles 23 and 24. And now they can point to the overly long shifts and lack of hazard pay and personal protective equipment experienced by thousands of workers in COVID-19 economies, as well as to the ensuing high US unemployment figures in May 2020 of forty million and counting.

Article 25
Standard of Living and Social Security

The economic equality of my conception [of life] does not
mean that everyone will literally have the same amount. It
simply means that everybody should have enough for his or
her needs. . . . The real meaning of economic equality is "To
each according to his need." That is the definition of Marx.
If a single man demands as much as a man with wife and
four children, that will be a violation of economic equality.

—Mahatma Gandhi

You only find out who is swimming naked when the tide
goes out. So it is with pandemics. . . . You find out which
countries have taken governance seriously and which have
not. You find out who has a health care system that can
manage a once-in-a-century crisis and who doesn't.

—Thomas Friedman, *New York Times*, April 8, 2020, A25

(1) *Everyone has the right to a standard of living adequate for the health
and well-being of himself and of his family, including, food, clothing,
housing and medical care and necessary social services and the right
to security in the event of unemployment, sickness, disability,
widowhood, old age or other lack of livelihood in circumstances
beyond his control.*

(2) *Motherhood and childhood are entitled to special care and assistance.
All children, whether born in or out of wedlock, shall enjoy the same
social protection.*

Because Article 25(1) includes two lists of rights, I titled this commentary "Standard of Living and Social Security." Both lists seem aimed at a
worker "himself and his family." However, given the emphasis on nondiscrimination throughout the text of the declaration, there can be no
doubt that the human rights mentioned here were also meant to apply
to women as heads of families and to single people without a family to
care for. The opening use of the term "everyone" says as much. The
"censors" from the Commission on the Status of Women overlooked this
limiting phrase, as well as the "his" before the word "control." The social

security list in 25(1) lacks the adjective "social" because the drafters did not want to confuse the reader by having that phrase (which also occurs in UD 22) occur twice.

Other than his own socialist ideology, John Humphrey's list for UD 25(1)'s standard of living rights (to "food, clothing, housing and medical care") was inspired by constitutional phrases like "hygienic living conditions" and "low cost dwellings" (Cuba); "cheap houses" (Bolivia and Costa Rica); "sanitary dwellings" (Chile); "cheap housing" (Guatemala); "inexpensive and hygienic houses" (Mexico); and others (E/CN.4/AC.1/3/Add.1). These Latin nations clearly copied each other, and Humphrey copied them in his H35 ("Everyone has the right to medical care. The state shall promote public health and safety.") and in his H42 ("Everyone has the right to good food and housing and to live in surroundings that are pleasant and healthy"). In the First Session of the commission, an interesting exchange occurred between Hansa Mehta of India and Valentin Tepliakov of the USSR. Mehta wanted H35 to speak of "the right to health" because "the individual expects not merely medical care from the State but also such preventive measures as would protect his health," to which use Tepliakov objected that "health as a general expression is too wide and depends on many, many circumstances from the very day of the beginning of one's life" (E/CN.4/AC.1/3/Add.1/285). The right to "necessary social services" was added to this standard-of-living list in the Third Session when Chairperson Eleanor Roosevelt of the United States suggested "social services" be added "to make it clear that the term 'social security' encompassed the right to services as well as to economic protection" (E/CN.4/SR.66/13). Upon the suggestion of Panama, Humphrey had also added "food" to the list.

The delegate of Panama repeated points made in the "statement of essential human rights" submitted in April 1946 to the UN Economic and Social Council, Article 14 of which read as follows: "Everyone has the right to adequate food and housing. The state has the duty to take such measures as may be necessary to ensure that all its residents have an opportunity to obtain these essentials" (E/HR.3/12). The comment to this article pointed out that "food had not been dealt with in constitutional instruments hitherto . . ." and that "it might be sufficient for the state to protect its residents against diseased or unwholesome food and to ensure a continuous flow of food at prices within his reach. With respect to housing, it may be sufficient for the state by the exercise of its regulatory power to ensure that adequate housing shall be available at prices within the reach of all its residents" (ibid.). "What is adequate food and housing," they added, " must be determined at any given time in the light of developing knowledge and of the . . . resources within a country," and even then an individual "was entitled only to what is reasonable under the circumstances" (ibid.13). No one objected to Humphrey turning these observations into questions of human rights in his H35 and H42. Both the Panamanians and Humphrey may well have approved of the opening Gandhi quote in this essay to help us think about the scope of the challenge before us.

But my reader will understand that not all UD drafters had the same views on all the rights spelled out in 25(1). North Atlantic nations were less eager than socialist and communist ones to accept these "new" human rights as full-fledged members of the human rights family. Both France and the United States submitted adaptations of the Constitution of the World Health Organization to the First Drafting Session. It adopted this US version: "Everyone, without distinction of economic and social condition, has the right to the preservation of his health to the highest attainable standard of health. The responsibility of the State and community for the health and safety of its people can be fulfilled only by provision of adequate health and social measures" (E/CN.4/AC.1/SR.14/8). Note that the rights to food and housing are missing here and that the language is more that of social policy than of human rights. Even today in the United States the rights on either list of Article 25(1) are seen more as a matter of public policy than as a matter of rights, let alone of human rights.

The Soviet Union objected to this borrowing from the World Health Organization. In the Working Group of the Second Session, Alexandre Bogomolov argued that that language was "too general" and that it should be clearly stated that "it was the responsibility of the State to guarantee to the individual cheap and accessible medical assistance and to take general measures for the protection of his health" (E/CN.4/AC.2/SR.8/9). France agreed. The Russian point about "adequate medical assistance to the poorer classes" was echoed by the Commission on the Status of Women, which argued that it was "the duty of the State to provide medical care to the poorer classes, especially workers" (ibid.10). The language of rights was weakened again in the full Second Session when the UK delegation succeeded (in a vote of eight to two with five abstentions) in connecting the rights to "food, clothing, housing and medical care" to "the resources which the State or the community can provide" (E/CN.4/SR.40/16).

The Third Session of the commission was eager to keep the declaration as short as possible. As part of this goal, submissions were made to merge the previously discussed standard-of-living list with a social security list the drafters had also been discussing. In an exchange between Alexei Pavlov and Roosevelt about which country had the better health care system, the latter suggested there be "an exchange of medical missions between the two countries" (E/CN.4/SR.66/15). At one point the

International Labour Organization put this text up for adoption: "Everyone has the right to a standard of living and to social services adequate for the health and well-being of himself and his family and to social security, including protection in the event of unemployment, sickness, disability, old age or other lack of livelihood in circumstances beyond his control" (E/CN.4/SR.71/2). The USSR pointed out that specific mention of the rights to "housing and medical care" were still missing, to which China added that all four original standard-of-living rights (to housing, medical care, food, and clothing) should be reinserted into the article (ibid.). After a lengthy Soviet attack on US housing conditions that described how "millions of young people were forced to live in slums" (ibid., 8), separate Soviet paragraphs, one on the right to housing and one on the right to medical care, were rejected in votes of six to four with three abstentions and seven to four with four abstentions.

Having supported his Soviet colleague in proposing the reinsertion of the rights to housing and medical care, the Chinese delegate Peng-Chun Chang additionally proposed the reinstitution of the entire list to "food, clothing, housing and medical care." He twice rose to specifically defend the rights to "food and clothing." Geoffrey Wilson from the United Kingdom did not see a need for the inclusion of these two rights and wanted them to be voted on separately, which was done. Chang responded that he "did not see what possible objection there could be to that phrase when millions of people throughout the world were deprived of food and clothing" (E/CN.4/SR.71/13). Just before the vote, Roberto Fontaina of Uruguay also said he did not see the need for these rights to be mentioned since "the phrase 'standard of living for health and well-being' was sufficiently clear" (ibid.). Chang did not agree: "The question involved concerned not only the quantity but also the quality of food. [He] . . . did not understand the wish to avoid the two principal factors of an adequate standard of living" (ibid., 14). After these pleadings, the rights to food and clothing were accepted for inclusion in the standard-of-living list and the whole list of "food and clothing, housing and medical care" (social services already being there) was adopted by twelve votes to none, with two abstentions (ibid.), meaning no one voted against 25(1)'s standard-of-living list of human rights.

The merger of the standard-of-living list and the social security list was now complete. As to that second list itself, not a great deal was added to Humphrey's H41 ("Everyone has the right to social security. The State shall maintain effective arrangements for the prevention of unemployment and for insurance against the risks of unemployment, accident, disability, sickness, old age, and other involuntary or undeserved loss of livelihood."). You can see that this is very close to what we have in 25(1). These kinds of rights can be found in many socialist and communist constitutions of the 1940s from which Humphrey borrowed. The UD drafters turned them into *human* rights by stipulating that "everyone" has them and not just workers or employees. While the list itself was fairly standard and not much discussed, the simple label "security" created a great deal of ideological handwringing. In my account of Article 22, I explained that the label "social justice" proposed by Syria for that article was rejected and never proposed for 25(1)'s list, where, in any case, it would have been objected to by North Atlantic delegations.

When René Cassin put Humphrey's articles H35 and H42 into just one social security article, he also added this second paragraph to UD 25: "Mothers and children have the right to special regard, care and resources" (E/CN.4/W.2/Rev.2). The significant uptick in domestic abuse calls concerning women and children during our pandemic "stay-at-home" orders makes us applaud Cassin's addition. Wanting to make the best of this overlap with UD 16(3) on family protection, Afanasi Stepanenko from Byelorussia suggested to the Working Group of the Second Session that the sentence "Mothers and children are entitled to protection and assistance by the State" be added to 16(3) instead. Bodil Begtrup from Denmark objected on behalf of the Women's Commission because she "would prefer to see mothers' rights and the protection of children" dealt with separately (E/CN.4/AC.2/SR.6/2), suggesting it be placed with provisions for social security in Article 25, which was done. When Begtrup proposed that mothers and children be separated in different sentences and that the word "mothers" be replaced by "motherhood" "in order to cover the prenatal state" (ibid., 8), Roosevelt agreed and brought this text to a vote: "Motherhood shall be granted special care and assistance. Children are similarly entitled to special care and assistance" (ibid.). The Third Session changed this to "Mother and child have the right to special care and assistance."

In the Third Committee, Yugoslavia's proposal (A/C.3/233) to give equal rights to illegitimate children led Norway to propose that "children born out of wedlock are equal in rights born in marriage and shall enjoy the same social protection" (A/C.3/344). Mohammed Habib from India welcomed the Norwegian amendment "in the firm conviction that the sins of the parents should not be visited upon the children" (A/C.3/SR.144/578). The Third Committee also restored the abstract language that "motherhood and childhood are entitled to special care and assistance." It clearly did not want to tie the human rights of children to any kind of narrow definition of the family, in which they might get entrapped or which might leave some children unprotected.

At the time that the Third Committee was discussing these rights of children, UNICEF chair Ludwik Rajchman reported that only 6 percent of those eligible for aid had received it and consequently "the infant mortality rate had reached an abnormally high level in those countries" (A/C.3/SR.169/796). By November 15, 1948, the office of United Nations Secretary General had collected $30 million in its Appeal for Children campaign. At the time of my writing this, more than eight hundred thousand children have died in the war in Yemen and millions more are suffering from severe malnutrition and will soon succumb to death by starvation.

If you add up all the human rights mentioned in UD 25—the standard-of-living and social security lists in 25(1) and the rights of children in 25(2)—you have got every person covered with human rights from cradle to grave. To make that a reality, we need to face up to the challenge of economic inequality that Gandhi talks about in *My Life Is My Message* when he quotes Karl Marx's famous slogan "From each according to his ability and to each according to his needs." As you can see, Gandhi only takes the last half of that phrase because the point he is making is the same as the one of Article 25, which is that in times of need, every one of us needs to be cared for by others who acknowledge those needs and have a duty to see to them. My hope is that COVID-19 has made us more caring citizens in a more caring state. In the words of Roger Cohen, "If this plague that cares not a whit for the class or the status of its victims cannot teach solidarity over individualistic excess, nothing will. If this continent-hopping pathogen cannot demonstrate the precarious interconnected-ness of the planet, nothing will" (*New York Times*, April 4, 2020, A22).

Article 26
The Right to an Education

Education is the great engine of personal development. It is through education that the daughter of a peasant can become a doctor, that the son of a mine worker can become the head of the mine . . . , that a child of farm workers can become the president of a great nation. It is what we make out of what we have, not what we are given, that separates one person from another.

—Nelson Mandela

"How much does a teardrop weigh?" one asks. The other answers: "Depends. A willful child's teardrop weighs less than the wind, but that of a starving child weighs more than the world."

—Gianni Rodari

---

(1) *Everyone has the right to education. Education shall be free, at least in the elementary and fundamental stages. Elementary education shall be compulsory. Technical and professional education shall be made generally available and higher education shall be equally accessible on the basis of merit.*

(2) *Education shall be directed to the full development of the human personality and to the strengthening of respect for human rights and fundamental freedoms. It shall promote understanding, tolerance and friendship among all nations, racial or religious groups, and shall further the activities of the United Nations for the maintenance of peace.*

(3) *Parents have a prior right to choose the kind of education that shall be given to their children.*

The first paragraph of 26(1) contains five components of the right to an education that were not controversial: the generic right itself, that it be free, that it be compulsory, that it include access to technical and professional training, and that higher education be made available to all on the basis of merit. From the start, the idea that everyone has the right to a primary education that is free and compulsory elicited a consensus among the drafters. Manuel de J. Quijano, the delegate from Panama, had perused John Humphrey's constitutional survey and "pointed out that the constitutions of forty countries proclaimed the principle of free and compulsory education. In those countries everyone without distinction whatsoever had the right to primary education," he said (E/CN.4/ SR.67/9). (Later we will see that the addition of 26(3) complicates this consensus on the term "compulsory.") The professional, technical, and university training of 26(2) were not controversial either because the drafters realized that any kind of education would serve the purposes of both the individual and society.

The American Federation of Labor explained its use of the phrase "to the full development of the human personality" as follows: "The more rights enjoyed by individuals and the more individuals for whom these rights of free development are safeguarded, the more democratic any society will be" (E/C.4/W.8/2). Many nations, too, yoked the benefits for the individual to the benefits for society. Brazilian delegate Austregesilo de Athayde told his colleagues on the Third Committee that "the right to an education was indisputable," for without it "the individual could not develop his personality, which was the aim of human life and the foundation of society" (A/C.3/SR.147/597). Referring to the war that had just ended, Philippine delegate Melchior Aquino observed that "the events of recent years have shown that an enlightened and well-informed public constituted the best defense of democracy and progress" (ibid., 593).

An important part of this link between individual benefit and social utility almost got lost. In his early draft on the right to an education, Humphrey had not included the general availability of technical and professional education. But in the First Drafting Session, René Cassin from France corrected that by adding at the end of his Article 46, "Vocational and technical training shall be generalized" (E/CN.4/AC.1/W.2/ Rev.1). Then for some reason this right was dropped in all three sessions of the commission, not to be reinserted in the article until in the Third Committee. Enrique V. Corominas, the delegate from Argentina, complained that the article made no mention "of modern educational trends such as vocational training and the development of technical aptitudes; it should not be forgotten," he said, "that industrial workers had ceased to be artisans and were becoming technicians. Free development of natural talents would form better members of society and raise the level of culture" (A/C.3/SR.146/581). Cassin, too, pointed out that "between elementary education and higher education there was room for technical and vocational training" and suggested that "technical and professional training shall be made generally available," which was done (A/C.3/ SR.147/586). Phrases like "generally available" and "equally accessible" also point to this dual purpose of the right to an education.

Since each nation on earth seeks to imbue its citizens with its own brand of civic education, the UD drafters could not very well prescribe any particular brand of civic education to the whole world. So in Article 26(2) they give us general principles or guidelines. When the nuts-and-bolts paragraph of 26(1) arrived at the Working Group of the Second Session, the representative of the World Jewish Congress, Alexander Easterman, immediately noticed that "the article on education provided a technical framework of education, but contained nothing about the spirit governing education which was an essential element. Neglect of this principle in Germany had been the main cause of two catastrophic wars." He proposed that this paragraph be added to the article: "This education shall be directed to the full development of the human personality, to strengthening respect for human rights and fundamental freedoms and shall combat the spirit of intolerance and hatred against other nations or racial or religious groups everywhere" (E/CN.4/AC.2/SR.8/3–4). Except for the reference to UN peace activities added later, this is pretty much what we have.

When in the Third Session this entire 26(2) was threatened with deletion, the United Nations Educational, Scientific and Cultural Organization representative Pierre Lebar "warned the Commission against such a step." "He cited the example of Germany where under the Hitler regime education had been admirably organized but had, nevertheless, produced disastrous results. It was absolutely necessary that education to which everyone was entitled should strengthen respect for the rights set forth in the Declaration and combat the spirit of intolerance" (E/CN.4/SR.67/12). He was immediately supported by Franz Bienenfeld, representing the World Jewish Congress. Bienenfeld reminded the drafters that in the Second Session they had agreed that something had to be said about the goal and spirit of the educational enterprise. Deleting 26(2) broke that promise. He continued: "As the representative of UNESCO had pointed out, education in Germany and other fascist countries had been carried out in compliance with the principle of education for everyone; yet the doctrine on which that education had been founded had led to two world wars. If the Declaration failed to define the spirit in which future generations were to be educated, it would lose its value as a guide for humanity" (ibid., 13).

The Third Session adopted this Chinese-Yugoslav text for Article 26's second paragraph: "Education shall be directed to the full development of the human personality, and to the strengthening of respect for human rights and fundamental freedoms and to the promotion of international goodwill and to the combating of the spirit of intolerance and hatred against other nations or racial or religious groups" (E/CN.4/SR.69/9).

In the Third Committee the Mexican and US delegations wanted to change this negative tone of "intolerance" and "hatred" to the more positive goal of the "promotion of understanding, tolerance, and friendship among peoples, as well as the activities of the United Nations for the maintenance of peace" (A/C.3/356). France and Lebanon responded that the spirit of intolerance and hatred "unfortunately did exist and would not be eradicated by being passed over in silence" (A/C.4/SR.147/587). As a result the committee decided to broaden the educational goal by keeping both the negative and positive way of stating that goal. Just before the vote, Lebanon asked that "all peoples" be replaced by "all nations, racial and religious groups," which was done and gave us most of the 26(2) we have.

All along there had been rumblings about the reference in 26(1) to "compulsory" education. After the 26(2) discussions on the guiding spirit of education, delegations came to realize that an unqualified compulsory education system would give the state too much power over the lives of children. In the Third Committee three amendments were presented that sought to balance the power of the state in 26(1) with the "priority" or "prior" right of parents. Lebanon offered a simple text: "Parents have a priority right to choose the kind of education that shall be given to their children" (A/C.3/260). (The Style Committee changed this to "prior right.") The Dutch delegation proposed a slightly longer one: "The primary responsibility for the education of the child rests with the family. Parents have the right to determine the kind of education their children should receive" (A/C.3/263). Denmark submitted an amendment that focused on the rights of racial, national, religious, or linguistic groups to establish their own schools (A/C.3/250). This proposal was withdrawn shortly after it was proposed and was resubmitted when the Third Committee came to discuss and ultimately rejected an article specifically devoted to the rights of members of minority groups.

The rationales given by the Dutch and Lebanese delegations were similar and based on the poisonous influence Nazism had had on the German educational system and on those of the occupied nations. Dutchman Leo Josephus Cornelis Beaufort argued that "parents would be unable to bear the primary responsibility unless they were able to choose the kind of education their children would have. Nazi Germany, where the Hitler Youth deprived parents of control over their children, had provided an experience which should never be permitted to recur" (A/C.3/SR.146/582).

He was supported by Begum Shaista Ikramullah from Pakistan, who thought it was "essential to guarantee freedom to choose education, a principle flagrantly violated by the Nazis" (A/C.3/SR.146/584), and by

Adrian Carton de Wiart, the Belgian representative, who pointed out that the "Netherlands representative had expressed the horror which the Nazi-occupied countries still felt at the thought that the State could compel children to be deformed morally and intellectually by the doctrine of the party in power" (A/C.3/SR.147/594). Lebanon sought to win over some doubters by making the point that 26(3) would serve as balance to the power that the state was given in 26(1): "It was important to proclaim the rights of parents. By stating that education was compulsory, the state would be authorized to force parents to send their children to school. Were the parents not entitled, on the other hand, to select the school to which they would send their children, and the type of education they intended to give them? The Lebanese amendment was intended to simply assert that right" (ibid., 598). It was adopted in a vote of seventeen to three with seven abstentions (ibid., 605).

The communist delegations saw no need for 26(3) since, as USSR drafter Alexei Pavlov put it, "A child had an absolute right to an education, independently of the wishes of its parents. Education should be compulsory because a child could not claim the right as it had no strength to defend it" (A/C.3/SR.148/605). This lack of a parental "prior right" is no surprise for an authoritarian system, but the three negative votes from France, the United Kingdom, and the United States do call for an explanation. The United Kingdom "opposed the Lebanese and Netherlands amendment; the basic text [=26(1)] did not exclude parents from the right to choose their children's education. Also, a specific mention of the rights and duties of the family was inappropriate in a declaration of universal rights" (A/C.3/SR.146/585). France, too, pointed out that "there was nothing in paragraph 1 that threatened the freedom and rights of parents" (A/C.3/SR.147/586).

The United States also argued that "the text in no way opposed the existence of private schools. . . . A number of delegations were anxious that the right of parents to govern the education of their children should be explicitly mentioned." But that was "difficult," said Eleanor Roosevelt, "since it was also necessary to take the interests of children and of the State into account. The amendments suggested were designed to avert situations such as prevailed in Nazi countries where education, which was entirely under state control, tended to atrophy children's intellectual faculties. No object could be of more legitimate concern, but the provisions of article 23 [=26] were drafted with a precision which left no opening for misunderstanding." She also felt that 26(3) encouraged the danger of parents wanting "to supervise school curricula, which clearly might have undesirable consequences. On that ground the US delegation would vote against the amendment submitted" (A/C.3/SR.147/590).

The Dutch delegation reiterated that "the inalienable right of parents" to choose the kind of education their children are to receive should be explicitly mentioned because "during the last war it had been violated with dreadful consequences" (A/C.3/SR.147/598). As I said, this third paragraph of Article 26 was adopted by seventeen to thirteen votes with seven abstentions (ibid., 605).

Article 27
Participation in Culture

We are, at almost every point of our day, immersed in
cultural diversity: faces, clothes, smells, attitudes, values,
traditions, behaviours, beliefs, rituals.

    —Randa Abdel-Fattah

In States inhabited by a substantial number of persons of a
race, language or religion other than those of the majority
of the population, persons belonging to such ethnic,
linguistic or religious minorities shall have the right, as far as
compatible with public order and security, to establish and
maintain schools and cultural or religious institutions and to
use their own language in the Press, in public assembly and
before the courts and other authorities of the State.

    —Set-aside UD article

---

(1) *Everyone has the right freely to participate in the cultural life of the
community, to enjoy the arts and to share in scientific advancement
and its benefits.*

(2) *Everyone has the right to the protection of the moral and material
interests resulting from any scientific, literary or artistic production of
which he is the author.*

It would not surprise me if either of the two paragraphs of this article
struck the reader as counterintuitive. If there are to be human rights to
participation in culture, should we not first think of the rights of members of minority groups whose personal identities do *not* blend in with
the main culture, as indicated in the article in the epigraph that the
drafters rejected? Yet article 27(1) only talks about everyone's right to
"participate in *the* cultural life of *the* community," as if there is only one
cultural tradition, that being the majoritarian one that is fed to its par-
ticipants through a national language, holidays, festivals, school calen-
dars, curricula, and other official ways. Also, few of my readers will count
themselves among 27(2)'s creators of scientific, literary, or artistic works
from which they expect to receive honors or other benefits. Let me answer the most pressing question first.

There is a very good reason why the opening right "to participate in
the culture of *the* community" did not strike the UD drafters as an affront

to members of minority groups, as it may strike us today. At the time the drafters were considering this UD 27, they had every reason to think the declaration would also include the "set-aside" article that I quoted in the epigraph. John Humphrey took that other one over from Hans Lauterpacht, who in 1945 had published a book entitled *An International Bill of the Rights of Man*. Lauterpacht had felt that because Hitler had used minority rights protection as a pretext to invade Poland, the United Nations Charter had gone overboard in its neglect of minority rights. He felt the inclusion of what was his Article 12 in the new international bill gave the UN a chance to redress the balance. Humphrey agreed.

The quoted version of the Lauterpacht-Humphrey article made it to the Second Session of the Human Rights Commission, where, due to a bad ruling by the chair, it was "left aside" and not formally included, though it had been "retained" earlier. It would take us too far afield if I related the details of this sorry story (see my *Universal Declaration of Human Rights: Origins, Drafting, and Intent* [Philadelphia: University of Pennsylvania Press, 1999], section 7.4). Suffice it to say that it never had strong support and that—though the votes were there—the communists, who were its main supporters, did a poor job of corralling the votes to stave off its final defeat in the Third Committee, mostly due to assimilationist opposition from Latin nations.

The reader should know that in 1966 the United Nations corrected this error of omission when it adopted Article 27 of the International Covenant on Civil and Political Rights. This 1966 article does not make minority groups, as such, the bearers of these human rights. It instead uses the term "persons," as did the rejected 1948 one that I cited at the start. The covenant's correction reads like this: "In those States, in which ethnic, religious or linguistic persons belonging to such minorities shall not be denied the right, in community with other members of their group, to enjoy their own culture, to profess and practice their own religion, or to use their own language." At the time of this writing, it has been ratified by more than 150 nations worldwide.

As to the proper story of UD Article 27, when Humphrey did his survey of constitutions to help support this human right to participation in culture, he did not find much material. There was no constitutional precedent for this as a civil or human right. A couple of constitutions stated that the "artistic, historic, and archeological wealth of the Nation" had to be safeguarded by the nation (Bolivia, Art.163) or that "the sciences, letters, and arts are free" (Brazil, Art.173), but Humphrey found no template for the UD's individual human right to participation in culture. A few nations spoke of culture in the context of the right to an education without separating out a right to cultural participation. Yugoslavia came closest with its Article 37(2), stating that "the State assists science and art with a view to developing the people's culture and prosperity," but again no mention was made of an individual's human right to this assistance. Only two countries submitted statements on this right to the commission. Chile stressed what we find in 27(2) and the United States suggested that the commission should consider the right "to enjoy minimum standards of economic, social and cultural well-being" (AC.1/3/Add.1/336).

During the initial drafting stages, Humphrey's Article 44 ("Everyone has the right to participate in the cultural life of the community, to enjoy the arts and to share in the benefits of science" [E/CN.4/AC.1/11/49]) was adopted without much discussion. He was a specialist in Latin American affairs and surely knew about the Ninth International Conference of American States that was to be held in Bogotá, Colombia, in the summer of 1948. It explains where he got his H44. That conference of twenty-one American states adopted what is called the Bogotá Declaration, which was held up by some of these nations as a model for the UD to follow.

Article 13 of the Bogotá Declaration reads like this: "Every person has the right to take part in the cultural life of the community, to enjoy the arts, and to participate in the benefits that result from intellectual progress, especially scientific discoveries. He likewise has the right to the protection of his moral and material interests as regards his inventions or any literary, scientific, or artistic works of which he is the author" (E/CN.4/122/4). You can see that our UD 27 owes a lot to this text. The connection was made explicit when, in the Third Session of the commission, René Cassin of France wanted to add to Humphrey's H44 this second sentence: "Everyone is also entitled to the protection of the moral and material interests relating to the inventions or any literary, scientific or artistic work of which he is the creator." He then "stated that the Bogota Conference had adopted a similar provision" (E/CN.4/SR.70/6). He received immediate backup for this addition from Chile, which was "gratified that it was based on the Bogota Declaration," and Uruguay's Roberto Fontaina, who "pointed out that the Declaration of Human Rights had made provisions for the rights of other groups but had left the intellectual worker without protection" (ibid., 7). Even so, the French amendment was rejected by six votes to five, with five abstentions (ibid.)

The *Third Committee* took up the Bogotá cause. The first sentence was "fixed" when Cuba and China saw to it that "to enjoy the arts and to share in scientific achievement"—which is what had come down from the Third Session—was made to look more like the Bogotá text to become our 27(1): "to enjoy the arts and to share in scientific advancement and its benefits." Jorge Carrera Andrade from Ecuador pointed out that "it was important to establish . . . the State's obligation to render works of art and intellectual creations accessible to the people by granting admission without charge to all museums and libraries and, above all, by extending public education," thus linking this UD article to Article 26 on education (A/C.3/SR.150/618). But he did not think it a good idea to also copy the second Bogotá sentence because "writers and inventors . . . formed only a small proportion of society" (ibid., 619).

Article 27's second paragraph, about the "protection of the moral and material interests" that result from "scientific, literary and artistic production," caused a stir when France, Cuba, Mexico, and China all proposed that the Third Committee add it to UD 27(1) (A/C.3/360/361). There were two views on a creator's right to his or her moral and material interests. Mexico, which also had taken the initiative at Bogotá, pointed out that the committee had "already recognized the rights of the wage earner, the family, the mother and the child; if it did not wish there to be a serious omission in the text it was drawing up it must now proclaim the rights of the individual as an intellectual worker, scientist or writer; in other words, the rights of all those who contributed to the progress and well-being of humanity" (A/C.3/SR.151/617). Cassin of France pointed out that its own proposal (A/C.3/244/Rrev.1), which had mentioned "moral and material interests," also went beyond the question of just royalties and patents because "many scientists attached great[er] importance to the spiritual side of their work than the profits they could gain from it; they only asked that their work should be recognized by future generations" (A/C.3/SR.151/620).

The other, narrower reading of 27(2) was that it "was out of place in the declaration, more especially since [it] dealt with a special aspect of the rights to property" (A/C.3/SR.151/621). This was the view of Uruguay and the United States, as well as the United Kingdom, which felt that "copyright was dealt with by special legislation and in international conventions; it was not a basic human right" (ibid., 624). The vote came to eighteen for, thirteen against, with ten abstentions. The whole of Article 27 was adopted by an overwhelming thirty-six to none, with four abstentions (ibid., 635).

Both paragraphs of UD 27 mention the benefits of science, which— just after the dropping of atomic bombs on Hiroshima and Nagasaki in August 1948—raised the question of the purpose of science. To that end the Soviet Union had submitted to the Third Committee to add to 27(1) this text: "The development of science must serve the interests of progress and democracy and the cause of international peace and co-operation" (E/800). This was the fall of 1948 and the Cold War was making itself felt. Delegations could not agree on the meaning of terms like "progress" and "democracy" that figured in the Soviet amendment. Belgium saw "in the USSR amendment . . . an attempt to assign science a political mission," and thought it better "to say that the aim of science was to search for truth" (A/C.3/SR.150/622), which would also help solidify 27(2). The United Kingdom also objected to the use of these two words, as "the conception of democracy and progress did not seem to be the same everywhere" (ibid., 625). While Argentina was sympathetic to the Soviet position, it "would, however, like the amendment to make no mention of 'democracy'" (ibid.). Cuba also felt that "science should remain entirely free" from any state interference, leaving room for 27(2) (A/C.3/SR.151/628).

The Soviet Union responded by "citing extracts from the United States Press [showing] that scientific research was controlled by military authorities and developed for military purposes" (A/C.3/SR.151/629). Eleanor Roosevelt responded for the United States by citing "a recent article in a USSR publication to the effect that all efforts of the Academy of Sciences should be directed towards the building of communism. The United States delegations did not agree that cultural activities such as literature, music or sciences should be directed" (A/C.3/SR.152/637). Poland argued that "there had been no divergence of views on that subject [of democracy] at the time when Poland had fought against Hitler in defense of democracy, when the whole world had applauded the victories of the Red Army, when President Roosevelt had proclaimed the four freedoms. Poland interpreted the word 'democracy' . . . in the same sense as Abraham Lincoln in his famous definition of government as being of the people, for the people, by the people. That is why it considered that science, if placed at the service of democracy, could not but promote the interests of humanity" (A/C.3/SR.151/631).

Alexei Pavlov asked that three roll-call votes be taken, first on science serving the interests of progress, then on its serving the cause of international peace and cooperation, and finally on its serving the cause of democracy. All three linkages were soundly rejected, putting more emphasis on the individual initiatives mentioned in 27(2) (A/C.3/SR.152/633–34). When various nations rose to explain why they had rejected these Soviet linkages, Pavlov pointed out that "it was illogical to include in Article 23 [=26] a definition of the purposes of education and to refuse in Article 25 [=27] to lay down a similar definition of the purposes of science" (ibid., 636). He was supported by Carrere Andrade of Ecuador, who said he "had voted in favour of the USSR amendment in the firm conviction that science should serve the interests of life rather than death, of peace rather than war. In so doing he had considered only the ideas, and not as other delegations appeared to have done, political matters" (A/C.3/SR.150/625). For similar reasons, Venezuela had abstained (ibid.). Lebanon had voted against the USSR amendment because that text had "confused the true aims of science with its accidental results. It was true that those results should be put to the service of peace and progress; to say that, however, without at the same time stating that the purpose of science was to enquire into the mysteries of nature in the search for truth was to distort the meaning of science" (A/C.3/SR.152/637–38).

Article 28
The Right to a (Good) World Order

I don't want you to listen to me, I want you to listen to the scientists. I want you to unite behind the science. And then I want you to take real action.

— Greta Thunberg

Yes, the "environment" is about polar bears, dolphins, redwood forests, and bees, but it is also about human beings—workers, consumers, families and community members.

— Bill Bigelow and Tim Swinehart

Everyone is entitled to a social and international order in which the rights and freedoms set forth in this Declaration can be fully realized.

In July 2015 human rights scholar Stephen Humphreys wrote in the *Open Global Rights Newsletter* that, "faced with an extraordinary, indeed existential, threat to the fulfilment of supposed 'internationally protected' human rights, on a global scale, human rights law and lawyers—and the human rights movement as a whole—has little useful to say and no obvious role to play," to which he added, "I hope I am wrong." In 2021 he would be mostly wrong. Members of the human rights movement are listening to Greta Thunberg and a host of others. I encountered some of the others in the second of the opening quotations, which I took from the introduction to the book of essays *A People's Curriculum for the Earth*. The essayists prepare human rights activists for "the Big Talk" they need to have with activists in the sustainability movement. All of us know that the whole thing is interconnected, plastic and poverty, facing climate chaos, burning the future (about coal and fracking), and teaching in a toxic world and then also in a nuclear world, as well as food, farming, and the earth, all of which are chapter headings of this publication by Rethinking Schools. You can learn about the sustainability movement at https://www.unsdsn.org.

Today the right to a healthy environment has been inserted in more than one hundred national constitutions. The abovementioned essays grapple with the question of whether protecting planet earth, and not just the humans who inhabit it, is the more urgent task. They discuss the overlap between protecting indigenous human rights and conservation efforts; they pass on lessons from litigating for the Amazon; they ask who legitimately can defend the rights of nature; they tell us how to litigate the right to a sustainable climate system and teach us about rights as a response to ecological collapse; and they ask whether human and non-human rights converge or conflict. The UN Environmental Rights Initiative gives you interesting ways to contact others who want to preserve this planet. Alternatively, you can read the reports of the Special Rapporteur on Human Rights and the Environment, a position in the Office of the UN High Commissioner for Human Rights. These reports speak about human rights and climate change's impact on humans, other animals, and the vegetative world.

As I said in my Statement of Purpose at the start of the book, when it comes to human rights activism, we all need to make our own local and personal connections. In the case of Article 28, that means being good recyclers, educating ourselves on climate change issues, and engaging with others in political action. That then leads to economic and political action, sharing and implementing the high moral ground spelled out in the Universal Declaration.

Article 28 aims at a "social and international order" in which *our own* (because we are "born with" them) human rights and freedoms can be *fully* realized. The full realization of our twenty-first-century human rights cannot happen if we ignore major international threats to any kind of life on Earth simply because the drafters in the 1940s did not much think about that larger threat. These are *our* human rights, and Article 28 talks about *our* future generations. That means the world order we build must be one as we who are living now envision it and not as does some previous generation that faced different crises from the ones we do. In our day, human rights and sustainability cannot be separated from each other.

These issues were not on the radar of the visionaries who wrote the Universal Declaration in the late 1940s. They faced other problems and threats. As internationalists, they worked at creating a new international order in at least four ways. First, they created a new international *political* order when they replaced the old League of Nations with the new United Nations. Second, they put the world order on new *economic* foundations by creating the International Monetary Fund, the World Bank, and what in 1994 became the World Trade Organization. Third, the Nuremberg and Tokyo war crimes trials (see UD 11) were the beginning of a new *criminal* international order. Fourth, the drafting and adopting of the Universal Declaration of Human Rights in 1948 was the first step toward a new international *moral and legal* order. You see that these 1940s visionaries were not twiddling their thumbs while the world lay in ruins.

But they had no inkling of the climate crisis that haunts us today. They did not know, in the words of Thomas Friedman, that "pandemics are no longer just biological—they are geopolitical, financial and atmospheric, too. And we will suffer increasing consequences unless we start behaving differently and treating Mother Earth differently" (*New York Times*, May 31, 2020, SR. 5). The 1940s visionaries could not have known that the world order they created would be rapidly disintegrating and being dismantled before our eyes in the 2020s. It turns out, then, that we in the twenty-first century are tasked to create our own new world order as we want to imagine it. That basically is what UD Article 28 tells us to do, just so long as we built our new world order in such a way that "the rights and freedoms set forth in this Declaration can be fully realized."

The article was first proposed by Lebanon when the Third Session of the commission considered it as an alternative to what became Article 22, which now serves as an introduction to the social, economic, and cultural rights of the declaration. At that time the adjective "good" was already in the UD text that called for a "good social and international order." The Soviet Union liked the article but proposed that the adjective "good" be taken out. It repeated its request in the Third Committee. This Soviet pressure for a leaner text led to an interesting dialogue that rings a bell in the progressive ears of some of us.

The Soviet Union wanted the word "good" deleted because it took the presence of the term to be a reference to an international capitalist rather than to an international socialist order, which the Soviets preferred. As Alexei Pavlov of the USSR pointed out, "As long as society was divided into exploiters and the exploited, as long as there was private ownership of the means of production, the social order could not possibly be a good one" (A/C.3/SR.152/638), which is why he wanted to see the term "good" removed. During the onset of the Cold War and into today, these two views of our world order, the socialist order—which is not the same as a communist one—and the capitalist one, were competing for attention. And the communists did not want the Universal Declaration to tip the scales of moral valuation one way or the other. Apparently the communist delegations associated the use of the word "good" with a capitalist world order, though the records leave that an open issue. "It would be preferable," Pavlov said, "to avoid an ideological discussion and to delete the word 'good' because it represented an evaluation which the new [socialist-communist] democracies, in the name of millions of workers and indigenous inhabitants of colonies, in the name of posterity felt bound to reject" (ibid., 639). Just before the vote, he reiterated that "the aspirations of the masses were usually associated with the socialist order with its lack of class distinction, exploitation or slavery. The capitalist order was one of the most dangerous for the masses and the efforts of its protagonists would not be able to save it. The desire for socialism and its realization in certain countries could not be ignored and, therefore, it should be referred to in connexion with a 'good social and international order.' Any such suggestion, however, would give rise to an ideological discussion, and he had, therefore, contented himself with suggesting the deletion of the word 'good'" instead of claiming it for his own preferred world order (ibid., 641). Since neither side should claim the term, it was deleted by thirty-four votes to two with two abstentions (ibid., 642).

While they expressed doubts about Pavlov's reasoning, most delegations saw the point he was making and voted for the deletion. As Eleanor Roosevelt, speaking for the United States, put it, "Any order which permitted individuals to achieve the rights and freedoms set out in the declaration would obviously be a good one and the adoption of the USSR amendment would not mean the endorsement of any particular political or social system" (A/C.3/SR.152/640). Ralph Maybank of Canada was supported by the Norwegian, Peruvian, and UK representatives. He pointed out that "if the vote were to be taken on the basis of the USSR representative's arguments, however, he would not be able to vote for it. Should the rights set forth in the declaration be achieved, the social and international order would be good, whether it came within the framework of capitalism, communism, feudalism, or any other system. On that understanding he would vote for the USSR amendment" (ibid.). This is the very point I have been making in this commentary—namely, that the declaration gives us a list of moral rights that transcend or stand above particular religious, political, economic, and even domestic and international jurisprudential systems and it judges those systems to be good or bad. The key is that all the rights set forth in the declaration are to be fully realized before any order, whether domestic or international, is to be called good.

Uruguay voted for the USSR amendment not just because it improved the form of the article but, more importantly, "the article itself was necessary because it allowed the individual a voice in international affairs" (A/C.3/SR.152/640). Normally we think of the international order as one that is created and maintained mostly by the Member States of the United Nations. These states supposedly are the only entities that have rights and duties within the international order overseen by the UN. They make and maintain that order. Instead Uruguay correctly saw that Article 28 gives us, as the individuals we are, also a role to play in this mostly state-run human rights regime. If you are so lucky as to live in Europe, Latin America, or Africa, you can go to a regional international human rights court and have your case heard. Obviously a great deal of work remains to be done to give legal human rights recourse to every living human being. In most of the world, including the areas where a skeletal human rights system is in place, that remains an aspirational goal. But our progress depends on how many people join the human rights movement.

The phraseology of UD 28 ("social and international order") is fortuitous, for climate justice that for us in the twenty-first century is the most pressing international problem was not on the radar of the 1940s visionaries. It is now up to us to expand, strengthen, and create new climatological, geopolitical, financial, and atmospheric dimensions of the international order begun by these visionaries. If we do that and create a world order in which "the rights and freedoms set forth in this Declaration can be fully realized," then, under whatever political banner we do that, the resulting social and international order will be a good one. Given how hopeless and uncertain things often seem, Vaclav Havel, the playwright who became president of Czechoslovakia, gives us a good motto to go by: "Hope," he writes, "is definitely not the same thing as optimism. It's not the conviction that something will turn out well, but the conviction that something makes sense, regardless of how it turns out" (*Disturbing the Peace* [New York: Alfred Knopf, 1986], 181–82).

Article 29
Duties as Limitations

A Declaration of Rights is, by reciprocity, a Declaration of
Duties also. Whatever is my right as a man, is also the right
of another; and it becomes my duty to guarantee, as well as
to possess.

 —Thomas Paine

"Human rights" are a fine thing, but how can we make
ourselves sure that our rights do not expand at the expense
of the rights of others. A society with unlimited rights is
incapable of standing to adversity. If we do not wish to be
ruled by a coercive authority, then each of us must rein
himself in. . . . A stable society is achieved not by balancing
opposing forces but by conscious self-limitation: by the
principle that we are always duty-bound to defer to the sense
of moral justice.

 —Aleksandr Solzhenitsyn

---

(1) *Everyone has duties to the community in which alone the free and full
development of his personality is possible.*

(2) *In the exercise of his rights and freedoms, everyone shall be subject only
to such limitations as are determined by law solely for the purpose of
securing due recognition and respect for the rights and freedoms of
others and of meeting the just requirements of morality, public order
and the general welfare in a democratic society.*

(3) *These rights and freedoms may in no case be exercised contrary to the
purposes and principles of the United Nations.*

Halfway through the Third Committee discussions of this article, the
Dutch delegate "noted" that "the debate on Article 27 [=29] had shown
that the rights of the individual are not absolute" (A/C.3/SR.154/655).
As my opening quotes suggest, rights and duties—just like high and low,
beautiful and ugly, or day and night—go together. Where one of a pair
like this occurs, the other one is needed to explain the first, which is why
I have taken some liberties with the length of this essay on duties.

 The constitutions that John Humphrey surveyed contained mostly examples of residents' duties to pay taxes, serve in the military (when applicable), and be generally law abiding. Only China's (Art.23), France's

(Art.4), Paraguay's (Art.35), and Turkey's (Art.68) constitutions imposed limitations based on the rights and freedoms that other people have, as our 29(2) also says is the case.

Both Humphrey and René Cassin began their lists not with rights but with duties. Humphrey began with everyone having "a duty to the State and to the (international society) United Nations. He must accept his just share of responsibilities for the performance of such social duties and his share of such common sacrifices as may contribute to the common good" (AC.1/3). His idea that we would have duties to the state brought forth a strong reaction from Charles Habib Malik of Lebanon, who observed that in the late 1940s "men had no need for protection against kings or dictators, but rather against a new form of tyranny of the *State* over the individual whom it was the duty of the Commission to protect" (E/CN.4/SR.9/3; original italics). Alluding to Hitler's Third Reich and other kinds of authoritarianism, he questioned "whether an individual owed such a duty of loyalty regardless of the characteristics of his State" (E/CN.4//AC.1/SR.3/9).

As a result, Cassin dropped all references to the state in his rewrites. He submitted four communitarian-type opening articles (AC.1/W.2/Rev.2), the first one being that "all men are brothers. Being endowed with reason, members of one family, they are free and possess equal dignity and rights." Those ideas were moved to our preamble and to Article 1. Cassin's second article spoke of a duty *of* (not to) society to help everyone "develop his spirit, mind and body," which idea we find in UD Articles 22, 26, and 29(1). Our 29(2) shows up in Cassin's third article: "Man is essentially social and has fundamental duties to his fellow men. The rights of each are therefore limited by the rights of others." And in his fourth: "In the exercise of his rights, everyone is limited by the rights of others." Our 29(3), about owing duties to the principles of the United Nations, was added very late in the process.

It was immediately apparent that the UD drafters wanted to collapse these four Cassin articles into one or two. The Drafting Committee decided to keep Cassin's first article in reserve and adopted this collapsed text for the other three: "These rights are limited only by the equal rights of others. Man also owes duties to society, through which he is enabled to develop his spirit, mind and body in wider freedom" (E/CN.4/SR.13/4). Upon the urging of Panama and the Philippines, the Second Session of the commission decided to put "the State" back into the article by inserting that our rights are limited by "the just requirements of the democratic State" (E/CN.4/SR.2/8). That insertion was disputed in the Third Session. After an intense debate, the chairperson appointed a subcommittee consisting of Australia, China, France, Lebanon, India, and the United Kingdom. It came up with a two-paragraph article: "(1) Everyone has duties to the community which enables him freely to develop his personality," and "(2) In the exercise of his rights, everyone shall be subject only to such limitations as are necessary to secure due recognition and respect for the rights of others and the requirements of general welfare in a democratic society" (E/CN.4/SR.52/2). As you can see, this subcommittee replaced "democratic state"—which was a very controversial phrase during the onset of the Cold War—with the less controversial "democratic society." When called upon to explain what it meant by the phrase "general welfare in a democratic society," at the suggestion of Egypt, the committee added the terms "morality" and "public order" as qualifications of such a society (E/CN.4/SR.74/11). This gives us our 29(1) and (2).

Given that our possession of human rights is limited by our own duties and by the rights of others, you might ask why this article on duties is at the very end of the declaration instead of at the start with other basic principles. It was moved to the end in the Third Session upon the suggestion of Peng-Chun Chang of China. "An article which dealt with the limitations on the exercise of the rights and freedoms proclaimed in the Declaration should not," it said, "appear at the beginning of the Declaration before those rights and freedoms themselves had been set forth" (E/CN.4/SR.77/2). Egypt argued that "Article 2 was among the articles that set forth general principles and, as such, should appear at the beginning of the Declaration" (ibid.). The Soviet Union agreed with the United Kingdom that "the reader should know from the outset that the rights and freedoms set forth in the Declaration were to be enjoyed within the framework of society." So did Belgium (ibid., 3). The proposal to make 29 the "penultimate article" carried by a vote of eight to seven with one abstention (ibid., 3). The eight positive votes came from Egypt, the United States, Lebanon, Australia, Chile, France, India, Panama, the Philippines, and Uruguay. They all felt, in the words of Salvador Lopez of the Philippines, that "since they were dealing with a Declaration on Human Rights, the rights of the individual should be stressed before his duties to society" (ibid., 3).

The Third Committee held revealing discussions and votes. I comment on the most interesting ones for each of UD 29's three paragraphs. For 29(1) the Third Committee received this from the commission: "Everyone has duties to the community which enable him freely to develop his personality." Cuba (A/C.3/261) proposed four additional paragraphs about the relationship of rights and duties that were too long to be viable. Just before votes on all the paragraphs were to be taken, Australia "suggested inserting the phrase 'in which alone the free and full development of his personality is possible' into this first paragraph after the word 'community'" (A/C.3/SR.154/658).

Fernand Dehousse of Belgium, supported by Greece, objected that it might mistakenly be thought that "the individual could only develop his personality within the framework of society; it was, however, only necessary to recall the famous book by Daniel Defoe, *Robinson Crusoe*, to find proof of the contrary." He also did not think the text should imply "it was the duty of society to develop the human being's personality," for countries had different views on that matter (A/C.3/SR.154/659). Sensing difficulties, Alan Watt of Australia said that "his delegation would not insist on its proposal" (ibid.). However, Alexei Pavlov of the USSR "thought . . . that the text proposed by the Australian representative was important in that it stressed the harmonious relations that should exist between the individual and the society in which he lived." He felt that the word "alone" "rightly stressed the fact that the individual could not fully develop his personality outside of society. The example of *Robinson Crusoe*, far from being convincing, had shown, on the contrary, that man could not live and develop his personality without the aid of society. Robinson had, in fact, had at his disposal the products of human industry and culture, namely the tools and books he had found on the wreck of the ship. . . . In view of the fact that the Australian delegation had withdrawn it, he would take it up in the name of his own delegation" (ibid., 659–60).

This Australian-USSR proposal for 29(1) with the word "alone" in it was adopted by thirty-five votes to none with six abstentions. And so it happened that one of the most important words in the declaration was the result of a wonderful collaborative effort. Article 29(1) protects the declaration against critics who claim that our modern concept of human rights is too individualistic and even atomistic; that it is based on an idea of what a human being is that flies in the face of social and psychological realities. As this unanimous vote shows, that is not what the UD drafters were thinking.

Most amendments to 29(2) had to do with adding to or subtracting from the limitations on the practice of human rights that were "necessary to secure due recognition and respect for the rights of others and the requirements of morality, public order and the general welfare in a democratic society." Upon the suggestion of Uruguay, the phrase "necessary to secure" was changed to "prescribed by law solely for the purpose of securing," after which came the list we now have (A/C.3/268). Justin Jimenez de Arechaga reasoned that "this amendment would protect personal liberty, in so far as the support of public opinion would be needed to limit human rights. It would always be easier for a Government to close down one newspaper than to have a general law censoring the Press. The latter measure . . . would arouse much greater reaction among the people of the country concerned" (A/C.3/SR.153/643). In spite of important opposition, the amendment was adopted by twenty-one votes to fifteen, with seven abstentions (A/C.3/SR.154/661).

As if directly addressing us in the early twenty-first century, the Dutch delegate pointed out that adding "by law" to 29(2) would not help protect human rights "in an authoritarian State, where legislative power was not independent of the executive power," but he did say he would vote for the addition (A/C.3/SR.154/656). In response to worries by the United States that this amendment would undercut the morality of human rights, Uruguay pointed out that "any limitations introduced by the State in defence of morality, public order and the general welfare must be justifiable on moral grounds; they must also have a legal form and be generally applicable" (A/C.3/SR.153/646).

France also felt that the phrase "by law" was too restrictive because limitations could also be imposed by "convention and judgments on individual cases" that would make such a limitation legitimate (A/C.3/SR.154/653). Its own amendment asked for the insertion of the term "legitimate" before the word "requirements" (A/C.3/345). Uruguay responded that "the free will of man was undeniably limited, if only by the demands of his conscience, the rules of positive morality, or standards set by social conventions" (A/C.3/SR.154/654). Jimenez de Arechaga reiterated his belief that "the principle should be adopted that limitations to be set by public authorities could only be set in accordance by pre-established standards, i.e. in accordance with provisions legally enacted" (ibid.). When the vote on inserting the term "legitimate" was taken, it passed by twenty-two to eight with eleven abstentions (ibid., 661). What the General Assembly on December 10 voted on contained the word "just" instead of "legitimate" and is therefore definitive.

The Soviet Union, having been rebuffed when it wanted to change the requirements of "the general welfare in a democratic society" in 29(2) to the requirements of a "democratic state," now proposed that the words "and also the corresponding requirements of the democratic state" be added at the end of that paragraph (E/800). As he had done with the introduction of the word "alone" into 29(1), Pavlov explained his country's new position by linking the concept of the individual to that of society and that concept in turn to that of the state. He pointed out that "it was impossible for the individual to be free of society, for man was a social being." Having embedded the individual in society, he added that "the proper co-ordination of the interests of the individual and society was only possible under a socialist regime. All the rights laid down in the declaration would be implemented in democratic societies by democratic states. The law was nothing without the machinery to implement it, and at the present time, that machinery was the State. It was impossible, therefore, to ignore the requirements of the democratic state" (A/C.3/SR.153/644). To the objections (which I record in the next paragraph), Pavlov responded that "the concepts of morality and public order were wider than the democratic State required. The concept of morality, in particular, was subject to various interpretations; the morality of a socialist regime was certainly of a higher order than that of a capitalist regime where man was exploited by man" (A/C.3/SR.154/655).

This USSR proposal to add limitations set by a "democratic state" was rejected by a vote of twenty-three to eight with nine abstentions (A/C.3/SR.154/663). Pavlov was right when he argued that the state plays a crucial role in the implementation of human rights. That is still true today, seventy-five years after the UD's adoption. But when that position is stated without further nuance, problems arise. Benigno Aquino of the Philippines put it this way: "The USSR amendment by raising the State above that society would destroy the intent and meaning of the article. Since the definition of 'the corresponding requirements' of a State would lie with that State, it could under terms of the USSR amendment annul all individual rights and freedoms contained in the declaration. Aquino was therefore strongly opposed to the amendment" (A/C.3/SR.153/649).

Little words can make a big difference. Watt of Australia pointed out that the commission's text spoke of "the requirements of morality, public order and the general welfare *in* a democratic society," while the Soviet amendment spoke of them as being "requirements *of* a democratic society and the corresponding requirements *of* a democratic state" (A/C.3/SR.154/657; original italics). The difference underscores what the objectors to the USSR amendment were saying. For they thought of the items "morality, public order and the general welfare" as independent forces in democratic societies and not as products of those societies and certainly not of democratic states, as Pavlov defined these terms. The majority of UD drafters wanted to maintain a distance between the moral norms of the declaration that might play a role in further spelling out what the "requirements of morality" might be.

At one point these other independent limitations were endangered because New Zealand asked for the deletion of the items "morality" and "public order" (A/C.3/267) from the list, leaving "the general welfare" in place. The New Zealand delegation "wondered whether it had been wise" to add these terms at the last moment in the Third Session, "for it was far from clear what those three expressions ["morality," "public order," and "general welfare"] were intended to mean. Did they not, in a sense, overlap; and had not an excess of public order often led to the infringement of human rights and freedoms?" (A/C.3/SR.153/645). Pablo Campos Ortiz of Mexico responded that these terms were necessary as independent forces that "were recognized by the laws of all nations; [and that] it was the concept of democracy that was still inadequately defined and unknown to jurisprudence" (A/C.3/ SR.153/649–50). Not long after this, the New Zealand delegation withdrew its amendment.

Both Article 29(3) and Article 30 originated in the Second Session of the commission when General Carlos Romulo from the Philippines proposed that "all laws in any State shall be in conformity with the purposes and principles of the United Nations as embodied in the Charter" (E/CN.4/SR.41/3). The phrase "all laws in any state shall be in conformity with" conflicted with the drafting rule that had been followed, not to mention the obligations of states in the declaration. Seconding what Pavlov had also said, William Hodgson from Australia argued that "the question of how national laws were in conformity with the Declaration had no bearing on the Declaration itself" (ibid., 5). Until the two legal international covenants, the International Covenant on Civil and Political Rights and the International Covenant on Economic, Social and Cultural Rights, came into force in 1976, that is indeed how the declaration functioned in world affairs. It was a moral banner that floated above and across national borders, hoping its inhabitants would see it and take action. Not wanting to make any reference to either the UN Charter or the declaration, the Third Session had deleted this paragraph.

Both France (A/C.3/345) and Egypt (A/C.3/264) successfully resurrected a different version of it when the Third Committee adopted our 29(3): "These rights and freedoms may in no case be exercised contrary to the purposes and principles of the United Nations." France said the paragraph "was intended to make clear that the individual belonged to the international community as well as to his own national society and that the interests of that organized international community were the same as his own" (A/C.3/SR.153/643). Aquino of the Philippines did not like any other amendments, but "he was in favour of the mention of the purposes and principles of the United Nations as suggested by the French representative" (A/C.3/SR.153/648). Belgium agreed but wanted it done in a separate paragraph, as was proposed by Egypt (ibid., 650). Australia considered the addition of 29(3) "most appropriate" (A/C.3/SR.154/658). To no one's surprise, this addition was added by a vote of thirty-four to two with six abstentions. At this point the minutes record that "Article 27 as a whole, as amended, was adopted by 41 votes to none, with one abstention. The whole of Article 29 was adopted unanimously by 41 votes to none, with only one abstention" (A/C.3/SR.154/664).

Article 30
Indestructible and Inherent

Human rights will be a powerful force for the transformation of reality when they are not simply understood as
externally defined norms of behavior but are lived as the
spontaneous manifestation of internalized values.
> —Daisaku Ikeda

I want to say to you . . . that we honestly face the fact that the
movement must address itself to the question of restructuring the whole of American society.
> —Martin Luther King Jr. to the Southern Christian
> Leadership Conference, 1967

---

*Nothing in this Declaration may be interpreted as implying for any
State, group or person any right to engage in any activity or to
perform any act aimed at the destruction of the rights and freedoms
set forth herein.*

The movement Dr. King is talking about in the above citation is the US civil
rights movement that, with the vigilante killing of Trayvon Martin in Flor-
ida in 2013, became the Black Lives Matter movement. After the murder of
George Floyd by a police officer in Minneapolis in May 2020, that movement became the largest-ever social protest movement in the United States,
with worldwide echoes. King had questioned "the capitalistic system" and
was looking for the "restructuring of the whole of American society." He
said he himself was "no communist" and he seemed to be searching for a
middle way between capitalism and some further left ideology.

Now, fifty-three years after King said this, much of the whole country
seems to be looking for that same middle way. On the weekend of July 4,
2020, the *New York Times* devoted its entire sixteen-page Sunday Review
section to a discussion of "how to save democracy from capitalism and
save capitalism from itself." Like King, this national US daily paper told
its readers that America had failed to live up to its founding promises of
equality for all: "Picture the nation as a pirate crew: In recent decades,
the owners of the ship have gradually claimed a larger share of the booty
at the expense of the crew. The annual sum that has shifted from workers
to owners now tops $1 trillion" (SR. 2). Not all developed nations have
this same kind of dangerous wealth gap.

Europeans also face a resurgence of authoritarian populism, but their societies are more fascist-proof than we are in the United States. After World War II, they created good safety nets, encapsulated their national-isms within the wider European Union, and in 1954 adopted the first re-gional convention on human rights with a special Human Rights Court attached where their citizens could lodge complaints against their own governments. Other continents (except for Asia) have similar courts. Right now US citizens have none of these things. Also, twenty-seven European states have jointly borrowed $750 billion to help weaker states during the COVID-19 crisis because they see this as a crisis without borders. We need the same kind of solidarity among nations across different continents to rebuild the international order that lies in tatters around us.

What King wanted and what thousands of Black Lives Matter march-ers also plead for is a third founding and total reorganization of this country. Having come to the end of this book, I want to repeat what I said at the start, which is that if we are going to have that kind of a totally new beginning, we should do it with human rights. Let us use the thirty articles of the UD as moral platforms for a reconstruction of our socie-ties and for revolutions in values wherever we live. The day before he died, John Lewis (another US civil rights icon) wrote, "Democracy is not a state. It is an act, and each generation must do its part to help build what we called the Beloved Community, a nation and world society at peace with itself" (*New York Times*, July 30, 2020, A23). Throughout these drafting stories, I often made nations and not just individual drafters the heroes. I do not know how you look at nations, but sometimes—as in these stories, where many nations spoke up and contributed—I ended up thinking of them as quasi-persons. My point was and still is that na-tions as such, working together, created the moral high ground from which we can bring about Lewis's "nation and world society at peace with itself." These human rights stories are applicable wherever my reader decides to make a difference. The 1940s visionaries who populate these stories fought for social, political, cultural, and economic reorganizations that cut as deeply as we today think we need to go.

Maya Angelou was spot-on when she said that "history, despite its wrenching pain, cannot be unlived, but if faced with courage need not be lived again." I think you might agree with me that today's Germany—which has figured in almost every one of this book's stories in a grossly negative fashion—as a nation exhibits the courage Angelou talks about. It has been a consistent leader in the postwar reconstruction of our world along the lines of the Universal Declaration. If they can do it, so can we.

As to the alleged indestructibility and inherence mentioned in the title of this final story, there is a difference between UD 30's overall indestructibility of human rights and UD 29(3) saying that "these rights and freedoms may in no case be exercised contrary to the purposes and principles of the United Nations." Their common origin lies in the drafters' desire to embed the individual in the international community as defined by the purposes and principles of the United Nations. But that does not go far enough, for some nation, state, person, or group could in a perverse way interpret the UN principles and purposes to allow for the violation of the rights spelled out in this declaration. That happens when human rights are violated for allegedly peaceful purposes. So Article 30 goes a step further when it says that "nothing in this Declaration"—not even a perverse reading of the UN principles and purposes mentioned in 29(3)—"may be interpreted" as a license to violate human rights.

Indestructibility points to inherence, for this blanket condemnation of any and every violation of the UD rights makes them in effect inherent in the human person. That is also what Article 1 means when it says we are "born with" them and what the preamble means when it calls them "inalienable" in "all members of the human family." This idea is the theme of my book *Inherent Human Rights Philosophical Roots of the Universal Declaration* (Philadelphia: University of Pennsylvania Press, 2009). When it celebrated the seventieth anniversary of the declaration in December 2018, the Office of the UN High Commissioner for Human Rights posted thirty articles, one on each UD article. It gave its essay on Article 30 this heading: "Rights Are Inalienable." I would insert "Human" before "Rights," for that is what sets the 1948 declaration apart from previous declarations and from ordinary city and states' rights, which are alienable rights in that our having them can easily be changed or taken away.

So the UD text has come full circle. It floats above world affairs as a moral banner that nations, persons, and groups need to look at and adhere to at pain of condemnation. Nothing can justify violation of any of the rights in this declaration. That does not mean that respect for human rights around the world was automatic. The high commissioner's office noted that what the UD drafters achieved in 1948 was "an astonishing achievement. In the midst of recovery from war, at the outset of the Cold War, with the United Nations in its infancy, the drafters transcended differences in language, nationality and culture—not completely, but to an extent unprecedented in international relations" (Art.30). As readers who have read some or all of the other essays in this book know, this did clearly happen. The document is the result of an amazing cooperative effort that was stitched together with difficult compromises.

After that, with a great deal of yet more cooperative effort, the international community took eighteen years to adopt the 1966 International Covenant on Economic, Social and Cultural Rights, which implemented most of the second half of the UD, and at the same time the one on civil and political rights, which implemented the first half of the UD text. Both of these came "into force" in 1977, meaning that enough countries had signed on to this legal implementation of all the UD articles, except Article 17 on property. In addition to these two international covenants of wide scope, the UN also sponsored numerous legal conventions on specific human rights mentioned in the UD—on the rights of women (1979), the rights of children (1989), and the rights of the disabled (2006)—as well as on torture (1984) and many other specific UD rights. The total today is close to two hundred human rights "instruments," as they are called.

Initially, when Charles Habib Malik of Lebanon proposed to the Second Session of the commission that "nothing in this Declaration shall be considered to recognize the right of any person to engage in any activity aimed at the destruction of any of the rights and freedoms prescribed herein" (E/CN.4/SR.41/7), he had left out the state as one of the possible violators of human rights. Since states were "the chief offenders against human rights," William Hodgson of Australia wanted to know why they had been left out (ibid., 8). Though Malik agreed with Hansa Mehta from India that "the declaration dealt with the rights of individuals and not of States," he accepted the correction, and the article as we have it was adopted in that Second Session by eight votes to seven (ibid.).

The discussion of this article overlapped with a discussion on a very similar article for the legally binding covenant that was also being considered but was dropped for a lack of time. In that other discussion, Eleanor Roosevelt of the United States expressed her doubts about the efficacy of the article. But she did point out that "Nazi Germany had appeared to be legally fulfilling the duties and obligations of the state, but in practice had been destroying all human rights and liberties" (E/CN.4/AC.1/SR.28/4). Malik of Lebanon, on the other hand, "considered that this was a most important article which simply aimed at rendering it impossible for any mischief-maker to invoke the Bill of Rights for his own protection while he was in the act of destroying or attempting to destroy the human rights of others" (ibid., 5). "He explained that the formulation of the article was based on the concept of checking and preventing the growth of nascent Nazi, fascist or other totalitarian ideologies" (ibid.).

When in the Third Session Chairperson Roosevelt from the United States proposed the deletion of Article 30, Alexei Pavlov of the USSR rose to make a legitimate complaint. He pointed out that during the deliberation of the articles, "provisions designed to eliminate the remains of nazism [sic] or fascism" had usually been rejected by the commission "on the pretext that they would be covered later by a general article. But the Commission was at present deleting those general articles" (E/CN.4/

SR.74/7). Pierre Ordonneau from France backed him up, saying that "it was essential that the Declaration should at least recall the dangers of nazism [*sic*]" (ibid., 8). In a vote of ten to one with two abstentions, the Third Session adopted the Lebanese text and sent it on to the Third Committee. Except that upon the recommendation of France it changed "shall be considered to recognize the right of any State etc." to "shall imply the recognition of the right of any State etc." (E/CN.4/SR.74/9).

In the Third Committee the French delegation (A/C.3/345) proposed that the term "group" be inserted between "State" and "person" because "experience had shown that it was rarely States or individuals that engaged in activities that aimed at the destruction of human rights; such activities in recent times had been pursued by groups sometimes acting on the instructions or with the connivance of states" (A/C.3/SR.155/666). The only noncommunist nation that spoke up on behalf of this French proposal was Belgium, which "was firmly convinced of the necessity to stop the activities of subversive groups and thus to prevent a repetition of the experience of a number of countries in the years immediately preceding the war" (ibid., 667). Pavlov of the USSR made that same point more explicitly when he argued that "experience had shown how dangerous were the Nazi groups which . . . by constant infiltration and propaganda had paved the way for the fascist regimes of Hitler and Mussolini" (A/C.3/SR.156/670). He also gave the example of the Ku Klux Klan, "whose activities were well known in the United States. Naturally," he added, "attempts were made to belittle the importance of those organizations on the ground that their membership was very small and their activity of little consequence. He recalled that the same attitude had prevailed concerning the fascist organizations of Hitler and Mussolini. The disastrous consequences of such indifference were unfortunately all too well known" (ibid., 671). This was followed by an equally impassioned speech from Stephen Demchenko, Pavlov's colleague from the Ukrainian Soviet Socialist Republic.

The word "group" was inserted by forty-two to zero votes with one abstention, meaning Article 30 was unanimously adopted (A/C.3/SR.156/672). The August 2017 neo-Nazi march and attack by a white supremacist group in Charlottesville, Virginia, comes to mind as a clear example of the need for this insertion. So does the January 6, 2020, attack by similar groups on the U.S. Capitol, which used to be the symbol of democracy around the world.

Having come to the end of this book, my opening epigraph to Article 30 from the Japanese writer Daisaku Ikeda invites comment. For "the transformation of reality" that the drafting stories I have told call for cannot happen unless human rights norms are "not simply understood as externally defined norms of behavior but are lived as the spontaneous manifestation of internalized values." Such internalization will not be as easy as it may seem to those of us already converted to the cause of human rights. Contemporary discussions urge us not simply not to be racist (or not to be sick), but to be consciously antiracist, as if trying to get over some illness or fighting off an addiction. That in turn calls for constant self-examination and for actively making connections between some article in the declaration and conditions on the ground. Throughout, I have nudged my readers to do just that in their local or national community or make contacts abroad.

Acknowledgments

The first person I need to thank is Rick Mikulski, government and social sciences librarian at Oregon State University in Portland. He knows more about how to find documents and citations in the United Nations Archives than anyone I know. It is very much with his help that the notes in this book are so accurate and traceable to their source.

I am always grateful to Drew University's Philosophy and Political Science Departments for giving me a wonderful work environment for many years. Many people have wanted me to do a more "popular" book on the Universal Declaration that would be accessible to readers who might not be scholars of the subject but are just interested in this iconic text and what it stands for. These include friends and family here and in the Netherlands. Three of these must be mentioned by name. I thank Lisa Jordan for her help with the openings of Articles 12 and 28 and my friend Paul Wehn for initially pushing me to make use of epigraphs to give my drafting stories more depth. And I thank my niece Marleen in Amsterdam, who years ago started her rooting for the creation of this book.

I have said it before, but it bears repeating that without the constant support from my wife and best friend, Nancy, this book, too, would not have been written. The stable environment that she has created over the years is an absolute necessity for an impatient fellow like me.

I thank all who, as the operative paragraph (or statement of purpose) would have it, have used my books on the UD for "teaching and education to promote respect for these rights and freedoms [so as] . . . to secure their universal and effective recognition" everywhere in the world.